Constructing Teacher Identities

Also available from Bloomsbury

Accent and Teacher Identity in Britain, Alex Baratta
Academic Working Lives, edited by Lynne Gornall, Caryn Cook, Lyn Daunton,
Jane Salisbury and Brychan Thomas
Transforming Teacher Education with Mobile Technologies, edited by
Kevin Burden and Amanda Naylor
Social Networks in Language Learning and Language Teaching, edited by
Avary Carhill-Poza and Naomi Kurata
Linguistic Landscapes Beyond the Language Classroom, edited by Greg Niedt
and Corinne A. Seals
The Sociopolitics of English Language Testing, edited by
Seyyed-Abdolhamid Mirhosseini and Peter I. De Costa
A New Perspective on Education in the Digital Age, Jesper Tække
and Michael Paulsen
Social Theory for Teacher Education Research, edited by Kathleen Nolan and
Jennifer Tupper
Navigating Teacher Education in Complex and Uncertain Times,
Carmen I. Mercado
Developing Culturally and Historically Sensitive Teacher Education, edited by
Yolanda Gayol, Patricia Rosas Chávez and Peter Smagorinsky
Knowledge, Policy and Practice in Teacher Education, edited by
Maria Teresa Tatto and Ian Menter

Constructing Teacher Identities

*How the Print Media Define and Represent
Teachers and Their Work*

Nicole Mockler

BLOOMSBURY ACADEMIC
LONDON · NEW YORK · OXFORD · NEW DELHI · SYDNEY

BLOOMSBURY ACADEMIC
Bloomsbury Publishing Plc
50 Bedford Square, London, WC1B 3DP, UK
1385 Broadway, New York, NY 10018, USA
29 Earlsfort Terrace, Dublin 2, Ireland

BLOOMSBURY, BLOOMSBURY ACADEMIC and the Diana logo are
trademarks of Bloomsbury Publishing Plc

First published in Great Britain 2022
Paperback edition published 2024

Copyright © Nicole Mockler, 2022

Nicole Mockler has asserted her right under the Copyright, Designs and
Patents Act, 1988, to be identified as Author of this work.

For legal purposes the Acknowledgements on pp. xviii–xx constitute an
extension of this copyright page.

Cover design: Charlotte James
Cover image © MBCheatham/Getty Images

All rights reserved. No part of this publication may be reproduced or transmitted
in any form or by any means, electronic or mechanical, including photocopying,
recording, or any information storage or retrieval system, without prior permission
in writing from the publishers.

Bloomsbury Publishing Plc does not have any control over, or responsibility for,
any third-party websites referred to or in this book. All internet addresses given in this
book were correct at the time of going to press. The author and publisher regret any
inconvenience caused if addresses have changed or sites have ceased to exist,
but can accept no responsibility for any such changes.

A catalogue record for this book is available from the British Library.

Library of Congress Cataloging-in-Publication Data
Names: Mockler, Nicole, author.
Title: Constructing teacher identities : how the print media define and
represent teachers and their work / Nicole Mockler.
Description: London ; New York : Bloomsbury Academic, 2022. |
Includes bibliographical references and index.
Identifiers: LCCN 2022003824 (print) | LCCN 2022003825 (ebook) |
ISBN 9781350129252 (hardback) | ISBN 9781350226968 (paperback) |
ISBN 9781350129269 (pdf) | ISBN 9781350132344 (epub)
Subjects: LCSH: Teachers–Press coverage–Australia. | Education in mass
media–Australia | Teachers–Australia–Public opinion. | Public opinion–Australia.
Classification: LCC LB2832.4.A88 M64 2022 (print) | LCC LB2832.4.A88 (ebook) |
DDC 371.100994–dc23/eng/20220302
LC record available at https://lccn.loc.gov/2022003824
LC ebook record available at https://lccn.loc.gov/2022003825

ISBN: HB: 978-1-3501-2925-2
PB: 978-1-3502-2696-8
ePDF: 978-1-3501-2926-9
eBook: 978-1-3501-3234-4

Typeset by Newgen KnowledgeWorks Pvt. Ltd., Chennai, India

To find out more about our authors and books visit www.bloomsbury.com
and sign up for our newsletters.

For Jack Mockler (1906–1994),
Who taught me many things, among them how to read the newspaper.

And for Elenie Poulos,
Who makes all things possible.

Acknowledgement of Country

Much of this book was written on the unceded Land of the Gadigal People of the Eora Nation, custodians of this Country since time immemorial.

I acknowledge the Traditional Owners of this land on which I am privileged to live and work, and pay respect, with gratitude, to Elders past and present, and to all Aboriginal and Torres Strait Islander peoples, guardians of the oldest living cultures in the world.

I am grateful for the generosity, patience and openness of my Aboriginal and Torres Strait Islander friends and colleagues, from whom I have learned so much over the years.

Always was, always will be, Aboriginal Land.

Contents

List of Figures		viii
List of Tables		ix
Foreword *Bob Lingard*		xii
Acknowledgements		xviii
1	Words Matter	1
2	The Australian Teacher Corpus	27
3	Change over Time	59
4	The 'Newspaper Effect' in the Australian Teacher Corpus	87
5	The Significance and Evolution of 'Quality' in the Australian Teacher Corpus	119
6	A Comparative View of Teachers in the Print Media	143
7	Teachers in the Print Media: Conclusions, Limitations, Prospects	165
References		177
Index		197

Figures

2.1	Media interests snapshot, September 2021	32
2.2	Total articles in the ATC by newspaper	37
2.3	Total articles in the ATC by year	37
2.4	Representation of different occupational groups in the Australian print media	38
3.1	Number of lexical keywords and unique keywords by annual sub-corpora	68
4.1	Percentage of articles in the ATC and AFR sub-corpus	97
5.1	Teacher quality, teaching quality and education quality by year	127

Tables

1.1	Inventory of Linguistic Devices Constructing Newsworthiness	16
2.1	Australian Newspaper Profiles	33
2.2	Australian Newspaper Readership, Twelve Months to March 2021	35
2.3	Top Thirty Most Frequent Words in the ATC, Ordered by Frequency	39
2.4	Top Thirty Most Frequent Lexical Words in the ATC, Ordered by Frequency	39
2.5	Top Thirty Keywords in the ATC as Compared to the NOW-AU Corpus, Ordered by Log Ratio	41
2.6	Keywords in the ATC, Organized by Category and Ordered by Log Ratio	42
2.7	Concordance Lines for *Performing*	43
2.8	Collocates of Teacher and Teachers in the ATC, Organized by Category and Ordered by MI	46
2.9	Concordance Lines for *New Teachers*	47
2.10	Concordance Lines for *Male* as a Collocate of *Teachers*	48
2.11	Top Fifteen Collocates of Male and Female in the ATC, Ordered by MI	48
2.12	Concordance Lines for *Models* as a Collocate of *Male*	48
2.13	Concordance Lines for *Models* as a Collocate of *Female*	49
2.14	Concordance Lines for *Teacher* as a Collocate of *Female*	50
2.15	Concordance Lines for *Public* as a Collocate of *Teachers*	51
2.16	Concordance Lines for *Quality* as a Collocate of *Teacher*/s	52
2.17	Concordance Lines for *Good* as a Collocate of *Teacher*/s	53
2.18	Concordance Lines for *Best* as a Collocate of *Teachers*	54
2.19	Concordance Lines for *Every* as a Collocate of *Teacher*	55
2.20	Concordance Lines for *Need* as a Collocate of *Teachers*	55
2.21	Concordance Lines for *Should* as a Collocate of *Teachers*	56
3.1	'Lockwords' in the Australian Teacher Corpus (Compared to NOW-AU), Ordered Alphabetically	61
3.2	Keywords in the ATC, Organized by Category and Ordered by Log Ratio, Diachronic Keywords in Bold	62
3.3	Keywords in the ATC: Changing Patterns over Time	63

3.4	Top Ten Collocates of *Performing* in the 1996, 2007 and 2019 Sub-corpora, Ordered by MI	65
3.5	Unique Keywords by Year (with Associated Events Noted)	70
3.6	Concordance Lines for *Gender* from the 2016 Sub-corpus	74
3.7	Concordance Lines for *Marriage* from the 2017 Sub-corpus	75
3.8	Concordance Lines for *Gay* from the 2018 Sub-corpus	76
3.9	Concordance Lines for *Faith* from the 2018 Sub-corpus	77
3.10	Diachronic Keywords by Year	78
3.11	Consistent Collocates of *Teacher* and *Teachers*, Ordered Alphabetically	81
3.12	Diachronic Collocates of *Teacher* (Top Ten per Year)	83
3.13	Diachronic Collocates of *Teachers* (Top Ten per Year)	84
4.1	Keywords for Newspaper Sub-corpora within the ATC, Ordered According to Log Ratio	89
4.2	Concordance Lines for *Controversial* in the *West Australian* Sub-corpus	93
4.3	Top Twenty Collocates for *Outcomes-Based* in the *West Australian*, Ordered by MI	93
4.4	Concordance Lines for *Instruction* in *The Australian* Sub-corpus	95
4.5	Concordance Lines for *Autonomy* in the *Australian Financial Review* Sub-corpus	99
4.6	Top Twenty-Five Collocates of *Teacher/s*, Organized by Newspaper Sub-corpora and Ordered by MI	100
4.7	Collocates Relating to Teacher Professionalism for Both *Teacher* and *Teachers*	102
4.8	Collocates Relating to Teacher Industrialism for Both *Teacher* and *Teachers*	103
4.9	Top Five Prototypical Texts for Each Newspaper Sub-corpus	106
4.10	Problem Frames in Use in the Prototypical Texts	116
5.1	Most Frequent Two- and Three-Word Clusters Including *Quality*	124
5.2	Five Most Frequent Word Clusters Including *Quality* in Each Annual Sub-corpus	125
5.3	Consistent Collocates of *Quality*, Ordered Alphabetically	127
5.4	Concordance Lines for *Teacher* as a Collocate of *Quality*	128
5.5	Concordance Lines for *Teaching* as a Collocate of *Quality*	128
5.6	Concordance Lines for *High* as a Collocate of *Quality*	129
5.7	Concordance Lines for *Poor* as a Collocate of *Quality*	129
5.8	Concordance Lines for *Improve* as a Collocate of *Quality*	130

5.9	Concordance Lines for *Ensure* as a Collocate of *Quality*	130
5.10	Concordance Lines for *Provide* as a Collocate of *Quality*	131
5.11	Concordance Lines for *Our* as a Collocate of *Quality*	131
5.12	*Quality of ...* in Prototypical Texts	132
6.1	Newspapers and Articles in the International Corpus	144
6.2	Top Fifty Keywords for Each International Sub-corpus, Organized by Thematic Group, Ordered by Log Ratio	146
6.3	Concordance Lines for *Disciplinary* in the NZ Sub-corpus	150
6.4	Concordance Lines for *Inappropriate* in the NZ Sub-corpus	151
6.5	Top Twenty Collocates of *Teacher* and *Teachers*, Organized by Country Sub-corpus and Ordered by MI	153
6.6	Consistent Collocates of *Teacher* and *Teachers*, Organized Alphabetically	154
6.7	Concordance Lines for *Former* as a Collocate of *Teacher*	155
6.8	Concordance Lines for *Every* as a Collocate of *Teacher*	156
6.9	Concordance Lines for *One* as a Collocate of *Teacher*	156
6.10	Concordance Lines for *Training* as a Collocate of *Teacher*	157
6.11	Concordance Lines for *Support* as a Collocate of *Teachers*	158
6.12	Concordance Lines for *Unions* as a Collocate of *Teachers*	159
6.13	Unique Collocates of *Teacher* and *Teachers*, Organized by Country Sub-corpus and Ordered by MI	160
6.14	Concordance Lines for *Evaluations* in the US Sub-corpus	161
6.15	Consistent Collocates of *Quality*, Ordered Alphabetically	162
6.16	Unique Collocates of *Quality*, Organized by Country Sub-corpus and Ordered by MI	163

Foreword

Nicole Mockler's *Constructing Teacher Identities: How the Print Media Define and Represent Teachers and Their Work* is predicated on the valid assumption that how the print media represent teachers and their work is an important factor in societal views of and regard for the teaching profession. It is also a factor in attracting clever young people to the profession and ensuring the longevity of teacher careers or otherwise on both counts, in addition to more material factors such as salary, working conditions and career opportunities. Additionally, of course, and as she rightly notes, everyone has been to school and so almost deems themselves as experts on teachers, their work and also on schooling. This situation is different from that of other professions.

Media constructions of teachers and their work are also situated against particular socio-political and cultural-discursive contexts, which continue to change and morph. Think here, for example, of the impact of Covid and remote teaching of students at home and the seeming respect this has built in some media contexts for teachers and acknowledgement of the demanding complexity of their work. As another example: at the time of writing this foreword there has been much media coverage in the *Sydney Morning Herald* of a teacher shortage in New South Wales and a high incidence of out-of-field teaching. The New South Wales Teachers' Federation, the union representing teachers, has played an important role in precipitating that coverage so as to strengthen political pressure on the New South Wales government.

Most teachers and educational researchers generally have a feeling about this representation work of the media and its effects. Most often teachers have a sense of media teacher bashing, a feeling partially confirmed by Mockler's analysis. Certainly, in the political edge to print media representations of teachers, she notes that teachers are often the collateral damage in such negative reporting. There are also possibly different representations across different types of newspapers. For example, local newspapers in country towns often present more positive views of teachers and their work than do national and capital city-based, more mass circulation papers. Many such local papers in Australia, though, have closed down across the recent past.

What Mockler does and does so well in this book is draw upon a huge empirical database, notably sixty-five thousand print media articles in the Australian print media across the period from 1996 through to 2020. She offers an exceedingly thorough and systematic analysis of this purpose-built corpus (Australian Teacher Corpus – ATC), using corpus-linguistics, quantitative analysis and also some forensic and granular qualitative analyses. Mockler provides impeccable quantitative analysis, combined with insightful qualitative analyses. While the focus is on Australian media representations of teachers, she also provides some comparative analyses of such media representations in other Anglophone nations: the UK, the United States, Canada and New Zealand (see Chapter 6). Given Bourdieu's argument that there is a 'circular circulation' across media forms of articles/stories and also across nations in the context of some global media ownership, this comparative analysis is most insightful. While there is some global flow of media stories and types of stories, mediascapes, there are still important national and local elements to print media coverage and ownership. Today, Bourdieu's concept of circular circulation of media stories applies even more strongly across media types, from print media to social media, television and radio and in multiple directions across these entities, as well as across the globe.

Mockler makes the valid point that print media archives are perhaps less transient than the archival records of some of these other types of media; social media for example. She also makes the important point that while sales of print media might be in decline and the influence of social media rising, print media still help shape the work of politicians and public policy, as well as playing into popular opinion formation. This drop in sales and the emergence of online versions of newspapers, as well as newspapers that are only online such as the *Guardian Australia,* have seen print media sometimes referred to as legacy media.

Certain voices are heard in print media, while in comparison a wider range of voices is heard on social media, even though the aspired for democratic impulse of social media has not eventuated. Mockler's analysis shows that the voices of politicians and policy makers tend to dominate print media coverage of teachers. She also argues further analysis is required of this voice issue.

Importantly, the twenty-five-year time frame of the database and analyses enable Mockler to provide an empirically-informed account of changes in the representations of teachers over time. For example, the influential media trope of teacher quality and changing narratives about it over time.

As far as I am aware, this is the most extensive study of media representations of teachers and their work and as such provides an important baseline for future research of multiple kinds. While the focus is mainly Australian print media representations, the methodology, the analytical framework utilized and the insights have broader applicability, while also setting the stage for future comparative analyses. This is an exemplary research on media representations of teachers in its empirical base, its theoretical framing (practice architectures, media framing, linguistic devices for creating newsworthiness) and its methodology, that is, corpus-assisted discourse analysis. On the latter, Mockler traverses corpus analytic approaches in the social sciences, including methods for corpus analysis (see Chapter 2).

I strongly commend Nicole Mockler on the transparency of the methodology that framed the study and her openness to outlining the decisions she made at various points of the analysis of the Australian Teacher Corpus, of necessity focusing on some things and neglecting others. This is an ideal example of the difference between good quality social science research and a stage play, an opera or film, say; while the former makes public and transparent its processes of data collection and analysis, warts and all, the latter seek to hide as far as possible the tricks involved in their representations of reality, eschewing the making public of such strategies. Research is always and at all times, partial; selections and decisions have to be made. Furthermore, transparency is central to the trustworthiness of research. Mockler's research and her book are exemplary in this way: transparent and thus trustworthy, and all the better for acknowledging the selective decisions made and shortcomings of the research. Chapter 7 is very good on these very points. As Mockler honestly notes: she has provided *an* account of the Australian Teacher Corpus, but a justifiable one. She also concedes some weaknesses in the corpus (duplications, absences).

The analyses proffered by this book call out for comparative analyses of print media representations of teachers in different national and subnational contexts. They also demand comparative analysis of social media and representations of teachers and their work (cf. Baroutsis and Lingard 2019) and the processes of 'deep mediatization' associated with social media (Hepp 2019). Research on print media and its impact on education policy, for example, has utilized the concept of mediatization, the ways the logics of practice of the journalist field affect the policy production field, education policy as media release. Mockler's analysis demonstrates how mediatized representations of teachers play into and help frame societal and public views of teachers, interwoven with changing sociopolitical contexts and dominant cultural discourses.

Foreword xv

Recent research on mediatization and the impact of social media talks of 'deep mediatization' (Hepp 2019), whereby involvement in social media includes surveillance simultaneously with the expression of multiple voices on politics and policy, ideas captured in talk of 'surveillance capitalism' (Zuboff 2019) and 'data colonisation' (Couldry and Mejias 2019). Mockler's account demands a similar comparative analysis of the social mediatization of representations of the teaching profession and the work of teachers. The complementarity of legacy and social media and the melange of their effects also calls out for further research. There is also a need for analysis of online news media. Related, as she points out, is a call for analysis of multimodal representations of teachers in the media, including images and additionally research on broadcast coverage. I would also like to see an analysis of the Australian Teacher Corpus regarding the policy effects of these media representations.

What then are the major 'findings' of Mockler's research? The first is the sheer volume/numbers of articles published in the twenty-five-year time frame about teachers and their work. There are many more articles about teachers than about other professions. The amount of coverage granted to matters of schooling teachers and their work is also variable across time. So, the analysis demonstrates how there was a real upsurge in coverage during the federal governments of Gillard and Rudd (2007–13), the period of the so-called 'education revolution' (see Savage 2021; Reid 2019). Mockler notes as well the political edge to stories about teachers with the profession often becoming the collateral damage from particular, often negative media coverage. She suggests these findings are similar to media representation of teachers in the other Anglophone nations she deals with. The exception – the Australian idiosyncrasy – is the heavy focus in the Australian print media on teacher quality and teacher education in the latter half of the twenty-five years which are the time frame for her analysis. Much of the coverage is negative in relation to teacher quality and teacher shortages. This coverage of these topics is greatest, she points out, in the two national papers, Murdoch's *The Australian* and Nine Media's *Australian Financial Review*. There is a logic here in that the federal or national government funds and sets policy for universities where teacher education occurs and thus teacher education becomes a matter of national concern for national newspapers. Yet she notes that further analysis of the Australian Teacher Corpus in relation to teacher education is required. The analysis shows a focus on early career teachers across the time frame of the research, but with a changing emphasis from teacher shortages to teacher quality in relation to recruitment to the profession. Mockler also rightly documents the concentration of media ownership in Australia, which carries implications for how teachers are represented in these papers and their political and policy effects. Maybe future comparative research might deal with nations with highly concentrated media ownership such as Australia and with nations where this is less so.

This is a significant book on print media representations of teachers in Australia, 1996–2020. It adds to the quite small body of published books on cognate topics, for example, Baroutsis, Riddle and Thomson's (2019) edited collection, *Education Research and the Media*, David Berliner and Bruce Biddle's (1996) much older US-focused, *The Manufactured Crisis*, Michelle Stack's (2016) higher education-focused, *Global University Rankings and the Mediatization of Higher Education* and Ilana Synder's (2008), *The Literacy Wars: Why Teaching Children to Read and Write Is a Battleground in Australia*. The book also supplements the many journal articles on her topic, including several by Mockler herself.

Mockler's book, however, is of a different order to these books and journal articles with its very large database and its detailed quantitative and qualitative analyses. Her analysis differs from these worthy texts in its systematicity, its scope and scale and in its focus on media representations of teachers. The analyses proffered are insightful and establish a significant baseline for much further research. While Mockler rightly eschews suggestions that media logics (cf. 'media mentalities', Baroutsis, 2019) of the representations of teachers have a simple, direct and linear impact on the public imaginary of teachers and their work, her account certainly demonstrates that these representations are significant in constituting the public imaginary about teachers and schooling. These representations have political effects with print media remaining significant for both politicians and policy makers.

Nicole Mockler's exemplary, empirically and theoretically informed account will be of interest to those researching the media, media representations of teachers, those interested in corpus analysis, but there ought to be broader interest amongst those who work for enhancing the status and the standing of teachers, including teacher unions, teacher professional associations, teacher educators, educational researchers and parent groups. Teachers are central to our futures – touch the future, teach – and media representations are one contributing factor relating to how we might progressively conceive of teachers and work for such futures where all young people have access to quality schooling. Mockler also provides ample and compelling evidence for how we might strategize to challenge unhelpful, dishonest and negative representations of teachers and their work towards enhancing progressive possibilities for teachers, teaching and schooling.

Professor Bob Lingard
Institute for Learning Sciences and Teacher Education
Australian Catholic University
and Emeritus Professor
The University of Queensland

Acknowledgements

This book has been a long time coming and I have been the beneficiary of a great deal of generous support along the way.

I was awarded a University of Sydney Research Accelerator (SOAR) Fellowship for 2018–19, and it was during this time that this research was conceptualized and begun. Without this support it is hard to imagine designing and executing such an ambitious project as a sole researcher, and I am deeply grateful to the university for this opportunity.

Professor Monika Bednarek of the Department of Linguistics at the University of Sydney is owed a special 'thank you'. I am greatly indebted to her for being so open to a random and probably quite audacious request from a then-unknown education academic to audit her corpus linguistics course some years ago. Monika is an outstanding teacher and scholar, and has not only shared her knowledge and exacting expertise with me but also generously introduced me to her colleagues and networks in Australia and elsewhere. I am deeply appreciative of her warm encouragement of this project since the beginning, and of her friendship over the years.

In 2018, I attended the Lancaster Corpus Linguistics Summer School, which supported my development in corpus-assisted methods at a critical time in the development of this research. There I was fortunate to meet Professor Tony McEnery, who generously encouraged this non-linguist to pursue what was at the time a nascent idea for a large-scale project.

Dr Christopher Norton of the University of Leeds helped me to build the first iteration of the Australian Teacher Corpus by creating a bespoke python script, and was patiently open to my many requests for tweaks along the way.

Harris Manchester College at the University of Oxford provided a vibrant scholarly community and a safe haven for writing in Michaelmas Term of the 2019–20 academic year. Thanks are due to Reverend Professor Jane Shaw, College Principal, and Dr Sarah Ogilvie, Senior Research Fellow in Linguistics, for their warm welcome in 2019 and their ongoing friendship and support. Thanks are also due to Professors Diane Mayer and Jo-Anne Baird and colleagues within the Department of Education at Oxford, who hosted me as visiting scholar in 2019.

Acknowledgements xix

My colleagues in the Sydney School of Education and Social Work at the University of Sydney have supported this project in many ways. My 'Friday Writing Group' colleagues, Dr Kathryn Bartimote, Dr Nikki Brunker, Associate Professor Cathie Burgess, Associate Professor Ilektra Spandagou and Dr Matthew Thomas have provided constructive and detailed feedback on chapters in development. Professor Kalervo Gulson and Drs Remy Low and Vic Rawlings have additionally provided ongoing moral support and encouragement, as has my long-term partner-in-crime, Professor Susan Groundwater-Smith.

Emeritus Professor Barbara Kamler is the writing mentor every academic needs. She has contributed greatly to this book through a carefully calibrated combination of 'tough love', sharp blue pencil and a persistent (but essential) 'so what?' I am not sure that there will be enough 'outrage and passion' in this final version to keep her happy, and there are definitely more concordance tables than she would have liked, but I hope that in the end she will see the mark she has made on this work.

My colleagues and friends Professor Helen Proctor and Dr Meghan Stacey have read and provided feedback on every word of this manuscript, and I fear I have racked up a debt to them that would take several lifetimes to acquit. They have both provided the perfect balance of 'love your work but hate this paragraph', and never once asked why I was torturing them with my long drafty sentences.

The two anonymous reviewers of the manuscript engaged carefully and thoughtfully with the text and provided constructive feedback that enabled me to sharpen the manuscript ahead of publication, and I am greatly indebted to them for their time and effort.

Many thanks to Professor Bob Lingard, who has long been a generous mentor and supporter of my work, for his contribution in writing the foreword. I have also been the beneficiary of many long and interesting conversations about education with senior scholars and mentors Professors John Furlong, Stephen Kemmis, Ian Menter and the late Geoff Whitty over the years, and I thank all of them for their time and support.

Since the very beginning of my career in education, I've been fortunate to have been led by women who were and are powerful role models and mentors as outstanding educators, leaders and researchers, and this work is in part a reflection of their active encouragement to me to 'do my thing'. They include Barbara Stone, Leoni Degenhardt and Professors Judyth Sachs, Jenny Gore, Diane Mayer and Deb Hayes, and their support over the years has enriched my work.

xx *Acknowledgements*

My lifelong teaching friends continue to keep me grounded, generously affirm that my work is important beyond the academy, and also have been known to give me a reality check from the trenches when needed. They include Serena Vecchiet, and the 'SecEd Gals' of the University of Sydney Class of 1991: Alyssa Roach, Amanda Johnstone, Ariana Ryan, Cath Donnelly, Cathy Player, Heather Beddie, Kim Elith, Melanie Van Der Meer and Tracy MacMillan, still some of the most outstanding teachers I know. They also include Sharon Brien and Joanne Hack, passionate educators and frequent and fearless interlocutors both, who keep me honest.

Finally, Elenie Poulos has been a source of inspiration and support for almost as many years as are covered in the Australian Teacher Corpus. In this project, and all those that have come before it, her belief in me and her constant encouragement to keep going have made everything possible. Thank you.

1

Words Matter

I've been a 'news hound' for most of my life. I remember as a child spending school holidays at my grandparents' house, examining the front page of the newspapers that arrived daily – there were four daily newspapers in Sydney at the time – wondering how it was that the same event could raise such completely different outrage in the three different papers. Around the same time I was fascinated by *Behind the News*, the long-running Australian public television show that aims to give children insight into how news stories are created. For a while in my teens I toyed with the idea of becoming a journalist, but the lure of a seemingly 'safe' profession like teaching was strong for a first-in-family university student, made safer by the time I finished my degree in the recession of the early 1990s. I've remained an avid newspaper reader, however, and the advent of the internet, where everything from the *New York Times* and *Washington Post* to the *Daily Mail* is available in real time, has only fed the addiction.

In my years as a school teacher, I became interested in how my profession was characterized in the media, and this was something I took up in my doctoral research (Mockler 2008), examining how a selection of prominent Australian education journalists represented teachers and their work. In the years since my doctorate I have pursued this interest, initially using news framing analysis to explore constructions of education and teachers in small collections of texts (e.g. Mockler 2013, 2014, 2016), and more recently employing corpus-assisted methods to examine patterns and chart shifting constructions over time on a larger scale (e.g. Mockler 2020a, 2020b; Mockler and Groundwater-Smith 2018). My interest in the discursive construction of teachers in the print media – and the way in which these representations form part of the cultural-discursive 'arrangements' of teachers' work (Kemmis et al. 2014) eventually brought me to the research that is the subject of this book.

In *The Archaeology of Knowledge*, Foucault wrote of the complex relationship between words and discourses, arguing that while discourses are comprised of 'signs', they are ultimately more than can be rendered or represented in words:

> 'Words and things' is the entirely serious title of a problem; it is the ironic title of a work that modifies its own form, displaces its own data, and reveals, at the end of the day, a quite different task. A task that consists of not – of no longer – treating discourses as groups of signs (signifying elements referring to contents or representations) but as practices that systematically form the objects of which they speak. (1972: 49)

The starting point for this book is thus the idea that the way we speak in the public space about things that matter to our society, like education, has implications for those things, and consequently, for society as a whole. While they do not tell the whole story, for discourses are more than words, words are nevertheless important. Of all public policy areas, education is a particularly fertile space for public discussion as it provides a rare common experience that most of us share. The vast majority of people alive today within any Western society went to school themselves, and send or have at some point sent their children to school. Consequently, most of us have a first-hand understanding of school, for better or worse. The policy areas of health or immigration, for example, do not hold such extended connections experienced by virtually all citizens in the same way as education (although since early 2020 the area of health has taken on renewed interest due to the Covid-19 pandemic). Consequently, politicians in Western democracies often use education and education policy as touchstones for building connection with members of their electorates and communities, and both this and the high level of community knowledge of and interest in education translates into an abundance of media coverage, particularly in the print media.

Much of this media coverage focuses on teachers, the human faces of education and schooling, and understandably so. To start with, the 'human interest' factor is high: most of us can name, from our own experience, a good and/or not-so-good teacher who made an impact on us as a young person. Second, collectively and individually, teachers are charged with the responsibility of supporting the next generation academically and socially, and thus their practices – most often understood through the lens of common sense – are a matter of interest more broadly. Third, the growth of what sociologist of education Marianne Larsen has called 'the discourse of teacher centrality', 'one of the most revered and abiding cultural myths associated with education: the assumption that the key to educational success lies with the teacher' (2010: 208) is also responsible. Teachers are increasingly positioned as both saviours and demons within this discourse, answerable for aspects of education well beyond their sphere of influence, and for this reason also, media coverage of education-related issues often places teachers front and centre.

In early 2020, the issue of 'teacher quality', a media 'go to' for some years now (Mockler 2020b), once again became a fixation of both capital city daily newspapers in my home state of New South Wales (NSW). This followed the release of a NSW parliamentary report substantially authored by Mark Latham, then a recently elected MP from far-right nationalist party Pauline Hanson's One Nation. The report advocated the introduction of a school inspectorate to undertake 'regular inspections of classroom practices, teacher quality and school management' (NSW Legislative Council Portfolio Committee No. 3 – Education 2020: viii), and has given rise to media commentary such as this, from a former Liberal (conservative) Party staffer turned journalist:

> A new NSW Parliamentary report found last week our schools are failing. It's not that our schools are under-staffed or under-funded or under-equipped. Indeed, there have never been more teachers, more funding and better equipment yet despite the record billions being thrown at the problem, the reality is that Australia is going backwards on almost every measure against our international competitors.
>
> And it [sic] hardly surprising when you consider who is teaching our children.
>
> …
>
> Yet across most of Australia, poor principals and mediocre teachers can't be removed; we subsidize comparative failure, not success; and we persist with teaching methods that we know don't work; or at least don't work for all students, like whole-word language training rather than phonics, and child centred learning rather than teaching that's driven by a teacher with a sound grasp of the fundamentals.
>
> Is it any wonder that Labor thinks it can make un-costed climate policies when our kids are being told that nothing is more important than cutting emissions to save the planet. Academically deficient teachers lead to inadequately educated young adults and ultimately even poorer decision making in government. (Credlin 2020)

The way we discuss teachers and teaching in the public space shapes, over time, the way we come to regard teachers, the beliefs and assumptions we hold about who they are, what they do and why they do it. Beyond our own school experience, the print media makes a most significant contribution to our broad social understanding of schooling and teachers' work (Mills and Keddie 2010). And consequently, the way teachers and schools are represented in the print media matters greatly to the way societies understand and value (or otherwise) teachers. This has flow-on effects to the way teachers understand their role and their importance to society, the way potential teachers feel about becoming a teacher, and the way current teachers feel about remaining in the classroom.

The aim of this book is to explore these representations over time in a very wide-ranging way, using the Australian print media as a case-in-point. It reports on research based on the Australian Teacher Corpus (ATC), a collection of over sixty-five thousand print media articles, purpose built for this research, which employs techniques of corpus-assisted discourse analysis. The book aims to develop a comprehensive picture of representations of teachers in the Australian print media over the past quarter-century and to contrast these with media representations of teachers in other Anglophone countries, namely the UK, United States, Canada and New Zealand.

This introductory chapter locates the research conceptually and methodologically. First, it provides an overview of the field of research on media discourses of education, both in Australia and elsewhere. Here it focuses on the particular themes taken up in this research, the scope of the research, both temporal and geographical, and the conceptual and methodological approaches taken. It seeks to build a case through this discussion for research that takes a 'wide-angled' longitudinal or diachronic view with a particular focus on print media.

Second, it introduces three sets of conceptual and methodological tools used as touchstones and resources in the book. The theory of practice architectures (Kemmis and Grootenboer 2008), which provides a conceptual frame for thinking about the relationship between the print media and teachers' work and for understanding the relationship between discourse and practice, is the first of these. In introducing the theory of practice architectures here, I consider briefly how media coverage contributes (both directly and indirectly) to the cultural-discursive, material-economic and social-political arrangements that frame and govern teachers' work, using this to inform a case for research of this scope and scale.

This discussion is followed by a meso-level discussion of two other tools used within the book. One is that of media framing, and here I draw on the seminal work of scholars such as Goffman (1974) and Gamson and Modigliani (1987, 1989) along with more recent work such as that of Altheide (2013) and Scheufele and Scheufele (2013) to explore the role of language in the framing and conveying of meaning within the media. Next, the concept of 'news values', and the creation of 'newsworthiness' by media organizations, is introduced, and here I draw especially on the work of Bednarek and Caple (e.g. 2012b, 2014, 2017). While the book aims to provide neither a framing analysis nor a discursive news values analysis (Bednarek and Caple 2017), I use both of these conceptual tools at different points in the discussion in Chapters 2 to 6.

Finally, turning to method, and mindful that the approach taken here may be very new to some readers, the concept of corpus-assisted discourse analysis is introduced, via a concise overview of corpus linguistic methods, and a brief explanation of each of the four key techniques used in the analysis presented. The chapter then concludes with an outline of the remainder of the book.

Understanding media discourses of education as a research problem

It seems somewhat obvious to say that the landscape of the media is currently in flux. In an age where social media has seen some of the power of 'traditional media' displaced (De Waal and Schoenbach 2010) and where the print media, and in particular newspapers, have seen their readership decline (Thurman and Fletcher 2019), one could be forgiven for asking why a book such as this would focus on representations in newspapers.

Part of the answer to this question lies in the role that newspapers play in the shaping of both public policy (Lidberg 2019) and popular opinion (Fahey, Weissert and Uttermark 2018). For example, broadsheet newspapers such as *The Australian* are understood to continue to play an important role in influencing politicians and policymakers, despite their relatively small and decreasing readership (Waller and McCallum 2016). Furthermore, the print media plays a part in influencing and informing other parts of the news media, including radio, television and social media: while this relationship is far from unidirectional, the influence of newspapers in this regard remains well established (Conboy and Eldridge 2017). Finally, transcripts and archives notwithstanding, the print media provides a more permanent and less transient record of both media attention and public discourse than other forms of media, as well as an accessible, searchable record.

Research on education and the media

While representations of education and teachers in popular culture, such as films, television and novels, have been the subject of a number of books over the past thirty years (Dalton and Linder 2019; Fisher, Harris and Jarvis 2008; Weber and Mitchell 1995) representations in newspapers and other news and print media have not been investigated in the same sustained manner. A small but growing field of scholarship has emerged, however, comprising studies that explore the relationship between education and the news media. This work, which usually focuses on small groups of print or other media texts, has explored different aspects of education, schooling and teachers' work as reflected in the media and has utilized an array of tools including critical discourse analysis, media framing analysis and, in recent years, corpus-assisted analysis and social network analysis. The field has also explored the complex interplay between media discourses and the shaping of education policy in a range of different national contexts including Australia, the UK and the United States. The emergence and widespread adoption over the past decade or so of social media, and the engagement of both educators and the general public on social media on topics related to schooling, teaching and education has brought about a shift in this relationship between media discourses and public policy. By way of situating the research reported in this book, here I will offer a brief overview of this field as it stands today. This account of the field is not intended to be a comprehensive mapping of research on education and the media – for this see, for example, Baroutsis (2019a) and Mockler (2019b) – but rather a snapshot of the current field that identifies the intended contribution of this book.

Much of the field focuses on the representation of teachers, schooling and education in mainstream media texts, most usually print media. Often, critical discourse or other forms of analysis are used to identify dominant 'narratives' (Thomson et al. 2003), 'propositions' (Shine 2015a) or 'identities' (Alhamdan et al.) at work in a selected group of media texts, usually bounded temporally, geographically and sometimes by media outlet. An example of this is Shine and O'Donoghue's (2013b) examination of representations of teachers in reporting on standardized testing in one Australian newspaper between 1997 and 2001, in which they identify 5 propositions in 106 media texts. These are: 'teachers and schools are to blame for declining educational standards'; 'teachers resist accountability measures aimed at improving educational standards because they fear being compared'; 'teachers are under pressure and testing aimed at improving educational standards increases that pressure'; 'teachers will undermine the testing process if testing is enforced' and 'teachers legitimate their opposition to standardized testing by claiming that it has no educational value' (Shine and O'Donoghue 2013b: 390–3). Punakallio and Dervin's (2015) exploration of media representations of Finnish teachers via an exploration of eighty-one front-page headlines in tabloid newspaper *Ilta-Sanomat* from 2000 to 2013 identified two 'interpretive repertoires' within the texts, 'the traditional teacher' and 'the vulnerable teacher'; and two key themes: violence and threats against teachers and teacher immorality. Similarly, Thomson et al.'s (2003) study, based on analysis of forty-three randomly sampled articles from the US print media between 1999 and 2002 about the US principal shortage identified a dichotomy at work within the texts, with principals depicted either as overworked, underpaid and undervalued or as the 'saviour-principal'.

These studies, as examples of those that focus on representations of teachers in the print media, highlight that teachers have often been represented in the media, across geographical boundaries and over time, in ways that play to common sense understandings of 'good' and 'bad' teachers. These images of teachers perhaps resonate with readers of newspapers, invoking memories of their own school days. They also tend to connect with dominant images of teachers in popular culture, from *The Simpsons*' Mrs Krabappel to Mr Keating of *Dead Poets' Society*. Such representations inform what Weber and Mitchell (1995; Weber 2006) refer to as the 'cumulative cultural text of "teacher"'.

Further to those studies that focus specifically on representations of teachers, a group of studies addresses media representations of education more generally, including schooling and other aspects of education systems. MacMillan's (2002) exploration of front-page news stories about education in the British tabloid press in 1998 highlighted the mobilization of particular themes and narratives of 'falling standards' and 'moral decline', which 'regularly form the basis for discussions in the press about who is to be held responsible for a decline in standards, not only within education, but, more generally, within society as a whole' (MacMillan 2002: 28). Cohen's well-cited study (2010) examined 170 news articles from the *Chicago Tribune* from 2006 and 2007, and identified dominant counter discourses of accountability and caring within these texts. Rönnberg, Lindgren and Segerholm's (2013) exploration of representations of Swedish school inspection in eighty articles from Swedish newspapers from 2003 to 2010 identified four metaphors of inspectorate as *watchdog, lapdog, mad dog* and *guide dog* at work in the texts. In Australia, Baroutsis (2016) used both interviews with teachers and media articles to explore the framing of 'school performance', identifying three dominant frames that rank performance, decontextualize performance and residualize public schools.

With the growing importance of international and national standardized testing over the past two decades, including the Organisation for Economic Co-operation and Development's (OECD's) Programme for International

Student Assessment (PISA), and the Trends in International Mathematics and Science Study (TIMSS) and Progress in International Reading Literacy Study (PIRLS), both run by the International Association for the Evaluation of Educational Achievement (IEA), representations of these programmes in the media have become a research focus. Stack's (2006, 2007) work in Canada, Mons and Pons's (2009) in France, Takayama's (2008, 2010) in Japan, Yemini and Gordon's (2017) in Israel and Baroutsis and Lingard's (2017) in Australia are all examples of this emerging focus. Waldow, Takayama and Sung have also undertaken comparative work in Australia, Germany and South Korea (Takayama, Waldow and Sung 2013; Waldow, Takayama and Sung 2014). Much of this work focuses not only on representations of the testing programmes themselves but also on the implied quality of the local school system, often pointing to manifestations of 'PISA panic' (Alexander 2012) in the media.

Indeed, looking broadly at work on representations of education in news media discourses, the deployment of panic and crisis emerges strongly. In particular, the two crises of 'teacher quality' (Alhamdan et al. 2014; Keogh and Garrick 2011; Mockler 2014; Shine 2015b; Shine and O'Donoghue 2013b; Ulmer 2016) and of ever-diminishing educational standards (Baroutsis 2016; Blackmore and Thorpe 2003; Cabalin 2015; McLeod 1989; Mockler 2016; Pettigrew and MacLure 1997; Stack 2007; Takayama 2010; Thomas 2003; Warmington and Murphy 2004) are found to dominate news coverage of education. Broadly, this research understands crises of education to play a central role in shaping media representations across time and location, and consequently in shaping public discourses of education, an example of what David Altheide (1997) has conceptualized as 'the problem frame'.

Perspectives on media influence – on the general public, on teachers, on policy – are less common in the research literature. In a relatively early but influential work, Wallace (1993) explored the news reporting of an evaluation report on the implementation of child-centred reforms emanating from the Plowden report in the UK. Based on his examination of newspaper articles, TV programmes and interviews, Wallace argues that 'the media play a supporting role in the conduct of this debate [around progressive education] within the public arena through the articulation of particular myths, and by bringing opposing myths into derision' (1993: 334). In Australia a decade later, Blackmore and Thorpe (2003) explored the role of the print media in mediating education policy in Victoria, at a time of radical reform. Their interviews with school principals whose schools had been the subject of media reports, content analysis of newspaper articles, interviews with editors and journalists, focus group interviews with public school teachers and interviews with principals and educational researchers who provided comment to the media generated evidence for the practical impact of media discourses on teachers' and principals' work. Their work also highlighted the complexity of the production of media discourses around education and the contested role of journalists and media outlets in this production.

Turning to the role of the print media in actively shaping public policy, McLeod (1989) and subsequently Gill (1994) explored both the reporting and shaping of curriculum change in Victoria in the late 1980s, with particular attention to the portrayal of different voices in the media, construed as 'a cautionary tale about the role the media may choose to play in shaping issues of public importance' (Gill 1994: 111). Lingard and Rawolle (2004) have theorized this shaping of issues of public importance using Bourdieu's tools of field, habitus and logics of practice (1990) arguing that *cross field effects* of the logics of practice of journalism have given rise to the mediatization of education policy. Rawolle (2010) has argued for the utility of the notion of mediatization in terms of practice and practice effects, as a methodological and theoretical resource, arguing that mediatization 'provides a way to highlight how partial media debates over education policy are and the potential effects that this may have on democratic decision making' (Rawolle 2010: 36). Phelan and Salter (2019) work with a similar conceptual frame, utilizing field theory to explore the relationship between journalistic *habitus*, logics of practice and conceptualizations of public education, while Baroutsis (2019b) uses the concepts of media logic and mediatization to explore the practices – both institutional and journalistic – that give rise to particular manifestations of education reporting. Elsewhere, Lingard has reflected on the media attention around the release of the My School website[1] in January 2010 suggesting that the government had effectively used the density of media coverage to 'circumvent teacher union opposition to the publication of the National Assessment Program – Literacy and Numeracy (NAPLAN) data, in effect working a different politics in the information age' (2010: 130).

The way in which education policy is framed by the media is the focus of a small number of studies. This includes Tamir and Davison's (2011) work, which takes a historical perspective, analysing media coverage of New Jersey education policy debates in 1985, and exploring the means by which economic and political elites might be seen to benefit from and in turn shape the reporting of education

---

[1] myschool.edu.au is an Australian Curriculum, Assessment and Reporting Authority website, which houses and makes publicly available comparative information about Australian primary and secondary schools, including standardized test results.

policy. The role of politicians and media commentators in shaping 'spin' is the focus of Hattam, Prosser and Brady's (2009) study, which explores the interplay of 'backlash politics' and the mediatization of education policy in Australia in the 2000s. Franklin (2004) investigated the interaction of the media and political interests through news management in the UK and the influence of this in the shaping of education policy. Through a focus on a small number of media texts related to specific policy events, these studies all shed light on the means by which the print media spin, constitute and/or otherwise shape education policy.

While this field, stretching across representational work and media influence work, is an international one, with scholarship emerging from the United States (Chesky and Goldstein 2016; Cohen 2010; Ulmer 2016), the UK (MacMillan 2002; Thomson et al. 2003; Warmington and Murphy 2004), Latin America (Cabalin 2015; Robert 2012), Europe (Erss and Kalmus 2018; Punakallio and Dervin 2015; Rönnberg, Lindgren and Segerholm 2013) and the Middle East (Yemini and Gordon 2017), there is a higher concentration of research in this area emanating from Australia, and focusing on Australian texts (e.g. Blackmore and Thorpe 2003; Fenech and Wilkins 2017; Mills and Keddie 2010; Mockler 2013, 2016; Shine 2015a). This is perhaps a product of attention wrought in Australia because of the unusually high concentration of media ownership in this context (McNair et al. 2017), a topic of some discussion in Chapter 2. Additionally, a small amount of work has taken a comparative approach across two or more national contexts (Alhamdan et al. 2014; Blackmore and Thomson 2004; Mockler and Groundwater-Smith 2018; Waldow, Takayama and Sung 2014).

Other variations in the field concern methodological and analytical approaches, with a wide variety of different techniques employed. These include very close textual analysis of a small and very purposively selected collection of texts (Cabalin 2015; Keogh and Garrick 2011; Thomas 2003); news framing analysis, which typically uses a 'medium-range lens' and a larger purposive selection of articles (Baroutsis and Lingard 2017; Chesky and Goldstein 2016; Mockler 2014, 2016, 2019a); to wide-angled analysis of large groups of texts using computational or corpus-assisted techniques (Fenech and Wilkins 2017, 2019; Mockler 2020a, 2020b; Winburn, Winburn and Niemeyer 2014). While this latter approach, the central one taken in this book (accompanied by close analysis that employs the 'zoom lens') is relatively new in research on education and the media, the use of corpus-assisted approaches allows for emerging and historical patterns to be explored in context and is useful for exploring and investigating these patterns across large corpora of texts to build understanding of the construction and shape of media discourses 'writ large'.

This book aims to make a unique contribution to this field of research around education and media discourses. In taking a broad survey across all major newspapers in one national context, it seeks to explore the nuances of print media reporting on education issues in a way that a focus on a smaller selection of articles or a single outlet, no matter how significant and elegantly accomplished, cannot. In taking a longitudinal view over a twenty-five-year period, it seeks to place these nuances in context, to explore change over time and to identify both enduring and evolving concepts. Finally, in both surveying the patterns of language across the whole corpus and sub-sections of the corpus as well as taking a 'deeper dive' at some points in the analysis, through a close focus on context, it seeks to interrogate discourses surrounding teachers at both macro and micro levels. The book responds to calls from other researchers in the field to develop more sustained narratives and deeper understandings of representations of teachers in the media (Cohen 2010; Shine 2015b, 2020).

Conceptual and methodological resources

Media reporting on education and the practice architectures of teaching

Four decades ago, David Altheide and Robert Snow (1979) developed the notion of 'media logic', the term they gave to the particular form of communication used by the mass media and the processes through which information is communicated by the mass media to a given audience. The concept of media logic contends that media forms shape and guide media content, and in turn are powerful in shaping public understandings of 'the way things are'. Altheide argues that 'the institutional media forms not only help shape and guide content and numerous everyday life activities, but also that audiences-as-actors normalize these forms and use them as reality maintenance tools' (2013: 225). In relation to education, these 'reality maintenance tools' coalesce with readers' own narratives of education, schools and teachers, connecting with the 'apprenticeship of observation' (Lortie 1975) served by most members of the general public and which ensures that they work with a base narrative drawn from their own experience. Furthermore, this experience is shaped into personal narratives by the constantly emerging 'cumulative cultural text' (Weber 2006; Weber and Mitchell 1995) of education and schooling.

Beyond the ways in which media narratives impact and influence teachers, school and system leaders and policymakers on an individual and personal level, this book is interested in the interplay between the media and the 'practice architectures' of teaching on a macro or systemic level. The theory of practice architectures has been developed iteratively by Australian academic Stephen Kemmis and colleagues over the past fifteen years (see, e.g. Kemmis 2017, 2019; Kemmis and Grootenboer 2008; Kemmis et al. 2014; Mahon, Francisco and Kemmis 2017). Informed by the philosophy of Wittgenstein and building on the site-ontological work of Theodore Schatzki (2002), the theory of practice architectures holds that *practices*, comprising *bundles* of *sayings*, *doings*, and *relatings* are held in place in different sites of practice by *arrangements*. These arrangements are understood as variously *cultural-discursive*, *material-economic* and *social-political* and practices are understood as ever-enmeshed with, and enabled and constrained by these arrangements.

Cultural-discursive arrangements

are the resources (in the broad sense of the word) that prefigure and make possible particular *sayings* in a practice, for example, languages and discourses used in and about a practice (Kemmis et al. 2014). They can constrain and/or enable what it is relevant and appropriate to say (and think) in performing, describing, interpreting, or justifying the practice. (Mahon et al.2017: 9)

Material-economic arrangements

are resources (e.g., aspects of the physical environment, financial resources and funding arrangements, human and non-human entities, schedules, division of labour arrangements), that make possible, or shape the *doings* of a practice by affecting what, when, how, and by whom something can be done. (Mahon et al. 2017: 10)

Social-political arrangements

are the arrangements or resources (e.g., organisational rules; social solidarities; hierarchies; community, familial, and organisational relationships) that shape how people relate in a practice to other people and to non-human objects; they enable and constrain the *relatings* of a practice. (Mahon et al. 2017: 10)

Media discourses of education are clearly not responsible for shaping the practice architectures of teaching in their entirety – unmistakably there is much more at play on societal, systems, and local levels that impact the arrangements that frame teaching practice. However, media discourses do play an important role in shaping the cultural-discursive arrangements that enable and constrain different types of teacher identities, dispositions and practices on a metalevel. They reflect what is both 'sayable' and 'unsayable' about teachers in the public forum and consequently influence broad understandings of what it is to be a teacher, and these contribute to the cultural-discursive arrangements within which teachers' practice is enacted. Additionally, media discourses indirectly and in different ways contribute to the material-economic and social-political arrangements that frame teaching. Entman's (2003) notion of 'cascading activation' suggests that agents operating at different 'levels' (e.g. politicians, policymakers, journalists, the media frames themselves and members of the public) form 'networks of association', 'among ideas, among people, and among the communicating symbols (words and images)' (Entman 2003: 419). Ideas are thus activated and transmitted throughout the 'levels', making use of particular material-economic and social-political arrangements, through a combination of communication means, one of which is media framing.

Media framing

Media framing concerns the mechanisms via which media messages are communicated, with obvious links to the shaping of popular opinion. The concept itself was first developed by Goffman (1974), and has since been advanced by scholars including Iyengar (1990, 1991) and Entman (1993, 2003). In a much-cited passage, Entman posits that media framing is about both selection and salience:

> To frame is to *select some aspects of a perceived reality and make them more salient in a communicating text, in such a way as to promote a particular problem definition, causal interpretation, moral evaluation, and/or treatment recommendation* for the item described. (Entman 1993: 51, emphasis in original)

Gamson and Modigliani's work has been influential in advancing framing analysis, conceptualizing a frame (and its relationship to policy) as

> a central organizing idea or story line that provides meaning to an unfolding strip of events, weaving a connection among them. The frame suggests what the controversy is about, the essence of the issue. A frame generally implies a policy direction or implicit answer to what should be done about the issue. Sometimes more than one concrete policy position is consistent with a single frame. (1987: 143)

14 *Constructing Teacher Identities*

Frames make complex issues accessible to mass audiences by appealing to existing cognitive schemas (Scheufele and Tewksbury 2007). By way of exploring the constitution of frames, and thus suggesting approaches to understanding and analysing them, Gamson and Modigliani (1987, 1989) argued that frames were the central organizing ideas within what they called 'packages'. A package is constituted by the frame itself and associated 'framing devices' and 'reasoning devices' that together convey a particular perspective on an issue and suggest a congruent solution. In their words,

> a package offers a number of different condensing symbols that suggest the core frame and positions in shorthand, making it possible to display the package as a whole with a deft metaphor, catchphrase, or other symbolic device. (Gamson and Modigliani 1989: 3)

'Framing devices' include metaphors, exemplars, catchphrases, depictions and visual images, while 'reasoning devices' are defined as roots (causal analysis), consequences (effects) and appeals to principle (moral claims). Further, Gamson and Modigliani (1987, 1989) demonstrate that packages can be referenced through the use of these symbolic devices that invoke their central characteristics, holding a *signature* – a particular combination of elements that provide a 'shorthand' for the central ideas of the package. In this way, Gamson and Modigliani offer a series of conceptual tools for analysing and understanding media frames, which also function as a way of understanding the mechanisms via which media discourses shape cultural-discursive arrangements.

'Framing effects' (Druckman 2001) occur when the frames used by journalists and media outlets for example (which are in turn shaped by those used by policymakers and politicians) impact the formation of public opinion: when 'emphasis on a subset of potentially relevant considerations causes individuals to focus on these considerations when constructing their opinions' (Druckman 2001: 1042). The flows, then, from cultural-discursive arrangements directly impacted by media discourses, to material-economic and social-political ones, are complex, reflexive and iterative.

News values

The concept of news values has been around since at least the 1960s (Galtung and Ruge 1965), broadly defined as 'the criteria employed by journalists to measure and therefore "judge" the newsworthiness of events' (Richardson 2007: 91). News values 'are said to drive what makes the news' and thus support us in 'answering the question [of] why events make it into the news media' (Potts, Bednarek and Caple 2015: 150). Richardson argues:

> The precise manifestation of what these values *mean* to journalists sifting news from mere events is wholly dependent on the (imagined) preferences of the expected audience. Thus, the daily developments of the stock exchange are of significance to certain readers while daily developments in the lives of minor celebrities are thought significant to (perhaps) different readers. (Richardson 2007: 92)

Over time, a range of different lists and typologies of news values have been established by scholars of journalism, such as those offered by Bell (1991), Galtung and Ruge (1965) and Harcup and O'Neill (2001, 2017). Bednarek and Caple have observed an imprecision in the terminology used in many of these inventories, arguing that 'the kinds of concepts that researchers list as *news values* are clearly not of the same kind … and it is questionable whether they all be covered by the same term' (2012b: 40). They argue for a more precise identification of news values that includes negativity, timeliness, proximity, prominence/eliteness, consonance, impact, novelty/unexpectedness, superlativeness and personalization, and excludes 'values' identified by others that relate more to what they refer to as 'news writing objectives' or 'news cycle/ market factors' than to newsworthiness as such.

Bednarek and Caple argue that news values have largely remained the province of scholarship in journalism and media studies, and are generally underutilized in critical discourse analysis of media texts, including corpus-based or corpus-assisted approaches (Bednarek and Caple 2014; Caple and Bednarek 2013). While acknowledging that news values have material (related to the material reality of an event and its consequent potential news value), cognitive (related to the beliefs of producers and consumers of news about news values), social (related to the use of news values as selection criteria for news stories by journalists) and discursive (related to the communication of news values) dimensions, they mount a particular case for attention to the discursive construction of news values. To this end, Bednarek (2016) poses a range of linguistic devices to support such discursive analysis, along with some examples of each. These devices are presented in Table 1.1.

News values, the concept of newsworthiness and the associated linguistic resources are used at different points in this book as a touchstone for

16 *Constructing Teacher Identities*

Table 1.1 Inventory of Linguistic Devices Constructing Newsworthiness

Consonance ([stereo] typical)	References to stereotypical attributes or preconceptions Assessments of expectedness/typicality Similarity with past Explicit references to general knowledge/traditions
Eliteness (of high status or fame)	Various status markers, including: role labels; status-indicating adjectives; recognized names; descriptions of achievement/fame; use by news actors/sources of specialized/technical terminology, high-status accent or sociolect [esp. in broadcast news]
Impact (having significant effects or consequences)	Assessments of significance Representation of actual or non-actual significant/relevant consequences, including abstract, material or mental effects
Negativity/positivity (negative/positive)	References to negative/positive emotion and attitude Negative/positive evaluative Negative/positive lexis Descriptions of negative (e.g. norm-breaking) or positive behaviour
Personalization (having a personal/human face)	References to 'ordinary' people, their emotions, experiences use by news actors/sources of 'everyday' spoken language, accent, sociolect [esp. in broadcast news]
Proximity (geographically or culturally near)	Explicit references to place or nationality near the target community References to the nation/community via deictics, generic place references, adjectives Inclusive first person plural pronouns Use by news actors/sources of (geographical) accent/dialect [esp. in broadcast news] cultural references
Superlativeness (of high intensity/large scope)	Intensifiers Quantifiers Intensified lexis Metaphor and simile Comparison Repetition Lexis of growth *only/just/alone/already* + time/distance or related lexis
Timeliness (recent, ongoing, about to happen, new, current, seasonal)	Temporal references Present and present perfect Implicit time references through lexis Reference to: current trends, seasonality, change/newness
Unexpectedness (unexpected)	Evaluations of unexpectedness References to surprise/expectations Comparisons that indicate unusuality References to unusual happenings

Source: Bednarek 2016, available at www.newsvaluesanalysis.com

understanding and contextualizing representations of teachers, getting to the issue of how different news values prominent in news stories about teachers link to particular representations of teachers and teaching. Along with 'framing devices' and 'reasoning devices', they are used to explore the linguistic aspects of the discursive construction of teachers. The analysis reported in this book is neither a framing analysis nor a discursive news values analysis; however, it uses techniques drawn from both at different points in exploring and explaining aspects of the ATC. The theory of practice architectures, and particularly the contribution of media discourses of education to the cultural-discursive arrangements that frame teachers' work is a further lens through which the ATC is viewed, in attempting to highlight the ways in which 'words matter' when it comes to public and other understandings of teachers and their work.

Analysing media texts

This book makes use of corpus-assisted discourse analysis techniques. As Baker (2006) has noted, such an approach utilizes methodological and analytical tools from the fields of both corpus linguistics and discourse studies. The book employs both quantitative and qualitative approaches to investigate and highlight the way that media discourses relating to education, and specifically to teachers, are constructed and maintained through language. While the research is not shaped as a Foucauldian study, it does work with a definition of discourse informed by Foucault's conceptualization of discourse as 'practices which systematically form the objects of which they speak' (1972: 49). By taking a corpus-assisted approach, we go deep into the language while remembering that discourse is 'language-in-action, and investigating it requires attention both to language and to action' (Blommaert 2005: 2). By working between corpus-assisted methods, and critical discourse analysis, this work attempts to attend both to language and to action.

Corpus linguistics and corpus-assisted discourse analysis

Working from the premise that 'the language looks different when you look at a lot of it at once' (Sinclair 1991: xvii), corpus-based approaches to discourse analysis use corpora, or large collections of texts, assembled electronically, to explore the role of language in the shaping of discourses. Corpora can be either purpose built for a research project, such as the corpus central to this book, the ATC, or general or national in nature, such as the British National Corpus (BNC), a hundred-million word corpus of written and spoken British English, first developed in 1994 and currently being updated (Love et al. 2017) or the Corpus of Contemporary American English (COCA) (2008), a corpus of 560 million words of written and spoken American English. Research that employs these general or national corpora often does so by using them as a 'reference corpus' against which to compare a smaller 'study corpus'. At different points in the analysis presented in this book, the ATC will be compared using the Corpus of News on the Web (NOW) (Davies 2016-) as a reference corpus, by way of establishing how far the language patterns identified in the ATC are similar to and different from those in use in Australian news media texts more broadly.

While, as noted above, educational research utilizing corpus-assisted methods to explore media texts is still quite rare, with the work of Fenech and Wilkins (2017, 2019) and some of my own recent work (Mockler and Groundwater-Smith 2018; Mockler 2020a, 2020b) providing an exception to this, the use of corpus-assisted methods in media analysis more broadly is quite common. Baker, for example, has extensively researched representations of Islam in the British print media, both individually and with colleagues (Baker 2010; Baker and McEnery 2019; Baker, Gabrielatos and McEnery 2013), along with representations of masculinity, similarly in the British print media (Baker and Levon 2015, 2016), using corpus-assisted discourse analysis. Media discourses around climate change (Grundmann and Krishnamurthy 2010), North Korea (Kim 2014) Aboriginal and Torres Strait Islander people(s) (Bednarek 2020), feminism (Jaworska and Krishnamurthy 2012), obesity (Brookes and Baker 2021) and diabetes (Bednarek and Carr 2020) represent some of the other diverse areas on which this focus has been brought to bear. In education, beyond media analysis, corpus-assisted methods have recently been used by scholars in relation to political speeches (Cohen 2021; Spicksley 2021), while Bokhove and Sims (2021) have used sentiment analysis on their corpus of some seventeen thousand OfSTED school inspection reports in the UK.

It is not my intention here to provide a comprehensive overview of corpus assisted approaches and methods – such as is provided elsewhere (see, e.g. Baker 2006; Brezina 2018; Hunston 2002) – however, it is necessary to provide an introduction to the four key tools used in the analysis presented in this book. The tools are employed in different ways throughout the book and each chapter begins with a brief introduction explaining the specifics of the analysis reported on in the chapter.

Word frequency

Word frequency is a very blunt instrument, and I am cognizant both of the pitfalls of relying too heavily on it, such as those laid out by Egbert and colleagues (Burch, Egbert and Biber 2017; Egbert and Biber 2019), and of the importance of attending to other measures. Analysis of word and word cluster frequencies is often used in this book, however, as a 'way in' to more complex analysis. As a means of gaining an initial idea of the 'shape' of the data, frequencies of both individual words and word clusters of between two and five words are often generated as a starting point for analysis, against the questions that each chapter sets out to address.

Collocation analysis

Firth (1957: 20) famously wrote, 'You shall know a lot about a word from the company it keeps', and understanding this 'company' is the aim of collocation analysis. Collocation analysis is explained by Baker (2006: 95–6) in the following way:

> All words co-occur with each other to some degree. However, when a word regularly appears near another word, and the relationship is statistically significant in some way, then such co-occurrences are referred to as collocates and the phenomena of certain words frequently occurring next to or near each other is collocation.

Collocation analysis explores significant and frequently co-occurring words in relation to 'the associations and connotations they have, and therefore the assumptions they embody' (Stubbs 1996: 172). As a tool for discourse analysis, collocation analysis provides insight into the discourse or semantic *prosody* of a concept. Louw defines semantic prosody as 'an aura of meaning by which a form is imbued by its collocates' (1993: 157), those words that frequently co-occur with the word in question. Louw furthermore argues that the capacity to systematically investigate semantic prosody provides the most compelling argument for the creation of large corpora, as the characteristics of discourse prosodies, critical to understanding discourses themselves, 'will only be revealed and be seen to stabilize once the content of a prosody can be collected extensively' (Louw 1993: 164). The ATC represents an attempt to construct one such extensive collection. The corpus comprises all articles published in the twelve Australian national and capital city daily newspapers that include three or more mentions of the word teacher and/or teachers, over the twenty-five-year period from January 1996 to December 2020. Chapter 2 provides an overview of the construction and shape of the ATC. While generalizations will not be able to be made about discourse prosody beyond Australian print media texts, the census nature of the corpus means that it is possible to make claims about the discourse prosody of different terms with respect to the Australian print media over this extended time frame.

In this research, collocation between a 'node word' or search term and other words has been investigated using WordSmith Tools 8 (Scott 2020b) and an intersection of two statistical measures, one related to statistical significance and one related to strength of association. The Mutual Information (MI) measure reflects the collocational strength of the relationship between words, with higher MI scores indicating stronger relationships: MI 'aims to measure the amount of information that the observation of one word gives about the likely occurrence of the other' (Gómez 2013: 204). Hunston (2002) indicates that MI scores of over 3 suggest the presence of collocation, however, she also notes that as MI does not take into account the size of the corpus under analysis, it alone does not provide adequate evidence of collocation. Similarly, McEnery, Xiao and Tono (2006: 56) argue that 'collocational strength is not always reliable in identifying meaningful collocations. We also need to know the amount of evidence available for a collocation'. They thus suggest drawing on the recommendation of Church and colleagues (Church et al. 1994), that both MI, which measures collocational strength, and the t-score, which reflects the confidence with which we can conclude that there is indeed an association (and which takes into account the size of the corpus under examination), be used in identifying collocates. In this analysis, an intersection of these two measures has been used, where words with both an MI score greater than 3 and a t-score greater than 2 have been identified as collocates of the search term. The collocation analysis was conducted using a 4:4 window (i.e. four words on either side of the search term or 'node word'), which is a common span to use in exploring linguistic collocations (Scott and Tribble 2006; Sinclair, Jones and Daley 1969). By way of narrowing the focus in situations where this technique identified a very large group of collocates, I often selected collocates that appeared with the node word in at least 1 per cent of instances of the node word's appearance in the corpus or sub-corpus. In this, I was led by a desire to understand the prevailing patterns of collocation in the ATC and what they showed about representation of teachers and their work. Where collocates are presented in table form in this book, unless otherwise noted (or in the case of collocates common to more than one sub-corpora), they are ordered according to MI values.

Keyword analysis

In corpus linguistics, *keywords* are words that occur more often in one group of texts than another, in a statistically significant sense. They 'give robust indications of the text's *aboutness*, together with indicators of style' (Scott 2010: 43), and Baker (2006) argues that keywords go beyond frequency to indicate the *salience* of particular words across a group of texts. Keyword analysis employs a measure of 'keyness' usually in the form of a test of significance (such as the log-likelihood statistic and associated p-value), which indicates how confident we can be that a keyword's prominence in a corpus cannot be accounted for by chance alone. Keyword analysis provides an insight into important distinctions between texts and groups of texts, and conveys a sense of the 'aboutness' of a large group of texts. Keyword analysis works by comparing a study corpus with a reference corpus. A variety of keyword analyses are reported in this book. They include a comparison of the whole ATC with the Australian portion of the corpus of NOW (Davies 2016-), which includes over three billion words gathered using Google News from twenty countries on a daily basis and is available in both online and downloadable formats, comparisons of smaller sub-corpora of the ATC (sectioned by year or media source) and finally comparisons of smaller corpora of media texts drawn from Australian, the United States, UK, Canadian and New Zealand contexts.

In this research the Bayesian Information Criterion, or BIC, has been used as an indicator of statistical significance, alongside Hardie's Log Ratio statistic (Hardie 2014), which is a measure of effect size. A high threshold was set for this analysis: to be identified as a keyword, a word must appear in at least 5 per cent of the texts in the ATC (or the sub-corpus under investigation) – this to attend to the issue of dispersion and ensure that the heavy use of a word in a small proportion of the texts within the corpus did not designate keyness. Wilson (2013) presents a very strong argument for using the Bayesian Information Criterion (BIC) to set statistical significance thresholds in keyness analysis (for further discussion, see also Gabrielatos 2018), and posits that BIC values over 10 suggest very strong evidence against the hypothesis that there is no real difference in the frequency of a word's use in the study corpus and the reference corpus. Accordingly, this is the threshold that has been used in this book. In terms of effect size, Hardie's Log Ratio, which takes into account the normalized frequency of a word in the study corpus and reference corpus, has been used, first because of its appropriateness for this kind of analysis (Gabrielatos 2018), second because of its interpretability: equal normalized frequencies in the reference and study corpora equate to a value of 0, while a value of 1 would indicate that the word is twice as frequent in the study corpus as in the reference corpus, and a value of 2 that the word is four times as frequent in the study corpus as in the reference corpus. In most cases, a threshold of 1.5 has been used to identify keywords. All keyword analysis undertaken in this study utilized WordSmith Tools 8 (Scott 2020b), which produces BIC and Log Ratio values. Where keywords are presented in table form in this book, unless otherwise indicated, they are ordered according to Log Ratio values.

At different points within the research, keywords were also used to identify prototypical texts from a sub-corpus of the ATC, using ProtAnt 1.2.1 (Anthony and Baker 2017), with these articles subjected to close analysis, using a thematic approach that drew on both framing and news values analysis.

Concordance analysis

Finally, close analysis of individual texts and collections of texts was conducted using concordance analysis. Extensive concordance analysis, manual examination of instances of frequent words, keywords, collocates and other words of interest in their context within the individual texts that comprise the ATC, was used. At each stage, preliminary findings were tested and verified via concordance analysis with a random selection of concordance lines used in instances where it was not feasible to examine the entire corpus. This systematic analysis ensured not only an understanding of quantifiable aspects of the relationship between language and discourse, but also the more subtle and nuanced aspects. AntConc 3.5.8 (Anthony 2019) was the primary concordance analysis tool used, although on occasion the concordance function of WordSmith Tools 8 (Scott 2020b) was also used. In this book, unless otherwise noted, all concordance tables include fifteen randomly selected lines – intended to give the reader a robust window on the data – generated by AntConc 3.5.8. Also unless otherwise noted, concordance tables are presented ordered alphabetically by the word immediately to the right of the node word, or, in the case of concordance tables for a word as a collocate of a node word, by the word immediately to the right of the collocate or node word.

Overview of the book

This chapter has sought to locate the research project on which this book is based, conceptually, methodologically and practically. The discussion which

Words Matter 23

has been opened up in this chapter will continue to unfold over the course of the book.

Chapter 2 introduces the ATC in more detail and presents a broad, overall analysis. Created for this study, the ATC comprises over sixty-five thousand media articles, encompassing approximately 45,000,000 words. As noted above, it contains all print media articles published in the Australian national and capital city daily newspapers that include at least three instances of the word 'teacher/s' over a twenty-five-year period, from January 1996 to December 2020, sourced using the Nexis database. The chapter introduces the ATC, discussing the general shape of the corpus (including distribution of articles in various sources) and then provides an overview of the whole corpus by exploring word and word cluster frequencies, keywords and collocations, along with associated concordance analysis. The chapter aims to develop a holistic picture of the ATC identifying a number of avenues for further inquiry which are picked up in the subsequent chapters.

Chapter 3 presents a diachronic or historical analysis of the ATC, exploring the way that print media discourses around Australian teachers have changed and remained constant over time, from the mid-1990s to 2020. Using the findings presented in Chapter 2 as a starting point, the analysis in this chapter identifies both static and changing ideas about teachers and their work as revealed in the corpus. It maps these changes historically onto shifts in relation to teachers' work over the same period, including those related to industrial issues and various waves of state-based, national and internationally influenced educational reforms.

Chapter 4 explores the differences and similarities between representations of teachers in the different newspapers within the ATC. As explained in more detail in Chapter 2, the print media landscape in Australia is bifurcated, with only one of the twelve national and capital city daily newspapers owned by an entity other than Murdoch's News Corp (which owns seven publications) or Nine Media[2] (which owns four). Furthermore, the newspapers differ in their scope, with two reporting predominantly on national issues and the remaining eight reporting on more local, state or territory-based issues. Eight of the twelve might be identified as what Baker, Gabrielatos and McEnery (2013) have referred to as 'right leaning', while the remainder might be identified using the same criteria as 'left leaning'. Four of the twelve are broadsheet publications (recognizing that this terminology has become problematic in recent years when most broadsheets

---

[2] A merger between Fairfax Media, the long-term previous owner of these newspapers, and Nine Media took place in 2018.

around the world have transitioned to Berliner size), while the other eight are tabloids. In this chapter, the nuances emerging from differences between the publications are explored. The discussion highlights similarities and differences in the discourses presented in different publications, considering what this means for perceptions of teachers within different reader communities.

The concept of 'teacher quality' has become a central one in Australian education policy discourses (Barnes 2021a, 2021b; Mockler 2020b) over the past twenty years. Chapter 5 traces the evolution of discourses of quality as in the ATC, from its early association with the beginnings of the professional standards movement in the late 1990s to its more recent use as a 'shorthand' (Gamson and Lasch 1983) for standards-based reform of the teaching profession and initial teacher education. This chapter presents a close diachronic analysis of 'quality' in the ATC from 1996 to 2020, tracking changes over this period in terms of usage, meaning and discursive constructions and mapping these historically against associated education policy reforms.

Chapter 6 steps away from the ATC, exploring similarities and differences in print media discourses surrounding teachers and their work in five Anglophone countries, namely Australia, Canada, New Zealand, the United States and the UK from 2016 to 2020. The chapter explores similarities and differences between the five international corpora and explores how these resonate with the findings presented in the previous chapters with respect to the ATC. The chapter explores both global trends in discourses of teachers and their work over this time period along with the shape of vernacularization (Rizvi and Lingard 2010) of these discourses in the five national contexts included in the analysis.

The final chapter draws together the analysis presented in the previous chapters to present some conclusions around representations of teachers in the print media. The chapter elaborates on the cultural-discursive, material-economic and social-political arrangements suggested and reinforced by the print media discourses identified in the analysis. It considers the contribution and limitations of the research, points to some paths left untrodden in this research and suggests future directions for work on education and the media, both with and beyond the ATC.

Conclusion

Media coverage about education, and specifically about teachers, shapes not only public attitudes towards teachers but also those of policymakers and politicians, and the attitudes of teachers themselves towards their profession and their work. This chapter has sought to provide a rationale for a book about print media discourses of education in Australia; to lay out the relationship of this work to that which has gone before; and to lay bare – albeit in a preliminary way – the particular approaches employed in this research. It has also suggested that the links between discourses and practices are more than incidental, with media discourses of education contributing to the shaping of teachers' practices through their impact on the cultural-discursive, material-economic and social-political arrangements that govern and frame their work. Ultimately, the book seeks to identify the shape and nature of media discourses of education as realized in the Australian print media and consider the implications of these for teachers' work and professional identities.

2

The Australian Teacher Corpus

Having laid out the background to the study and introduced some of the corpus-assisted techniques used in the analysis in Chapter 1, this chapter introduces the Australian Teacher Corpus (ATC). Custom designed for this study, the ATC contains 65,604 newspaper articles comprising 45,170,352 words published in major Australian newspapers between 1996 and 2020. In this chapter, I detail methods of creating the corpus, to lay bare the methodological and technical decisions taken in the course of this research, and introduce the shape of the ATC as a whole, utilizing the tools introduced in Chapter 1.

The ATC is an unusual and indeed, unique beast. While studies of media discourses of education often work with a purposefully selected group of texts and corpus-assisted studies often with a representative sample, my desire here was to create a complete and exhaustive collection of newspaper texts about teachers. I was inspired in this by a study conducted by Baker, Gabrielatos and McEnery (2013), in which they constructed a 143-million word corpus, comprising over 200,000 articles from the British press in order to explore representations of Islam in the public space. Their aim was to provide a systematic and 'complete' analysis of print media representations of Islam, with an eye to breaking open the way that racist and other discriminatory discourses were constructed and upheld in the media. The aim of this study was similar, but with respect to teachers. As discussed in Chapter 1, reporting on issues to do with teachers and teaching has been the subject of discussion both in academic literature and professional circles over a long period of time. What I wanted to achieve in this study was a systematic and 'complete' analysis of how discourses surrounding teachers and teaching have been constructed and sustained or changed over an extended period of time. The ATC is unique in both its scale and scope, comprising twenty-five years of coverage across all twelve Australian national and capital city daily newspapers.

The ATC: Practical, methodological and technical decisions in corpus construction

As the purpose of this study was to gain a broad-based understanding of discourses surrounding teachers and their work as well as a sense of changing discourses over time, the first phase of the study was given over to the construction of this very large corpus from the Australian print media. It is true to say that, at the outset, I underestimated the practical challenges of the task of creating the corpus, and the myriad decisions to be taken along the way which could impact the final product and thus the analysis. Two key decisions that emerged early on related to the scope of coverage (how many newspapers and which ones, from where?), and the time frame to use.

In relation to scope, school education in Australia is both a state/territory and national issue, and consequently, articles from each of the twelve Australian national or capital city daily newspapers (along with their weekend variants) were included in the corpus construction. The Australian Constitution gave the responsibility for schooling to the states and territories in 1901, meaning that each of the eight states and territories runs their own public education system and regulates curriculum, assessment and teaching standards for both government and non-government schools. At the same time, a national field of schooling has emerged in Australia since the 1970s (Lingard 2000; Lingard, O'Brien and Knight 1993; Savage and Lewis 2018; Savage and O'Connor 2015). In particular, the years since the election of the Rudd-Gillard Labor government in 2007 have seen the introduction of national curriculum, assessment regimes and teaching standards, which were previously developed and administered by the states. Over the same period, an ongoing national debate has taken place about school funding and the redistribution of funding on a national level in the interests of greater equity. Schooling and school systems, and consequently the work of teachers, have thus been both state and federal issues, and consequently the subject of coverage in both national and state-based newspapers over the period covered by the ATC. There are twelve national and capital city daily newspapers in Australia and in order to explore representations in not only the dominant east-coast states (which typically have the largest populations and newspapers with the highest readership), the decision was taken to include all twelve, including their weekend variants.

Because my interest was not only in representations of teachers but also in a diachronic analysis of change over time, it was important to cover a lengthy time frame. The corpus was thus extended back as far as feasible given the digitization of Australian newspapers from the late 1990s. At the time when the corpus was finalized, 1996 was the first full year where digitized versions of a critical mass of newspapers was available (most articles in eight out of the twelve newspapers in 1996, rising to nine in 1997), and thus this was taken as a starting point. The year 2020 was the last full year prior to the analysis of data and thus was taken as the final year for the corpus.

The Nexis database was used for data collection. To be included in the ATC, a newspaper article needed to include the word form teacher* (i.e. including both 'teacher' and 'teachers') at least three times. This parameter was used for two reasons. First, because the aim was to gain a very broad picture of discourses surrounding teachers, I did not want to confine the study to articles that were strictly about or focused entirely on teachers, or to expand it to those where only peripheral mentions of teacher/s were made. In my initial reading of a random selection of articles with only one or two mentions of teacher/s, I found these were often peripheral to discourses of teachers (e.g. naming a character in a film or television series). Conversely, articles with three mentions of teacher/s yielded more than a passing 'nod' to the profession, while not necessarily being exclusively focused on teachers. This seemed like a reasonable balance in the corpus construction process, and yielded a collection of articles that is largely focused on issues to do with teachers, teaching, schooling and education.

Additionally, I filtered articles to exclude those with a high level of similarity – this meant that duplicate articles published in the same newspaper were largely weeded out in the search, although further duplicates were identified and removed manually. Where articles had been syndicated and duplicates – or similar articles – were published across different publications, these were left in the corpus, as they were deemed to be representative of the density of representation. As such, they were considered to contribute in a different way to the discourses surrounding teachers to two identical articles published in different editions of the same newspaper on the same day.

Articles were downloaded from the Nexis database as individual Word documents in batches by year and outlet, and batch renamed to ensure they were easily identifiable with respect to their newspaper and year of publication. They were then converted into UTF-8 encoded text files by AntFileConverter 1.2.1 (Anthony 2017). A bespoke 'scrub' was created within the software program TextSoap 8.5 (Unmarked Software 2019) to tag the metadata within each article (this included the headline, byline, publication date and other details, image captions, where included, along with the load date). The aim was to exclude this material from the analysis, but render it still easily accessible and searchable. At this point, the files were saved in two versions for use with different corpus analysis software – a set of UTF-8 encoded .txt files for use with AntConc 3.5.8 (Anthony 2019) and ProtAnt 1.2.1 (Anthony and Baker 2017), and a set of UTF-16 files for use with WordSmith Tools 8 (Scott 2020b). While this process could have been simplified significantly by downloading the texts in large combined files rather than individual ones, this would have limited the analysis considerably. Attending to things other than sheer frequency of words (such as how far words were dispersed across articles either en masse or within a given year or publication) was deemed to be important (Egbert and Biber 2019). Ultimately, this has allowed for a better quality of analysis – a combination of 'macro' level and fine-grained analysis – than would otherwise have been possible.

I am aware that this description makes the corpus construction process seem relatively straightforward and streamlined. In reality, it was far more complicated, replete with 'two steps forward, one step back', due to not only the size and complexity of the corpus itself but also other factors beyond my control as a researcher. I began the process in June 2018, when I was a visiting scholar at the UCL Institute of Education, working with the Nexis UK database. At the time, batch downloading of individual articles was not possible on Nexis UK, so the articles were downloaded in bundles of up to five hundred and I engaged the services of Dr Christopher Norton at the University of Leeds to create a bespoke python script for the corpus, to split and rename the files and tag the metadata in each article. On my return to Australia in September 2018, it became apparent that there were significant differences between the Nexis UK database and the Australian Nexis database. At that point I elected to begin the process again with the Australian database, to ensure consistency within the corpus. The corpus (to the end of 2017) was completed by the end of 2018. In mid-2019, returning to Nexis to update the corpus for 2018, it became apparent that due to a major update in Nexis, this process would no longer work: the capacity to download .txt files had been removed, making it impossible to use the python script to clean and split the files. The Australian Nexis team was kind enough to allow me to access 'legacy Nexis' (which at that stage was still 'normal Nexis' in the UK and elsewhere in the world – Australia had been one of the first places to transition to 'new Nexis'), and again with Chris Norton's help the corpus was brought up to date.

With the advent of Covid-19, complications to work and life due to the pandemic meant the completion of the book had to be delayed until 2021. So in March 2020, I set about updating the corpus to the end of 2019. At this point, I hit a significant snag. The transition to 'new Nexis' had been completed worldwide and it was now impossible for the Nexis Australia team to provide legacy access. While it was consequently not possible to download .txt files for python processing, one of the excellent affordances of the fully transitioned Nexis was that individual files could be batch downloaded in a form easily convertible to .txt files. Upon applying the process outlined above to the 2019 files; however, it became apparent that the update to Nexis had also expanded the article pool captured by my search parameters significantly – I initially wondered why I had so many more articles than expected in the 2019 sample, and upon re-running the search on 2018...2017...2010...2004...1999 and so on, I discovered that across the board there were now more articles being captured by the search than there were in my previously-thought-to-be-perfectly-formed corpus.

At this point, I took the decision to go back to the beginning and rebuild the corpus from the ground up using the new Nexis database. I did this to ensure a level of consistency in the corpus and consequently trustworthiness in the research that is reported here. The construction of the current version of the ATC, then, was completed in early August 2020, and updated in January 2021 to include all articles that met the criteria published in 2020. The findings of earlier rounds of analysis on previous versions of the ATC were tested at each stage on the subsequent iterations of the corpus, and either updated or discarded depending on whether they still 'held'.

The landscape of newspapers and newspaper ownership in Australia

Media ownership, and particularly newspaper ownership, is highly concentrated in Australia, with companies historically founded and owned by a small number of wealthy families (such as the Murdochs and Packers) having controlled interests across print and broadcast media for decades. Figure 2.1 represents the main interests in Australian commercial television, radio and newspaper publishing as of September 2021. All twelve national and capital city daily newspapers in Australia could easily be plotted onto this snapshot, owned by three of these key players. The Nine Entertainment Company, which owns the influential Macquarie Radio Network and Channel Nine (one of three free-to-air commercial television channels), also owns the *Sydney Morning Herald*, *The Age* (Melbourne), the *Canberra Times* and the *Australian Financial Review* (national), through Nine Publishing. Seven West Media is the primary shareholder in Channel Seven (another of the commercial television channels) and the *West Australian* newspaper (Perth), while the remaining seven newspapers, the *Daily*

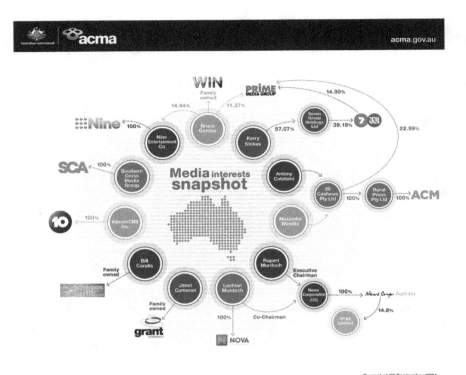

Figure 2.1 Media interests snapshot, September 2021 (ACMA 2021).
Source: Australian Communications and Media Authority © Commonwealth of Australia.

Telegraph (Sydney), the *Herald Sun* (Melbourne), *The Courier-Mail* (Brisbane), *The Mercury* (Hobart), *The Advertiser* (Adelaide), *Northern Territory News* (Darwin) and *The Australian* (national) are owned by Rupert Murdoch's News Corp Australia.

Over the past two decades, with the advent of online news and contraction of print newspaper readership, it has become increasingly difficult to categorize newspapers according to type. The classical broadsheet/tabloid distinction has become problematic as many broadsheet newspapers around the world, including in Australia, have moved to Berliner size (close to that of tabloids). Baker, Gabrielatos and McEnery (2013) argue that as a consequence of the breakdown of the broadsheet/tabloid distinction, a popular or populist/quality classification might be more appropriate; however, for ease of understanding, recognizing that this distinction is broadly understood and that newspapers have positioned themselves in such a way historically, I have chosen to retain

The Australian Teacher Corpus

Table 2.1 Australian Newspaper Profiles

Publication	Owner	Type	Orientation
The Australian/*The Weekend Australian*	News Corp Aust.	Broadsheet	Right-leaning
The Australian Financial Review	Nine Publishing	Broadsheet	Right-leaning
Daily Telegraph (Sydney)/*Sunday Telegraph*	News Corp Aust.	Tabloid	Right-leaning
Sydney Morning Herald/*Sun-Herald*	Nine Publishing	Broadsheet[a]	Left-leaning
The Age (Melbourne)/*Sunday Age*	Nine Publishing	Broadsheet[a]	Left-leaning
Herald-Sun (Melbourne)/*Sunday Herald*-Sun	News Corp Aust.	Tabloid	Right-leaning
The Courier-Mail (Brisbane)/*Sunday Mail* (Qld)	News Corp Aust.	Tabloid	Right-leaning
The Advertiser (Adelaide)/*Sunday Mail* (SA)	News Corp Aust.	Tabloid	Right-leaning
The West Australian (Perth)/*WA Saturday* /*Sunday Times*	Seven Group Holdings	Tabloid	Right-leaning
Hobart Mercury (Hobart)/*Sunday Tasmanian*	News Corp Aust.	Tabloid	Right-leaning
Northern Territory News (Darwin)/*Sunday Territorian*	News Corp Aust.	Tabloid	Right-leaning
Canberra Times (Canberra)	Nine Publishing	Broadsheet	Left-leaning

[a] Sunday variants of both the *Sydney Morning Herald* and *The Age* are tabloids.

the historical categorization here, at the same time recognizing that the terrain is becoming increasingly complex.

In Table 2.1, the twelve newspapers in this study have been characterized according to whether they, on balance and historically, subscribe more to a tabloid or broadsheet approach, based on the distinction offered by Baker et al. (2013). The tabloid approach includes a relatively strong focus on celebrity, sport and entertainment news, and stories, which tend to be relatively short, written in an informal style. The broadsheet approach is characterized by longer, more formal stories with relatively more political and social analysis and more international news. As Table 2.1 highlights, five of the twelve newspapers, including both national daily newspapers, might be categorized as broadsheet newspapers, with the remaining seven being tabloids. The two most populous capital cities, Sydney and Melbourne, each have two daily newspapers – one broadsheet and one tabloid – while the remaining six capital cities have one. With the exception of Canberra, the nation's capital and home to the Federal Parliament, the newspaper in all capital cities which have only one newspaper is a tabloid. Broadsheet newspapers are concentrated in the (most populous) south-eastern corner of Mainland Australia, and at the national level.

Similar to the broadsheet/tabloid distinction, the political orientations of the various newspapers are difficult to pin down. At any given time, political orientation lies at the confluence of factors such as ownership, editorship, perceived interests and advantage and so on. Additionally, newspapers often employ individual columnists or regularly publish op-eds by commentators of a divergent stance, making it difficult to categorize the newspaper on balance.

Reflecting on the problematic nature of this exercise, Baker et al. (2013) suggest the use of 'right-leaning'/'left-leaning' rather than conservative/liberal, left/right, a strategy used in Table 2.1, based on a reading of editorials over an extended period of time. Broadly speaking, Australian tabloids tend to be more right-leaning, along with the national broadsheets (one of which is Murdoch's flagship publication, *The Australian*), with the three capital city broadsheets being more left-leaning. At the time of writing, however, the Nine Publishing newspapers had been owned by Nine for only three years. As noted above, Nine also owns the Macquarie Radio Network, a hotbed of conservative populism in Sydney, Melbourne, Brisbane and Perth and home to a number of high-profile 'shock jocks', while Channel Nine television is known for sensationalist news reporting in its flagship programme, *A Current Affair*. Consequently, while these three newspapers are currently categorized as 'left-leaning', it remains to be seen whether Nine ownership will lead to the emergence of a more conservative orientation over the years to come.

Table 2.2 highlights 'average issue readership' figures for the newspapers in the study in the twelve months to March 2021. Readership broadly mirrors state and territory populations, with higher average readership levels in the New South Wales, Victorian and Queensland newspapers. The tabloid newspaper with the highest average readership across Monday to Saturday is the *Herald Sun*, while *The Australian* has the highest average readership of the broadsheets. Table 2.2 also provides evidence of the relatively large market share of the News Corp newspapers in *The Australian's* 63.7 per cent of average readership, as opposed to 25.8 per cent for Nine Publishing newspapers and 10.5 per cent for *The West Australian* (based on Monday to Friday figures).

Finally, while the newspapers' Monday to Friday and weekend variants have been bundled together for the purposes of analysis undertaken in this book, it is worth noting that most Australian newspapers (the *Australian Financial Review* and *Canberra Times* being the exceptions) have either a Sunday or weekend variant. These weekend variants tend to have a higher readership than the Monday to Friday editions. In most cases the weekend newspaper is consistent in form and orientation with the weekday editions, the exceptions being the broadsheet *Sydney Morning Herald* and *The Age* Sunday variants, the *Sun Herald* and the *Sunday Age*, both of which are tabloids.

Table 2.2 Australian Newspaper Readership, Twelve Months to March 2021

Publication	Monday-Friday	Saturday	Sunday
The Australian/*The Weekend Australian*	473,000	670,000	
The Australian Financial Review	162,000	158,000	
Daily Telegraph (**Sydney**)/*Sunday Telegraph*	453,000	495,000	783,000
Sydney Morning Herald/*Sun-Herald*	354,000	496,000	461,000
The Age (**Melbourne**)/*Sunday Age*	274,000	437,000	417,000
Herald-Sun (**Melbourne**)/*Sunday Herald-Sun*	563,000	653,000	749,000
The Courier-Mail (**Brisbane**)/*Sunday Mail* (Qld)	273,000	375,000	599,000
The Advertiser (**Adelaide**)/*Sunday Mail* (SA)	229,000	293,000	351,000
The West Australian (**Perth**)/*WA Saturday* /*Sunday Times*	339,000	409,000	394,000
Hobart Mercury (**Hobart**)/*Sunday Tasmanian*	42,000	51,000	40,000
Northern Territory News (**Darwin**)/*Sunday Territorian*	19,000	28,000	18,000
Canberra Times (**Canberra**)	43,000	46,000	36,000

Source: Roy Morgan, 2021, available at http://www.roymorgan.com/industries/media/readership/newspaper-readership).

Introducing the Australian Teacher Corpus

The ATC comprises 65,604 articles published in the twelve newspapers from January 1996 to December 2020. In total, the corpus comprises 45,170,352 words, or 'tokens' as they are known in corpus linguistic analysis. In taking a first look at the shape of the corpus, it is interesting to note that the articles are not evenly distributed across newspapers, and neither are they distributed evenly across the years covered by the corpus.

The average number of articles included in the ATC per newspaper is 5,469; however, six newspapers contributed significantly more articles to the corpus, while six others contributed less (Figure 2.2). The *Australian Financial Review*, for example, contributed the least number of articles to the ATC, suggesting that stories about teachers and education are perhaps regarded as less newsworthy by a newspaper focused on financial issues than more general publications. There was still, however, a large difference between general publications that might on the surface seem similar. For example, the Melbourne tabloid the *Herald Sun* contributed 625 articles less than the mean number of articles, while its Sydney counterpart, also owned by News Corp, contributed 2,142 more than the mean. This suggests that despite the two newspapers' similarity, what is deemed newsworthy by one is perhaps not necessarily deemed newsworthy by its stablemate. Conversely, the number of articles contributed by Melbourne and Sydney broadsheet counterparts, *The Age* and the *Sydney Morning Herald*, is roughly the same. This raises questions about the 'imagined audience' (Richardson 2007) of each newspaper and what constitutes newsworthiness in stories about teachers in different contexts, questions which will be taken up more extensively in Chapter 4.

In terms of the spread of articles over the twenty-five years of the corpus, Figure 2.3 highlights that this too is uneven. The average number of articles included in the corpus per year is 2,625. We see more attention paid to teachers in the Australian newspapers over the years 2004 to 2012, with a peak in 2008, the first full year of the federal Rudd-Gillard Labor government, and a year of concentrated attention on the government's 'education revolution'. Conversely, the years of the Abbott–Turnbull–Morrison Liberal government seem to be characterized by less attention to teachers in the Australian newspapers. In Chapter 3, a diachronic analysis of the corpus will shed light on some of the subtleties of these different distributions, but suffice for now to say that all years are not equal in terms of their representation in the corpus.

An important takeaway in relation to the shape of the ATC is the relative density of coverage. Remembering that the corpus includes only articles that use the word form teacher/s three times or more, these figures show that for every week of these twenty-five years, an average of 50.49 such articles was published in the twelve Australian newspapers. In 2008, the year with the largest number of articles, an average of 77.06 articles was published per week, and in this year, readers of *The Age* encountered an average of 11.02 articles in that publication alone, per week. Readers of *The Australian* in the same year encountered an average of 8.73 articles per week – one or two each day. Even in 2017, the year with the smallest number of articles in the corpus, an average of 36.37 articles was published each week, with the average number ranging from 4.53 in the *Sydney Morning Herald* to 1.31 in the *Australian Financial Review*. The point here is that media stories about teachers are a constant presence in Australian newspapers, even in time frames and newspapers where coverage is, on balance, lower than others.

By way of exploring how far this is reflected in newspaper coverage of stories relating to other occupational groups, such as public servants, accountants, nurses, lawyers and doctors, I ran a search using the same parameters: articles in the twelve national and capital city Australian newspapers, over the same time frame of 1 January 1996 to 31 December 2020. Figure 2.4 highlights the results of

The Australian Teacher Corpus 37

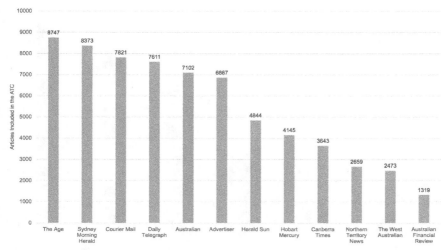

Figure 2.2 Total articles in the ATC by newspaper.

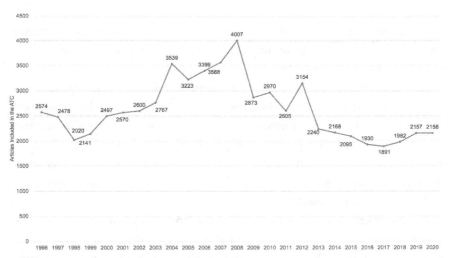

Figure 2.3 Total articles in the ATC by year.

this search. Of the five other occupational groups included,[1] the largest number of articles was those relating to teachers. The high-status occupational groups of doctors and lawyers came closest, while the occupational group of nurses, most closely associated with teachers as highly feminized, relatively low paid

---

[1] For doctors, it was necessary to filter out articles reporting on television programmes with 'doctor' in their title, such as *Doctor Who*, which accounted for a significant number of articles.

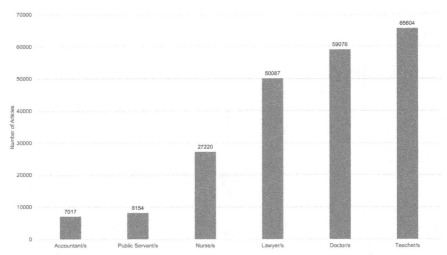

Figure 2.4 Representation of different occupational groups in the Australian print media (1996–2020).

'caring professions' which only in the last half-century have required tertiary preparation, were the focus of only 27,220 articles, that is 41.5 per cent of the 65,604 that focused on teachers.

This analysis is clearly a 'blunt instrument', in that it tells us nothing about the *types* of representations of the various occupational groups, but it does tell us that the Australian print media is, on balance, more interested in teachers than in any other of these groups – marginally so when it comes to doctors and lawyers, and far more when it comes to nurses, accountants and public servants. Presumably, Australian newspaper readers also have a high level of interest – and a connection to – teachers.

Having taken some time to consider the broad shape of the corpus, the remainder of this chapter will take a closer look inside the corpus itself. After a quick look at the most frequent words, it will explore the 'aboutness' of the corpus, through an analysis of keywords, and then, start addressing the question of how teachers are represented through an analysis of collocations.

The ATC: What's the corpus 'about'?

Beginning with a very basic exploration of the most frequent words within the ATC, Table 2.3 highlights the top thirty most frequent words in the corpus. As

The Australian Teacher Corpus

Table 2.3 Top Thirty Most Frequent Words in the ATC, Ordered by Frequency

the, to, and, of, a, in, is, for, that, it, with, on, was, are, be, as, at, school, I, teachers, he, have, said, they, not, their, by, but, students, from

Table 2.4 Top Thirty Most Frequent Lexical Words in the ATC, Ordered by Frequency

school, teachers, said, students, schools, education, year, teacher, one, says, children, years, government, people, parents, teaching, Mr, work, Australian, state, two, high, first, public, student, Australia, learning, last, day, good

is common, the vast majority of these words are grammatical rather than lexical and thus, as Baker (2006) notes, are perhaps better at denoting register than discourse. Of the thirty words, only four are non-grammatical, including three nouns (*school, teachers, students*) and one verb (*said*).

Table 2.4 includes the top thirty lexical words in the ATC, ordered by frequency. It highlights the prevalence of teachers and teaching, schools and education within the corpus, as well as the presence of governments within the discussion and a focus on both national (*Australian, Australia*) and state concerns. To develop an understanding of the collection of articles on a whole-corpus level, however, frequency analysis is only a first step.

As elaborated in Chapter 1, keyword analysis, which identifies and explores the words that appear relatively more frequently in a chosen corpus than in a broader 'reference' corpus, develops a sense of the 'aboutness' (Scott 2010) of the chosen corpus. Robust keyword analysis makes use of both significance testing and an effect size measure, which indicates the size of the statistically significant difference. In this case, in the light of the size of the corpus, I have used Bayesian Information Criterion (BIC) to set statistical significance thresholds, as suggested by both Wilson (2013) and Gabrielatos (2018), and Hardie's Log Ratio (2014) as the effect size measure. To 'make the cut' as keywords within this analysis, a word had to have a BIC value greater than 10 indicating very strong evidence that the normalized frequency difference is not due to chance (Wilson 2013), and a Log Ratio value of 1.5 or greater. A Log Ratio value of 1 means that the normalized frequency of the word in the study corpus is twice its normalized frequency in the reference corpus, while a Log Ratio value of 2 means that the normalized frequency in the study corpus is four times its normalized frequency in the reference corpus.

40   *Constructing Teacher Identities*

Furthermore, to be identified as a keyword, a word was required to appear in at least 5 per cent of the articles, or 3,282 articles. While on the one hand this created a high threshold and necessarily limited the number of keywords identified, on the other hand it attended to the issue of dispersion, ensuring that words identified as keywords were well dispersed in the corpus – that a word could not be identified as a keyword by being used many times in a relatively small proportion of articles. To generate keywords, the ATC was compared to a subsection of the corpus of the News on the Web (NOW) (Davies 2016-). The NOW corpus includes over three billion words gathered using Google News from twenty countries on a daily basis, and dates from 2010 to the present day, updated monthly. The subsection of NOW chosen comprised Australian news texts only, from 2010 to 2020 inclusive (referred to here as NOW-AU). This subsection includes over 750 million words in total, and over a million distinct word types.[2] The NOW corpus is available either via an online interface or as a downloadable collection of files. For this analysis, the downloadable files were used, and the keyword analysis was conducted using WordSmith Tools 8 (Scott, 2020b), which produces BIC and Log Ratio values.

This approach identified 105 keywords in the ATC. For the purpose of exploring the 'aboutness' of the corpus here, we will begin by considering the thirty top keywords, before moving to take a closer look at the broader group of keywords, organized into thematic groups. Table 2.5 contains the top thirty keywords for the entire ATC, 1996 to 2020. This list of keywords indicates that the corpus is strongly 'about' teachers, schooling and education, a finding which is hardly surprising (although perhaps also a little comforting to the architect of the corpus!). Interestingly, these words are all lexical as opposed to grammatical – a phenomenon consistent with the entire keyword list. This suggests that the ATC does not differ significantly from the NOW-AU corpus in terms of functional or grammatical words, and consequently, register.

While all of the top thirty keywords relate to education, they fall into different categories. Some are more about teachers and teaching (*teachers, teacher's, teacher, teaching, pupils, educators, students, teach, classes, taught, child's, student,*

---

[2] A limitation of the NOW corpus is that for copyright reasons in line with the United States Fair Use Law, ten words per two hundred words have been replaced with '@'. This effectively means that 95 per cent of the data are available without contravening copyright, and as the omissions occur 'blindly', all words are affected equally. For more information see https://www.corpusdata.org/limitations.asp.

The Australian Teacher Corpus 41

Table 2.5 Top Thirty Keywords in the ATC as Compared to the NOW-AU Corpus, Ordered by Log Ratio

teachers, teacher's, teacher, numeracy, principals, curriculum, classroom, literacy, teaching, maths, classrooms, pupils, schools, educators, school's, schooling, students, grammar, education, teach, school, secondary, educational, subjects, principal, taught, classes, child's, student, courses

courses), others are more about schools and schooling (*principals, classroom, classrooms, schools, schooling, school's, secondary, school, principal*), and still others are about what goes on in schools and classrooms (*numeracy, curriculum, literacy, maths, grammar, subjects*). Finally, some speak of education more broadly (*education, educational*).

In examining concordances for all 105 identified keywords, 6 key thematic groups emerged. These related variously to teachers, teaching, curriculum, schools, students, and teacher education, and each of these groups will be discussed briefly here. In presenting the keywords grouped in this way, I aim to provide some insight into the aboutness of the corpus by attending to its nuance, while at the same time recognizing that these categories are overlapping and thus somewhat arbitrary. Furthermore, concordance analysis showed that some, indeed most, keywords cut across two or more categories, and here I made an 'on balance' decision, based on the majority of uses as reflected in the concordance.

Table 2.6 highlights the keywords, organized by category and ordered according to Log Ratio. Keywords relating to teachers included not only those relating to individuals or groups of teachers, but to teachers as an occupational or industrial group, such as, *Federation* (relating to the New South Wales (NSW) Teachers Federation, the union for teachers in government schools in the state of NSW), *union, unions* and *association*. Only two adjectives used primarily to describe teachers appeared as keywords, namely *specialist*, for example, *specialist maths teachers* in primary and or secondary schools, and *male*. Both of these adjectives are commonly used with *shortage*, pointing to and often lamenting a *shortage* of *specialist* or *male* teachers. *Salary* and *pay* reflect the prominence of teachers' industrial negotiations over the two decades covered by the corpus, and also the recurring prospect of performance *pay* which, as we shall see in subsequent chapters, has emerged from time to time as a key policy issue. *Shortage* reflects a focus not only on shortages of particular types of teachers, but also ongoing and recurring concerns about prospective or current teacher shortages. *Profession* and *professional* most often refer to the teaching *profession* itself or *professional*

42   *Constructing Teacher Identities*

Table 2.6 Keywords in the ATC, Organized by Category and Ordered by Log Ratio

Teachers	teachers, teacher's, teacher, educators, profession, Federation, discipline, union, shortage, unions, salary, specialist, male, industrial, strike staff, pay, association
Teaching	classroom, teaching, classrooms, teach, taught, classes, learning, lessons, achievement, academic, lesson, class, standards, assessment, outcomes, tests, computer, performing, encouraged
Curriculum	numeracy, curriculum, literacy, maths, grammar, subjects, English, skills, language, science, reading, programs, arts, books, writes, write, writing, subject, knowledge
Schools	principals, schools, school's, schooling, school, secondary, principal, disadvantaged, primary, Catholic, college, department, funding
Student	pupils, students, child's, student, parents, children, parent, boys, studying, childhood, kids, child, girls, studies, boy, attend, adults
Teacher Education	courses, graduates, graduate, universities, qualified, training, university, trained
Other (Education)	education, educational
Other (non-Education)	letters, yesterday, mail, Howard, Victorian, state's, SA, government's, NSW

activities (such as professional development) for teachers. Finally, *discipline* refers predominantly not to academic disciplines, but to ongoing concerns about teachers' capacities to enact firm *discipline* and control of students within their classrooms, an enduring concern over the two decades of the corpus.

Teaching keywords include variants of the word form *teach*, including *teaching*, *teach* and *taught*, along with words associated with *learning*, namely *learn* and *learning*. Places and spaces within which teaching takes place also appear here, including *classroom/s*, *class/es*, and *lesson/s*, while a further set of keywords point to student and/or school performance. These include *achievement*, *academic*, which most often relates to academic *achievement* or academic *standards*, along with *outcomes*, *assessment*, *tests* and *performing*. The latter is a particularly interesting word, in that while it is sometimes used in tandem with arts, referring to either curriculum or co-curricular activities, *performing* also often refers to the performance of students, teachers or schools as represented on national and international tests. This is highlighted in Table 2.7, which shows randomly selected concordance lines for *performing*, sorted alphabetically by the word immediately to the right. Descriptors such as *high*, *low*, *best*, *worst*, *stronger* and *under* are most often used in these instances to categorize schools and people

The Australian Teacher Corpus   43

Table 2.7 Concordance Lines for *Performing*

suggests that the difference between a high-	**performing** and a low-performing teacher is substantial.
are well catered for through visual and	**performing** arts, languages other than English and technology
her before becoming a highly respected specialist	**performing** arts teacher. She was elevated further to
out of the 65 countries -- well behind high-	**performing** Asian systems as well the US and
but how their child's school is	**performing** compared to similar schools'. Opposition Leader
to know precisely how their child was	**performing** compared with others, has helped formulate the
sounded attractive. Take the nation's worst	**performing** education system, in terms of post-year 10
Year 7 students are the nation's worst-	**performing** in literacy and numeracy. According to 2004 test
campaign was absolutely about attracting high-	**performing** principals and teachers. '
lauded as having one of the best	**performing** school systems in the world, was envious
argument really says that students in low-	**performing** schools will be fine as long as
teacher directed classroom practice. In stronger	**performing** systems teachers are respected, well resourced
encouraged to leave the profession. 52 The best-	**performing** teachers in public schools should be paid
schools for teachers program gave about 1000 high-	**performing** teachers the chance to improve their skills
teachers in 52 schools identified as under-	**performing** to blame? Yes. But only to a

within them. This discourse of performance and its varying articulation over the past two decades is something to which we will return later in the book.

Nineteen keywords related to the category of *curriculum*. These include those broadly referring to the development of student knowledge and understanding, such as *subjects*, *skills*, *programs* (usually referring to particular or groups of teaching and learning programs), *knowledge* and *subject*, along with those specifically referencing particular disciplines or learning areas, including *numeracy, literacy, maths, grammar, English, science, language, reading, arts, books, write, writing*. It is worth noting here that with the exception of *arts*, the learning areas referenced here are all the so-called 'core' subject areas of English, mathematics and science, reflecting the importance these are accorded in the media and also in broader public discussions of curriculum and schooling.

School-related keywords include variants of the word form *school*, including *schools, schooling, school's, school*, along with the synonym *college*, used often in the non-government sector and also in some public school systems around Australia. *Principals, principal* and *department* (referencing various Departments of Education at federal and state/territory levels) are also represented here, related to different levels of school leadership and governance. The four adjectives *secondary, primary, disadvantaged* and *Catholic* are most often used as descriptors of schools and, on occasion, school systems or groups of schools. Examination of the concordance lines and sources for *disadvantaged* reveals that this word was relatively rare within the corpus until the early 2010s, when it became an integral part of the discourse around school *funding*, another of the keywords related to schools. The prevalence of *funding* as a keyword reflects the growing intensity of public discussions around the funding of schools in Australia over the past two decades, particularly in reference to disadvantaged schools and communities, and the diachronic analysis presented in Chapter 3 will provide more space for discussion of this shift.

Keywords relating to students include *pupils, students, student, child's, children, children's, kids* and *child*, along with *boys, girls* and *boy*. Keywords related to students' parents or guardians are also included here, namely *parents parent*, and *adults*, used most often within the corpus to point to adults other than teachers or parents involved in schooling in some way. *Studying, studies, attend* and *grade* – often used as an adjective with student, for example *Grade 3* student – reflect students' engagement in school, while the keyword *childhood* reflects the role of schooling as central to the lives and experiences of children.

Finally, eight keywords relate to teacher education, both pre-service teacher education through which teachers become qualified, and in-service teacher education, often referred to as teacher professional development and/or teacher professional learning. The increasing frequency of these keywords, namely *courses, graduates, graduate, universities, qualified, training, university* and *trained* over the second decade of the corpus, reflects growing media attention to teacher education over these years, and once again, the shifting attention to this phenomenon will be explored more expansively in the diachronic analysis presented in Chapter 3.

So, taking a bird's eye view, what do these keywords reveal in terms of the 'aboutness' of the corpus as a whole? We see here a corpus of texts focused clearly on teachers and their work, including the contexts within which they work, and the students and parents with whom they work. The keywords also resonate with the performative dimensions of contemporary teaching, reflecting policy reforms around teachers' work, performance and education over the past twenty years, and in terms of curriculum and assessment, with shifts towards 'core' curriculum and accountability through testing. Furthermore, manual examination of the keywords highlights that while some appear to be relatively consistent in terms of their appearance over the twenty-five years of the corpus, others have become far more prevalent in response to particular policies, events or trends within education over this period of time. In chapters to come, we will move to a closer examination of some clusters of keywords, along with a diachronic examination of keywords, exploring the changing nature of keywords over time along with lockwords, those that have endured as keywords over the duration.

The company teacher/s keep: Key collocations in the ATC

As noted in Chapter 1, the examination of collocation, or words frequently and consistently used together, sheds light on the 'discourse prosody' (Stubbs 2001) of particular words, the 'aura of meaning with which a form is imbued by its collocates' (Louw 1993: 157). In this initial analysis we will explore the collocations of *teacher* and *teachers* in the ATC as a whole, with particular attention to the adjectives consistently used in close proximity to *teacher* and *teachers*. This will provide a broad insight into the ways in which teachers are positioned within the texts. As noted in Chapter 1, I used a combination of the t-score and the Mutual Information statistic to identify collocates in the ATC. The collocation analysis was conducted using a 4:4 window (i.e. four words on either side of the search term or 'node word'). Additionally, to be identified as a collocate for discussion here, a word needed to appear within the 4:4 window in at least 1 per cent of appearances of the node word. For example, to be identified as a collocate of *teachers*, which appears 229,660 times in the ATC, a potential collocate had to appear 2,297 times within the 4:4 window. The discussion is thus focused on those collocates contributing significantly to the discourse prosody of teacher/s across the corpus as a whole.

Using this approach, fifty-four collocates were identified for *teachers* and thirty-eight for *teacher*, with eleven of these shared across the two search terms. Concordances were generated for all collocates, and on the basis of close examination of the concordances, the lexical collocates were inductively assigned to a thematic group. Table 2.8 highlights the collocates organized according to these groups.

Perhaps unexpectedly, the largest thematic grouping was that of 'teachers' work', which includes words related to schools, teaching, students and parents. This reflects the way in which teachers are often represented in the media in the context of broader discussions of education and schooling, student achievement, classrooms and school communities. It also reflects the ways in which teachers are often discussed in tandem with other 'educational stakeholders', with their interests sometimes represented as similar to, and sometimes competing with, those of students, parents and principals.

Of particular interest here among the lexical collocates, however, are those used to describe or position teachers, and in particular the adjectives and adjectival phrases that surround *teacher/s*. Some of the collocates within this category related to the age of students taught (high, primary, secondary), or subjects taught (English, maths, music, science). Others were adjectives used

46 *Constructing Teacher Identities*

Table 2.8 Collocates of Teacher and Teachers in the ATC, Organized by Category and Ordered by MI

	Teacher	Teachers
Teachers' work	parent, student, college, classroojm, school, class, education, year, years	principals, parents, classroom, students, work, schools, school
Types of teachers	former, head, primary, English, music, secondary, maths, high, science	male, primary, new, public, high
Quantitative markers	shortage, every, one	many, cent, more, per, all, some, most, two
Geographical markers		Queensland, NSW, state
Qualitative markers	quality, good	best, good
Industrial		Federation, union, president, pay
Professional	training	support, training
Voice	told, said	said
Grammatical words	who, another, was, your, had, her, his, has, being, been, after, with	were, are, who, need, have, should, will, other, for, their, would, and, our, also, being, than, from, with, had, not, how, can

to delineate particular types of teachers, such as male teachers, new teachers and public school teachers, all of which are of particular interest here. Of the 5,079 instances of *new* appearing as a collocate of *teachers*, 2,250 (44.3 per cent) were as part of the word cluster *new teachers*. Concordance analysis identified, as demonstrated in the extract provided in Table 2.9, that *new teachers* are characterized within the ATC as variously poorly equipped; challenged in their work; or an increasingly endangered species as a consequence of an impending or current teacher shortage. The discourse surrounding *new teachers* thus positions them as inherently problematic, either on account of their presence or their (potential or actual) absence.

This sense of shortage is also reflected in the concordance for *male* as a collocate of *teachers*, as highlighted in Table 2.10.

The concordance also highlights an assumption that more male teachers are required within the teaching profession, and a broad desire to attract more male teachers. The disparity between the proportion of male and female

The Australian Teacher Corpus

Table 2.9 Concordance Lines for *New Teachers*

"I'm under pressure to make our	**new teachers** able to teach online as well.
says the students are intrigued by their	**new teachers'** accents, and have a real curiosity
literacy and numeracy will ensure that our	**new teachers** are graduating with better skills that
	NEW teachers are ill-prepared for the realities
a noble profession" (The Age, 24/2). But when	**new teachers** are only offered one-year contracts,
no wonder that 47.9 per cent of	**new teachers** don't see themselves still teaching
study found that of all the challenges	**new teachers** face, handling parents is the toughest.
and impact negatively on student learning. "Most	**new teachers** have visited the school to become
the major reason for the increase in	**new teachers** needed every year," she said. "And
had a huge impact. Prof Johnson said	**new teachers** needed longer term, secure employment,
names - they can make things tricky for	**new teachers**. "Often our new teachers are also
also sit on selection panels to hire	**new teachers**. The students have high expectations of
teachers, and make it harder to recruit	**new teachers** to replace them. We already put
day unveil an $80 million proposal to entice 3000	**new teachers** to the profession with five-year
US it is estimated that two million	**new teachers** will be required in the next 10

teachers in different jurisdictions and sectors appears as an ongoing concern, along with a focus on the capacity and need for male teachers to act as role models for students, particularly boys. Further, it is interesting to note that, despite the well-documented feminization of teaching (see, e.g. Drudy 2008; Kelleher et al. 2011; Moreau 2019), *female* was not identified as a collocate of teacher or teachers within the ATC, and upon examination, that a stronger collocation exists between *female* and *male* and *female* and *student* than between *female* and *teacher*. In fact, an examination of the collocates of *male* and *female* within the ATC yields interesting findings with regard to gender in the corpus.

Table 2.11 includes the top fifteen collocates of both *male* and *female*. While a number of these collocates, represented in bold in Table 2.11, are shared between the two groups (*models, dominated, role*), concordance analysis highlighted that the relationship between the common collocates and the node words was not necessarily the same. In the case of *models*, for example, where the primary construction is *role models*, Tables 2.12 and 2.13 highlight the differing ways in which *male* and *female* collocations work, in context. As a collocate of *male*, *models* almost exclusively relates to the need for more male role models, for all children but particularly for boys. The lack of male role models in schools, a sign of the feminization of the teaching profession, is positioned as a problem that requires attention to the *shortage* or *lack* of male teachers. Where female role models are referenced in the ATC, this is more likely to occur alongside parallel mention of male role models, as highlighted in Table 2.13, where eight of fifteen concordance lines include reference to male role models. Over 61 per cent of the references in

Constructing Teacher Identities

Table 2.10 Concordance Lines for *Male* as a Collocate of *Teachers*

done on sentencing patterns in cases of	**male** and female **teachers** offending against students. 'What
the next decade with 40 per cent of	**teachers** in the **male**-dominated subjects nearing retirement.
brothers or first and second cousins. Our	**teachers**, mostly **male**, were strict but well liked
like to have one or two	**male** primary **teachers** through her son's six
opinion and common sense. The assertion that	**male teachers** are not the answer to all
in a good relationship environment.' Lyons says	**male teachers** are probably better suited to the
high school who showed me how great	**male teachers** can be.' While the 'intrinsic' value
that shows pupils will try harder for	**male teachers**. Children make more effort to please
said. 'There is no research suggesting that	**male teachers** contribute to better learning outcomes for
with girls, making it vital to attract	**male teachers**. 'Few would argue that male teachers
made up about 31 per cent. There were 9734	**male teachers** in the non-government sector -- about 30
not some politically correct utopia where all	**male teachers** just happen to be good teachers
are practical problems facing schools without	**male teachers**, such as the supervision of boys'
do not feel comfortable talking about with	**male teachers**,' Tamara said. 'You need someone who
inquiry into boys' education was more	**male teachers**, who are better role models and

Table 2.11 Top Fifteen Collocates of Male and Female in the ATC, Ordered by MI

Male	Female
models, **dominated**, female, scholarships, **role**, shortage, model, lack, numbers, positive, primary, teachers, number, boys, student	male, **dominated**, **models**, sex, student, aged, sexual, teacher, **role**, first, old, young, both, staff, teachers

Table 2.12 Concordance Lines for *Models* as a Collocate of *Male*

is a deficiency for many boys in	**male** role **models** and that is one of
mostly single-mother, families. Many had no	**male** role **models** at school. The dean of
with dysfunctional parenting and the absence of	**male** role **models** at home leaving classrooms looking
commentators who say young boys desperately need	**male** role **models**, especially given the explosion in
for a young boy to have no	**male** role **models** -- especially in the early years
to the education system to provide positive	**male** role **models** for children but the reality
inquiry had shown that a lack of	**male** role **models** had contributed to under-achievement
important to Labor than helping boys with	**male** role **models**,' Howard said incredulously. 'So much
there is general agreement that children need	**male** role **models** in schools. But it also
Simon Andrews warned the continuing lack of	**male** role **models** in primary schools was affecting
among teenage boys, especially those who lack	**male** role **models**, she says. There is compelling
motivation to read because of their macho-	**male** role **models**, the Queensland Association of State
good teachers. Putting aside the notion of	**male** role **models**, there are practical problems facing
and that, instead, these boys need strong	**male** role **models**. This argument has appeal for
there are decided educational benefits to having	**male** teachers as role **models**, said the committee. '

The Australian Teacher Corpus   49

Table 2.13 Concordance Lines for *Models* as a Collocate of *Female*

exposure to a variety of positive role	**models**, both male and **female**, but especially appropriate
important that they have very positive role	**models**, both male and **female**,' St Mary's
of society, rather than solely male and	**female** family role **models**. 'I think it's
is 'very significant. There are very few	(**female**) role **models** around the world'.
boys and girls needed both male and	**female** role **models**. 'Children from single-parent families
think is the answer.' Mr Tanner said	**female** role **models** could also help boys, and
is to have male as well as	**female** role **models** for young children in our
and females as long as you have	**female** role **models** in non-traditional areas (such
equally concerned about the small percentage of	**female** role **models** in corporate management and Parliament?
in the freezer. KS: Who were the	**female** role **models** in your life? Your mum,
for young children to have male and	**female** role **models**, particularly at a time when
girls' schooling was particularly low and positive	**female** role **models** rare. Boys and girls reported
thanks to the concerted STEM push and	**female** role **models** such as Simmons and Cathy
the young, should have both male and	**female** teachers as role **models** is valid. Even
have a mix of both male and	**female** teachers as role **models** at school and

the ATC to female role models (and it should also be noted that there are almost six times the number of collocations of *male* with *models* than of *female*) are accompanied by a reference to male role models, while less than 8 per cent of references to male role models were accompanied by one to female role models.

Additional to this differential use of the common collocates, a very different set of unique collocates emerges for the two groups. While the collocates of *male* are predominantly related to the shortage of male teachers and the desire to attract more men into the profession (*scholarships, shortage, lack, numbers, number*), the collocates of *female* have a somewhat sexual edge (*sexual, sex*) and also comprise adjectives used to describe women and girls (*aged, old, young*, mostly in this context describing female students). Concordance analysis on both sets of unique collocates highlighted that, consistent with the discussion of *models* above, male teachers are positioned within the ATC as both rare and much-needed additions to schools and systems. The key exception to this is in relation to sexual transgression: analysis of *sex* and *sexual* as collocates of *female* highlighted that these were often used in the ATC in relation to abuse of *female* students, usually, but not exclusively by male teachers. Furthermore, *female* is more strongly collocated with *teacher* than *teachers*, whereas the opposite is the case for *male*, which is more strongly collocated with *teachers* than with *teacher*. This reflects the phenomenon whereby *female* is used more within the ATC in reference to individuals while *male* is used more strongly within the ATC to refer to *male teachers* as a group, often in the context of lamenting the shortage thereof.

50 *Constructing Teacher Identities*

Table 2.14 Concordance Lines for *Teacher* as a Collocate of *Female*

all the excuses of this 28-year-old	**female** (a drama **teacher** no less) and probably
physical, fraud, and others. Cases included: A	**female** high school **teacher** who provided drugs to
A	**FEMALE** high school **teacher** who, according to court
interested in what skills and abilities a	**female** PE **teacher** might need to prosper and
vulnerable', a court has heard. A	**Female teacher** admits sex with student
to be continued. In another case, a	**female teacher** for 27 years had her registration suspended
Courier-Mail revealed last week that a	**female teacher**, 63, from Townsville died in Brisbane last
girl vomited and another student told his	**female teacher** he would not fetch the ball
the scissors across the room, striking the	**female teacher** in the face and cutting her.
a student infatuated with his much older	**female teacher** -- is a popular choice for European
parents rallied yesterday in support of a	**female teacher** removed from classroom duties and facing
IN September 2006, a	**female teacher** walking through the agricultural section of
with intentionally causing injury. A 48-YEAR-OLD	**female teacher** was sacked for medical certificate fraud.
was choked by a student and a	**female teacher** who had to be flown off
get as much attention from the	**teacher**.' While **female** teachers are important role models

The collocation of *teacher* with *female*, demonstrated in Table 2.14, highlights the particular circumstances under which teachers are described in the ATC as *female*. These include misdemeanors ranging from sexual abuse and assault of students to other illegal and/or inappropriate behaviour, death and instances where teachers might not be stereotypically expected to be female, such as in the case of physical education or agriculture. This provides a contrast to Table 2.10: the quality of being *male* is noteworthy for teachers, while it is noteworthy that a teacher is *female* only in extreme or unusual circumstances. Clearly, as is demonstrated by even this brief analysis, male and female teachers, and masculinity and femininity more generally, are represented and positioned quite differently in the ATC.

Concordance analysis for *public* as a collocate of *teachers* suggested that *public* often co-occurs with *teachers* in the context of discussion of industrial issues, including negotiation of pay and conditions, along with discussion of the affordances and constraints presented by public school systems. Table 2.15 also illustrates how *public* is used in the corpus both to delineate differences between teachers in public and other schools, and also on occasion to group public school teachers either with other teachers (such as *private* school teachers) and *public servants*. Concordance analysis for the collocate *government* indicated that it was most often employed as a synonym for *public*, doing similar work in this context to position teachers in *public* or *government* schools either with or in opposition to those in other, often *private*, schools.

Three geographical markers, *NSW*, *Queensland* and *state*, emerged as collocates of *teachers*, reflecting the federated nature of education systems in Australia, and

The Australian Teacher Corpus

Table 2.15 Concordance Lines for *Public* as a Collocate of *Teachers*

trying to spread big pay rises for	**teachers** and other **public** servants from state to
equate accommodation are still priorities for our	**public** education system. Individual teachers remain best placed
calls for a wide inquiry into the	**public** education system. NSW Teachers Federation president Sue
learnt that about 7,200 - or 9 per cent - of	**teachers** from **public** and non-government schools had
aside THE precarious contract system of hiring	**teachers** in **public** schools must be abolished. How
Why would a government which insists	**teachers** in the **public** system have such qualifications
13 per cent over three years won by	**teachers** last week. The **Public** Service Association's
was engaged to run a workshop on	**public** relations for teachers where staff were guided
Auburn West	**Public** School FORMER students/teachers/parents of Auburn
to introduce three-yearly criminal checks of	**public** school teachers. Currently Queensland teachers must pass
be married." Despite the concessions, private and	**public** school teachers will go ahead with a
the norm. Nor can principals in most	**public** schools choose the teachers they want or
schools to attract staff. In the Queensland	**public** system, teachers who opt to work in
as figures show 40 per cent of SA	**public** teachers aged under 45 are on short-term
report also reveals: 'About 19 per cent of	**public** teachers are on fixed-term contracts. 'Almost

the way in which much of the discussion of education and schooling in Australia is delineated according to the state or territory jurisdiction. A series of collocates reflect the positioning of teachers as both an industrial group (*federation*, *pay*, *president*, *union*), reflecting the significance of teachers' industrial negotiations and disputes over the two decades of the ATC, and a professional one (*support*, *training*), reflecting the complex professional learning and support needs of teachers. Two collocates (*said*, *told*) reflect the prevalence of different voices in the ATC, as revealed by concordance analysis and particularly the regularity with which sources (government, industrial and professional, along with others) are quoted in the media texts.

Two further groups of collocates offer an important insight into the positioning of teachers within the ATC and the discourse prosody of *teacher/s*, namely those that operate as qualitative markers with reference to teachers (*best*, *good*, *quality*) and those that have an essentializing edge, often used to make generalizations about teachers (*every*, *need*, *should*). The collocation analysis suggests that the *quality* of teachers themselves is a frequent concern across the ATC (see Table 2.16). Of the 1,991 collocations of *quality* with *teacher/s* in the ATC, 1,323 (66.4 per cent) are as part of the phrase *teacher quality*. A further 154 appear in *quality teacher* and a further 92 in *quality of the teacher*. While this will be the subject of a more lengthy discussion later in the book, and indeed is the focus of Chapter 5, suffice to say here that the discourse of *teacher quality*, strong in the ATC, discursively positions teachers as either of – or not of – quality. This discursive attention to teachers themselves rather than to their practices or their work more broadly repeatedly positions them as a problem

Constructing Teacher Identities

Table 2.16 Concordance Lines for *Quality* as a Collocate of *Teacher/s*

been written and said about the poor	**quality** of **teacher** graduates coming out of universities.
the	**quality** of **teacher** training courses has drawn a
trophy. To further emphasise the academy's	**quality**, principal **teacher** Lynda Herriman was one of
technology and high-skilled occupations. The	**Quality Teacher** Program is extended to 2004–05, with new
to improve student performance through high-	**quality teacher** training programs, increased investment and the
and includes other measures to improve	**teacher quality** and increase school autonomy without handing
Academic research has repeatedly pointed to	**teacher quality** as a far greater influence on
THE Federal Budget will target	**teacher quality** by investing $17 million to reduce the
undermine Queensland's current attempt to lift	**teacher quality**, especially among graduate teachers. The
recognised cornerstone of international success is	**teacher quality**. Every study shows teacher quality is
country, state governments are trying to boost	**teacher quality**. In NSW, Piccoli is instituting significant
formally register its teachers with a new	**Teacher Quality** Institute approved by the Legislative Assembly
plan under Ms Gillard's $550 million improving	**teacher quality** partnership. Some of the money can
direct extra funding for literacy, numeracy and	**teacher quality** programs to struggling schools. That's
in 2003, had failed, especially in boosting	**teacher quality**. While the key to a world-

requiring attention while at the same time feeding into the ongoing dichotomy of 'good' and 'bad' teachers. This preliminary finding is consistent with that of a previous corpus-assisted analysis, limited to a far smaller collection of articles that explicitly referenced teacher and/or teaching quality and to a four-year period, from 2014 to 2017 (Mockler 2020a). There, I found that when it came to *quality*, the discourse of *teacher quality* was particularly strong in relation to school teachers, while the phrase *teaching quality* was more often used in relation to teachers in tertiary education. The question of *quality*, specifically but not exclusively in relation to teachers, is an important one within the ATC, and one which will continue to emerge through the diachronic and other analysis and which, as noted above, will be the focus of the analysis presented in Chapter 5.

Good is a collocate of both *teacher* and *teachers*, and 2,396 of the 4,068 (58.9 per cent) collocations of *good* with *teacher/s* in the ATC appear in the phrase *good teacher/s*. As highlighted in Table 2.17, the *good teacher* is seldom nuanced or problematized within the texts contained in the ATC. The prevalence of *good* as a collocate of *teacher/s* does not on balance contribute to a positive discourse prosody for *teacher/s* within the corpus. In the majority of cases, the *good teacher* is contrasted, either explicitly or implicitly with 'other' (presumably, and sometimes clearly less good or indeed poor) teachers, meaning that even writing ostensibly about *good teachers* on occasion contributes to a negative discourse prosody.

Similarly, *best*, a collocate of *teachers* (see Table 2.18), is often used within the ATC to contrast the *best teachers* with other teachers, often with a view to justifying enhanced pay or other conditions for the profession's *best*. Again,

The Australian Teacher Corpus

Table 2.17 Concordance Lines for *Good* as a Collocate of *Teacher/s*

now is permanently injured.' Ms Rosevear said	teachers and staff had **good** relationships with the
through OK, and I wonder just how	'good' are the **teachers** in Singapore, Hong Kong,
the epitome of all that can be	**good** in **teachers**. Yet his predecessor at Blaketown
given access to good-quality schooling with	**good**-quality **teachers**. Notwithstanding that, a tendency for
fear maths. I can remember my grade 4	**teacher** rewarding the **good** students with jelly beans
the question - they would 'just prefer a	**good teacher'**. A simple answer is not to
the most important factor (at school). A	**good teacher** needs to have patience, kindness, empathy,
The report states: 'The difference between	**good teachers** and poor teachers can amount to
Victorian education. The deal doesn't recognise	**good teachers**, doesn't fix teacher shortages in
is wrong with paying on performance, if	**good teachers** go to our most challenging schools
get there where your teacher is. My	**teacher** was a **good** one because he brought
are up from 326, 423 to 334, 284 'Without	**good teachers**, we won't have students achieving
from leaving - and 89 per cent agreed that	**teachers** were doing a **good** job in difficult
president Heather Weber said experienced maths	**teachers** were often **good** at making maths interesting,
left teaching (with a package) were the	**good teachers** who knew they could get work

persistent referencing of the 'best teachers' within the ATC does not necessarily contribute to a positive discourse prosody for teacher/s and indeed, as demonstrated in Table 2.18, the 'best teachers' reference is often a shorthand to invoke the other, non-best teachers.

Essentially, *quality*, *good* and *best*, each strong within the ATC as collocates of *teacher/s*, lie at the heart of discourses that essentialize teachers into two groups (the 'good' and the 'bad'). They are thus also a tool used within the public space to flatten or simplify teachers' work in public discourse, denying complexity and complication in favour of a perspective that resonates with and reinforces the extensive experience of the majority of readers on the 'other side of the teacher's desk' (Lortie 1975). Additionally, they both reflect and play into the 'discourse of teacher centrality' (Larsen 2010), which was introduced in Chapter 1 and will be discussed further in relation to issues of *teacher quality* in Chapter 5. As tools within this discourse, these collocates, like the discourse itself, simultaneously elevate and deride teachers, working from an assumption that 'good teachers' and 'good teaching' are universally and consistently understood and experienced.

Finally, a number of other collocates were deemed to be of particular interest because of their emphatic edge, including *every*, *should* and *need*. The prevalence of these collocates within the ATC as collocates of *teacher* (in the case of *every*) and *teachers* (in the case of *need* and *should*) suggests something not only about the tone and register of articles within the corpus but also about the discourse prosody of *teacher/s*. Concordance tables for each of these three words are provided in Tables 2.19, 2.20 and 2.21, respectively.

54   *Constructing Teacher Identities*

Table 2.18 Concordance Lines for *Best* as a Collocate of *Teachers*

School where she was one of the	best and most dedicated teachers and a devoted
in NSW schools. Some of these	teachers are among the best in the state
BIGGEST CHANGES IN HONESTY AND INTEGRITY	BEST FIVE 1983 1993 2003 1 School teachers 55%
were willing to stand up for the	best interests of teachers and students. "We're
Making Time for Great Teaching, notes: "The	best professional development teachers can receive
three weeks and now we will be 80	teachers short. "The best and brightest education
sampled said they intended to become primary	teachers. So, how best to promote the status
research you might find some of the	best teachers in the poorest areas and some
social disadvantage. Its system for rewarding the"	best teachers" is a no-brainer: which postcodes
with the best teachers. To attract the	best, teachers must be well paid and the
from within those communities themselves? "The	best teachers of first peoples are first peoples,"
plan to increase the pay for the	best teachers up to $130,000. It's part of
time over his promise to make Victorian	teachers the best-paid in the country. The
by predator teachers" - should not implicate all	teachers. They do their best with limited resources,
needed to move to a system rewarding	teachers with the best classroom practice, professional

Every teacher accounts for 46.2 per cent of collocations of *every* with *teacher* in the ATC, while *teachers should* accounts for 56.3 per cent of the collocations of *should* with *teachers*.

Furthermore, *teachers need* accounts for 35.1 per cent of collocations of *need* with *teachers*. Many other constructions (e.g. *teachers in the ACT should, teachers and principals need, every beginning teacher*) operate as variants on these.

These three concordances highlight the homogenizing effect that these and other similar collocations have on teachers within the ATC. There is clearly no consistency across the corpus as to the object of what *every teacher* is, needs or should do, but the constructions imply legitimacy for a position that says that it is possible to make such statements about all teachers. Similar to the dichotomizing words discussed above, which pit 'good teachers' against 'poor teachers', they serve to flatten, de-complicate and deliberately obscure the complexity of teachers' work. They also have the effect of discounting the diversity of the teaching profession: with over 337,000 teachers currently working in public, Catholic and independent schools across the eight Australian states and territories (Australian Bureau of Statistics 2021), there is unlikely to be anything at all that *every* teacher *needs* or *should* do. The vast diversity of school and classroom contexts, not to mention differences between the needs and purposes of different groups of teachers, along with individual strengths, needs, dispositions, personal and professional experience and so on are negated here. Constructions such as these, which are very common across the ATC, play into and reinforce common sense

Table 2.19 Concordance Lines for *Every* as a Collocate of *Teacher*

home with his four children. And like	**every** accomplished **teacher**, he also understands the value
that anything less than a full-time	**teacher** aide for **every** Prep class is a
CEO has a support program that matches	**every** beginning **teacher** with a mentor and provides
on getting a properly trained specialist music	**teacher** into **every** school, someone who can teach
ever, ever stop -- ever. Learning as a	**teacher** just continues **every** year,' she says. 'There'
PETER Lindberg of Echuca (March 10) wants a	**teacher** stood down for **every** hour they go
not in a position to provide staff.	**Every teacher** and most of the education support
already working in the education system. And	**every teacher** assistant in the state will receive
huge burden to expect schools to evaluate	**every teacher**, every year. A profession-wide certification
six months of this year, Claasz explains,	**every teacher** had to spend the first 10 minutes
of Justice is squabbling over determining whether	**every teacher** in the state is fit to
subject come alive is the aim of	**every teacher**. Not enough teachers of legal studies
The private schools average 16 students for	**every teacher**, while government schools average 14.8 students
devices to do such a huge task.	**Every teacher** works with other teachers of that
I WISH I had a dollar for	**every** time I heard a **teacher** scream in

Table 2.20 Concordance Lines for *Need* as a Collocate of *Teachers*

violent and unpredictable behaviour,' she said. '	**Teachers** and principals **need** to understand how best
that Australia needs many more inspirational	**teachers**, and that we **need** the systems to
of teacher shortage already, we do not	**need** another 200 or 300 **teachers** ineligible to be standing
has forecast the move will create a	**need** for about 1800 Year 7 **teachers** to be retrained,
system. The Democrats alone recognised the	**need** for specialist **teachers** in primary schools. The
included in the curriculum and recognise the	**need** for **teachers** to be free to spend
the curriculum they are presenting. What students	**need** is for **teachers** to teach them what
Good	**teachers need** a good education and a worthwhile
wide range of skills and knowledge primary	**teachers need** across the curriculum, I'm not
their incomes are lowered. John Uren, Blackburn	**Teachers need** our help The mother who wrote
'should be based in part on what	**teachers need** rather than want to learn'. It'
footballers need recovery time after a match.	**Teachers need** recovery time after a term. It
need to be well supported financially and	**teachers need** to have the right training.' Mr
Ms Jan McMahon, said the government would	**need** to match the **teachers'** offer or face
system would be replaced with another, and	**teachers** would **need** the right of appeal to

understandings of teachers and teaching, invoking the audience's personal experience as students and/or parents and both summoning and enriching the cumulative cultural text of teacher in the public imaginary (Weber 2006). This is not to argue that every reference to teachers in the print media should offer a splendidly articulated and nuanced account of individual teachers and their work: merely that the strong presence of these homogenizing and essentializing discourses within the ATC points to embedded assumptions about teachers being a homogeneous group whose work is both simple and commonly understood.

56 *Constructing Teacher Identities*

Table 2.21 Concordance Lines for *Should* as a Collocate of *Teachers*

equal, and feels safer. Everyone thought that	**teachers** and students **should** respect each other. It
to parents to dictate how schools rules	**should** be applied. **Teachers** are there to teach,
showing 88 per cent of ACT residents believed	**teachers** in the ACT **should** be paid salaries
the subject ethos across. Teacher registration	**should** require deficient **teachers** to undertake mandated make-
education -- reading, writing and mathematics.	**Teachers should** be delivering on this reliable curriculum,
workers.' He said principals, counsellors and	**teachers should** be taught to recognise the potential
to class to trigger ideas and memories.	**Teachers should** bring in books and read the
Teaching standards PERHAPS prospective	**teachers should** complete the compulsory literacy and numeracy
assessments identified areas of need where these	**teachers should** could be used to best advantage
Cameron Arncliffe Here's the deal, kids	**Teachers should** have more time away from students,
also believes that parents as well as	**teachers should** have regular 'guided discussions' with children
made more relevant to students. He said	**teachers should** put less emphasis on requiring students
from the nation's first cross-border	**teachers' strike should** prepare for more industrial disruption.
try to resolve difficulties in attracting science	**teachers**. 'What **should** be done is that teachers
their therapy and educational entitlements. It is	**teachers** who **should** be complaining the loudest. They

Conclusion

This chapter has aimed to provide a holistic overview of the Australian Teacher Corpus, from making an argument for a focus on representations of teachers in the Australian print media on the basis of the relatively high density of press coverage, to locating the articles included in the ATC within the broader context of the newspapers within which they are located, the media landscape generally, and the historical time frame spanned. While it has aimed to provide an initial snapshot of representations of teachers, it has done so with the acknowledgement that the corpus itself is diverse, and that any broad 'findings' at this point require a closer examination that takes into account, for example, issues of dispersion over time and across publications. It is these more nuanced assessments that will fill the remaining chapters of the book.

At the whole-corpus level, this snapshot of the ATC, developed through keyword and collocation analysis, has highlighted, first, that the corpus is largely 'about' teachers. While this might seem to be an obvious observation – 'teacher/s' was, after all, the starting point for the construction of the corpus – it is nevertheless an important confirmation that the corpus is in fact about what it claims to be about. If the focus of this book is on representations and constructions of teachers in print media, a strong sense of the aboutness of the corpus as a whole as related to teachers and their work is an essential underpinning for what is to come.

Second, the analysis has highlighted that within the ATC, teachers are sorted and positioned in various ways according to characteristics that relate to whom and what they teach, to the work that happens in and beyond the classroom, to their performance in a professional capacity and to their involvement in industrial matters. In this sorting and positioning, some aspects of their work – such as those relating to 'core' subjects and classroom discipline – emerge as stronger than others on a whole-corpus level. Rather than an indicator of a 'hard and fast' research finding, this points to possible avenues for further exploration, and accordingly, this sorting and positioning and the aspects of teachers' work that dominate within the corpus will be a point for ongoing attention through the more segmented and focused analysis to come.

Third, in terms of discourse prosody, and acknowledging that broad-based generalizations about representations of *teacher/s* within the ATC would be unwise at this early point, the collocation analysis has highlighted some important starting points. The identification of qualitative markers such as *quality*, *good* and *best* as collocates of teacher/s highlights the prominence of 'quality' discourses, while the emergence of quantitative markers such as *every* and *all*, and imperatives such as *need* and *should* highlight both the all-encompassing and urgent tone of print media discussions of teachers. Indeed, this strong presence of both dichotomizing and homogenizing collocates within the corpus is one of the key findings of the whole-corpus analysis. It points to a very simplistic and 'flattened' representation of teachers and their work within the Australian print media, and this too will be the subject of more detailed exploration, through the diachronic and subsequent analysis.

Finally, the interesting initial findings around gender which emerged in this whole-corpus analysis also suggest possibilities for closer analysis. While much has been written about teaching as a feminized profession over the past three decades in particular (see, e.g. Basten 1997; Moreau 2019; Roulston and Mills 2000), gendered representations of teachers in the public space, and specifically in media discourses, has largely escaped attention. Consequently, this analysis suggests that an exploration of the gendered nature of representations of both teachers and students (for as we have seen in the collocation analysis, both are interrelated) might be a fruitful pathway for subsequent research.

Given the broad picture presented in this chapter of the ATC as a whole, a number of questions, beyond those outlined above, remain. One is around the changing nature of the corpus, and thus representations of teachers in the corpus over time. How far are the preliminary findings presented in this chapter consistently evident in the corpus over the years from 1996 to 2020 and how far are they temporal – or indeed cyclical – concerns? Another is around the sources of these observations – are teachers represented differently in different newspapers and different types of newspapers, for instance broadsheets and tabloids; News Corp-owned and Nine Publishing-owned; left-leaning and right-leaning? Another, given the federated nature of schooling provision and growing federal interference in schooling over the period of the corpus, relates to the balance of national and state concerns reported in the corpus and the positioning of teachers within these national/local discussions. And finally, another relates to the language of competition, performance and accountability in education, as they concern teachers and their work, which emerged within the keyword and collocation analysis presented here. All of these questions, which have been prompted by this preliminary analysis, point to fruitful possibilities for closer analysis. The exploration of some of these avenues, beginning with a diachronic exploration of the twenty-five annual sub-corpora, forms the substance of subsequent chapters of the book.

3

Change over Time

The analysis presented in Chapter 2 focused on the 'aboutness' of the Australian Teacher Corpus (ATC) as a single group of texts and the dominant representations of teachers that emerged while using a very wide-angled lens on the corpus. In this chapter a closer look is taken at the ATC, looking specifically at how both the 'aboutness' of the corpus and the representations of teachers contained within it have changed over time. A diachronic analysis, which explores change over time, will get to questions such as how far the 2020 texts are different from or similar to the 1996 texts in their representations of teachers, how representations have been consistent over the twenty-five-year period spanned by the ATC and how far they have changed. For this analysis, articles from each of the twenty-five calendar years spanned by the ATC were grouped together into what is known as a sub-corpus. The calendar year might be regarded as a somewhat arbitrary divide; however, it was used in this study largely because of the correspondence between the calendar year and the school year in Australia, which means that there is an annual 'rhythm' of reportage of schooling that corresponds with the calendar year, from 'back to school' stories in January to stories about student attainment and achievement in December. The calendar year has been used in this way in previous corpus-assisted studies, both within and beyond education (Baker, Gabrielatos and McEnery 2013; Mockler 2020b).

To produce the diachronic analysis, three strategies were used. First, extending from the keyword analysis presented in Chapter 2, keywords for each of the annual sub-corpora were identified, using the Australian portion of the corpus of News on the Web (NOW-AU) (Davies 2016-) as a reference corpus. This allowed for an exploration of how far the keywords identified within the ATC as a whole were key for the entire duration as opposed to key for some years

60   *Constructing Teacher Identities*

but not others, and consequently how far the 'aboutness' identified in Chapter 2 was consistent throughout the corpus.

A second keyword analysis was then undertaken, comparing each of the annual sub-corpora to the remaining twenty-four years of the ATC. This allowed for a finer-grained analysis of the more subtle nuances of the corpus – here the analysis focuses not on the differences between the collection of articles in the annual sub-corpus and news media stories generally, but between the collection of articles in the annual sub-corpus and other articles similarly focused on teachers, drawn from exactly the same publications but published in different years. The settings used in both types of keyword analysis were identical to those employed for Chapter 2, with Bayesian Information Criterion (BIC) values used as an indicator of significance and Hardie's Log Ratio (with a threshold value of 1.5) used as a measure of effect size. Once again, a word had to appear in 5 per cent of the texts in the sub-corpus to be identified as a keyword, to ensure that keywords were adequately dispersed throughout the sub-corpus.

The chapter takes the central findings of Chapter 2 with respect to 'aboutness' as a starting point, asking how far these findings are borne out in a year-by-year analysis of the ATC against the NOW-AU corpus. It then moves to an examination of the unique and more transient keywords identified in each annual sub-corpus when compared to the rest of the ATC. It concludes with an examination of the changing collocates for *teacher* and *teachers* over the twenty-five years of the ATC, and a consideration of what these, along with the consistent and changing keywords, show about the ATC and representations of teachers over time.

Mapping the big picture: The diachronic shape of the ATC compared to NOW-AU

Comparing each of the annual sub-corpora in the ATC to the NOW-AU corpus yielded fifty words that were key in all twenty-five sub-corpora, while a further forty-eight were key in thirteen or more of the twenty-five sub-corpora. This suggests, broadly, that there is a consistent 'aboutness' to the ATC; however, the question here is how far it reflects the 'top-level' findings presented in Chapter 2: how far are the keywords identified as central to the 'aboutness' of the ATC as a whole dispersed throughout the corpus as opposed to concentrated in a more truncated time frame?

'Lockwords' in the ATC

In his diachronic analysis of vocabulary change in British English from the 1930s to the early 2000s, Baker developed the concept of a 'lockword': 'a word which may change in its meaning or context of usage when we compare a set of diachronic corpora together, yet appears to be relatively static in terms of frequency' (Baker 2011: 66). The lockwords, or words which were key in all twenty-five years of the ATC, are presented in Table 3.1.

Perhaps unsurprisingly, twenty-five of the top thirty keywords across the ATC as a whole (see Table 2.5), emerged as lockwords. Of the remaining five, four (*numeracy, pupils, educators* and *child's*) were key in at least twenty-one of the twenty-five sub-corpora, spread over almost the full duration of the ATC: for example, *numeracy* was a keyword in twenty-one of the sub-corpora, the first in 1997 and the last in 2020. The remaining word, *grammar*, while key for the ATC as a whole, was key in only fifteen of the twenty-five sub-corpora, every year from 2004 to 2020 with the exceptions of 2013 and 2018. Concordance analysis highlighted that the usage of *grammar* is quite consistently split between reference to individual schools (e.g. *Sydney Grammar School*), which accounts for approximately a third of instances, and reference to grammar itself, particularly in the context of English teaching and student literacy. Additionally, it was difficult to identify from the concordance analysis a clear explanation as to why *grammar* did not appear as a keyword prior to 2004: both the usage and frequency appeared to be relatively similar across each of the twenty-five years of the ATC. Closer analysis of the frequency and keyword lists, however, highlighted that in each of the twenty-five years in which *grammar* was not identified as a keyword, it was because it was dispersed across slightly less than 5 per cent of the texts in the corpus (e.g. 4.92 per cent in 1998, 4.79 per cent in 2000 and 4.91 per cent in 2018), while the BIC and Log Ratio values would otherwise have identified it as a keyword. This is a salient illustration of how quantitative analysis needs to be supplemented with close textual analysis in corpus-based work.

Table 3.1 'Lockwords' in the Australian Teacher Corpus (Compared to NOW-AU), Ordered Alphabetically

---

academic, Catholic, child, children, children's, class, classes, classroom, classrooms, college, courses, curriculum. department, education, educational, English, girls, kids, language, learning, lessons, letters, literacy, maths, parent, parents, primary, principal, principals, profession, programs, reading, school, school's, schooling, schools, science, secondary, skills, student, students, studies, subjects, taught, teach, teacher, teacher's, teachers, teaching, union

---

62   *Constructing Teacher Identities*

Table 3.2 Keywords in the ATC, Organized by Category and Ordered by Log Ratio, Diachronic Keywords in Bold

Teachers	**teachers, teacher, teacher's, educators, profession, federation, discipline, union,** shortage, **unions,** salary, specialist, **male,** industrial, strike, **staff,** pay, **association**
Teaching	**classroom, teaching, classrooms, teach, taught, classes, learning, lessons, achievement, academic, lesson, class, standards, assessment, outcomes, tests,** computer, **performing, encouraged**
Curriculum	**numeracy, curriculum, literacy, maths, grammar, subjects, English, skills, language, science, reading, programs, arts, books,** writes, **write, writing, subject, knowledge**
School	**principals, schools, school's, schooling, school, secondary, principal,** disadvantaged, **primary, Catholic, college, department,** funding
Students	**pupils, students, child's, student, parents, children, parent, boys, studying, childhood, kids, child, girls, studies, boy, attend, adults**
Teacher education	**courses, graduates, graduate, universities, qualified, training, university, trained**

Diachronic keywords

The six categories of keywords presented in Chapter 2, namely teachers, teaching, curriculum, school, students and teacher education were also investigated diachronically. Table 3.2 highlights the ninety-four keywords in these six categories once again, with the eighty-five that were key in a majority of years, spread consistently across the sub-corpora, in bold.

Essentially, this analysis is consistent with the findings presented earlier. Only thirteen of the keywords used in Chapter 2 to represent the 'aboutness' of the ATC were found to have a pattern of decreasing or increasing importance within the corpus over time. These words, along with an indication of their keyword status in each year of the ATC, are presented in Table 3.3, organized within categories.

Taking first the category of *teachers*, the word *association*, key in each year of the corpus until 2011, and then once more in 2014, points to the decreasing importance of professional associations in the reporting of stories about teachers. *Association* appeared in 16 per cent of articles in the 1998 sub-corpus, most usually in the reporting of statements or responses from various principals' associations (such as the SA Primary Principals' Association, the New South Wales (NSW) Secondary Principals' Association and so on) and other professional associations for teachers (including the

Table 3.3 Keywords in the ATC: Changing Patterns over Time

		1996	1997	1998	1999	2000	2001	2002	2003	2004	2005	2006	2007	2008	2009	2010	2011	2012	2013	2014	2015	2016	2017	2018	2019	2020
Teachers	association	•	•	•	•	•	•	•	•	•	•	•	•	•	•	•	•			•						
	salary	•	•			•	•				•	•			•	•	•	•	•	•	•					
	pay	•					•				•	•		•	•	•	•		•	•	•					
	shortage				•	•	•	•	•	•	•			•	•	•										
	specialist							•	•								•	•	•	•	•	•	•	•		•
Teaching	computer	•	•	•	•	•	•	•	•		•		•	•	•											
	lesson					•				•						•	•	•	•	•	•	•	•	•	•	•
	outcomes					•				•	•	•	•	•	•	•	•	•	•	•	•	•	•	•	•	•
	performing												•	•	•	•	•	•	•	•	•	•	•	•	•	•
Schools	funding					•				•			•	•		•	•	•			•	•				
	disadvantaged												•	•	•	•	•	•	•	•		•	•		•	•
Teacher education	graduates			•	•	•	•				•	•	•	•	•	•	•	•	•	•	•	•		•	•	
	graduate			•	•	•	•				•	•	•		•	•	•	•	•	•	•	•		•	•	

English Teachers' Association of NSW, the Australian Science Teachers' Association and the TAFE (Technical and Further Education) Teachers' Association); and parent and community groups such as the Isolated Children's Parents' Association and the Parents and Citizens' Association. By 2018, this representation dropped to only 7 per cent of articles, similarly populated by the same groups. The question of representation of teachers' and school leaders' groups as voices of authority in newspaper articles about teachers and teaching is a significant line of inquiry which, while not explored in depth here, could be taken up in subsequent work, but this observation suggests a declining importance accorded to teachers' and principals' voices, and is consistent with recent work on teachers and the Australian print media (Mockler 2020a).

The prevalence of *salary* and *pay* in the sub-corpora from 1996 to 2012/2013 is reflective of shifting discussions of teachers' salaries over that time. The year 1996 saw the election of the Howard Liberal–National Coalition (Conservative) government at a federal level in Australia after thirteen years of Labor rule, during which time the Prices and Incomes Accord had been negotiated and re-negotiated between the Commonwealth government and the Australian Council of Trade Unions from 1983 onwards. The end of the accord, heralded by the election of the new government, saw protracted industrial negotiations between teachers and their employers in many Australian states and territories over 1996 and 1997, negotiations which periodically continued in different parts of Australia as new enterprise bargains were negotiated and struck into the 2000s. By 2011, 2012 and 2013, the prevalence of *pay* within the sub-corpora reflected not only ongoing wage negotiations, but also ongoing discussion in different state and territory jurisdictions about *performance pay* for teachers, an idea that was floated by then Prime Minister Julia Gillard, in May 2011 (Gillard 2011). Concordance and collocation analysis for *pay* in the combined 2011, 2012 and 2013 sub-corpora highlighted that *performance* was the second most frequent lexical collocate (after *teachers*) in this period, supplemented also by references to *merit pay, bonus pay* and *bonuses.*

Specialist was a keyword in 2001 and 2002 and then again for most years from 2010 to 2020. The early iteration of this within the ATC referred in roughly equal measures to the growth of specialist schools, mostly in NSW, that took place over this time and to the shortage of *specialist* teachers (e.g. language teachers) in the context of a broader teacher *shortage. Specialist* schools, many of which were partially or completely selective secondary schools, on the basis of academic or other (e.g. performing arts, sports) performance, were the subject of some debate in the early 2000s, before becoming almost seamlessly subsumed into the New South Wales (NSW) government system (Campbell and Sherington 2013; Campbell, Proctor and Sherington 2009). The growth in prevalence of *specialist* in the years from 2010 to 2020 is similarly reflective of education policy shifts – this time attempts to get more specialist teachers, particularly mathematics and science teachers, into primary schools in particular, which began during the years of the Rudd-Gillard Labor government and have been continued by the Liberal–National Coalition government since 2013 (Bourke, Mills and Siostrom 2020).

The 'teaching' keywords in Table 3.3 reflect first the late 1990s/early 2000s focus on the use of computers in schools and classrooms, including various state and territory initiatives early on in this period to influence teachers' engagement with Information and Communication Technology (ICT), through to the *Digital Education Revolution* (Australian Government Department of Education Employment and Workplace Relations 2010) of the Rudd-Gillard Labor government, which sought to provide a laptop computer for every child in an Australian school. Growing attention to formalized professional teaching standards and to teacher quality over the second half of the ATC was linked to the corresponding prevalence of both *outcomes* and *lesson*, where both student learning outcomes and the outcomes of schooling more broadly gained overage within the print media. *Lesson* planning/plans and *lesson* preparation were also topics with increasing coverage over the past decade in particular, linked often to stories about teacher workload.

Performing was a keyword in every ATC annual sub-corpus from 2007 to 2019, reflecting the increasing attention to performance – of teachers, students, schools, and school systems – in Australian education policy since the election of the Rudd-Gillard Labor government in 2007. By way of illustrating the rise and changing shape of this discourse of performance over the course of the twenty-five years covered by the ATC, Table 3.4 highlights the top ten collocates of *performing* in 1996 (when it was not a keyword), in 2007 (when it first became a keyword) and in 2019. The lexical collocates of 1996 point largely towards the performing arts: *Newtown* references Newtown High School of the Performing Arts in Sydney, as does *high* here. In 2007, *arts* was still the top collocate of *performing*, but the remaining nine collocates all relate to competition and performance. *High* here is generally about *high performing* rather than high schools. By 2019, *arts* is no longer one of the top ten collocates of *performing*, and all ten collocates relate in some way to competitive performance. Notably, five of the 2019 collocates relate directly to reportage of Australia's performance on international standardized tests: *Estonia, systems, Finland, Singapore* and *countries*, signalling how far Australia had come in terms of international competitiveness by 2019, and the 'reference societies' (Sellar and Lingard 2013) to which it was compared.

The final category for consideration is that of schools, where *funding* was a keyword in 2001, 2004, 2007, 2008, 2010 to 2013, 2016 and 2017. School funding in Australia is both particularly complex (Dowling 2008) and the subject of ongoing public debate (Rowe and Perry 2020), and the pattern of *funding* as a keyword reflects various policy shifts in school funding over this time. First, then Prime Minister John Howard's establishment and then

Table 3.4 Top Ten Collocates of *Performing* in the 1996, 2007 and 2019 Sub-corpora, Ordered by MI

1996	2007	2019
Newtown	arts	stronger
arts	poorly	Estonia
visual	rewards	systems
high	highest	Finland
how	aren't	world's
schools	low	Singapore
school	reward	top
state	systems	highest
are	high	countries
and	under	disadvantaged

re-authorization of the so-called Socio-Economic Status (SES) funding model for non-government schools in 2001 and 2004 respectively is reflected in the pattern. The SES model purportedly allocated proportionate funding to schools on the basis of the postcodes of students' homes, although by 2005 over half of all non-government schools were funded on the basis of 'funding guaranteed' or 'funding maintained', receiving 'an adjusted amount because a strict application of their SES score would have given these schools less funding' (Dowling 2008: 139). Two rounds of 'Gonski reviews' then took place in the 2010s. 'Gonski 1' was commissioned by the Rudd-Gillard government in 2010 and intended to be a once-in-a-generation review of school funding arrangements to ensure the equitable resourcing of Australian schools. The report was handed to the government in November 2011, by which time the education minister and later prime minister had, through her continued assurance that 'no school will lose a dollar' (Gillard 2010) effectively ensured 'funding maintained' status for all non-government schools, requiring a $6 billion injection of funds to achieve equity of funding for all schools. By the time the government response to the Gonski 1 report was announced, in September 2012, it came in the form of the *National Plan for School Improvement*, effectively pivoting the discussion from equity of funding to quality of teachers and schools (Mockler 2014). Discussion and debate around school funding continued until after the federal election in September 2013 in which the Rudd-Gillard government lost to the Liberal-National Coalition government. 'Gonski 2.0' was then commissioned by the Abbott–Turnbull–Morrison government in 2017, after considerable pressure from community-based groups around the realization of the aims of Gonski 1; however, Gonski 2 focused not on the creation and implementation of needs-based funding, but rather on how school funding might be best used to improve outcomes for students and schools.

Finally, *disadvantaged* was a keyword for each year of the ATC from 2007 to 2020 with the exceptions of 2015 and 2018. Addressing educational disadvantage was a key concern of the Australian Labor Party's Education Revolution (Commonwealth of Australia 2008), itself a key plank in the party's pre-election strategy in 2007. The attention to disadvantage, and in particular, *disadvantaged schools*, namely those schools inadequately funded, grew throughout the Labor years with the focus on school funding associated with the first Gonski review. The Abbott Liberal–National Coalition government, which came to power in 2013, inherited the ongoing community attention to educational disadvantage linked to Gonski 1, and particularly to questions of whether, how and when the reforms recommended by the review around 'needs-based funding' would be implemented, and at what cost. Despite the successful pivot between the two reviews on the part of the government from a focus on equity to a focus on quality (a pivot which had been well begun by the previous government, as noted above) (Mockler 2014), the discourse of disadvantage in relation to education has remained.

All in all, this diachronic comparison between the ATC and the NOW corpus has highlighted the relative stability of the ATC in terms of its focus (as highlighted in the large number of lockwords and other keywords in a large proportion of the sub-corpora). This is perhaps unsurprising given the relative stability, also, of schooling as a social institution over the past twenty-five years. It has also highlighted, however, some of the key changes in education policy and shifts in the way that education is discussed in the public space: growing emphases on performance and accountability, and on educational disadvantage are examples of these shifts that we can see reflected in the data. In order to take a more fine-grained look at these and other shifts within the ATC, however, we will now swap 'lenses' to explore the changing shape of the corpus at a closer, more 'zoomed-in' level.

Change over time in the ATC

In order to take a closer look at the changing aboutness of the ATC over time, each annual sub-corpus was compared to the remainder of the ATC. As noted above, this analysis allowed for a comparison not between articles in the ATC and general news media stories but rather a comparison between articles focused on teachers over time. This keyword analysis produced 149 lexical keywords over the twenty-five years of the ATC, of which 121 were unique to one year. The remaining twenty-eight keywords were key for between two and five years of the corpus, sometimes but not always in consecutive years. The discussion in this section will generally consider the unique keywords before moving to the diachronic ones, with some overlap where the two sets of keywords coalesce around a single issue or focus. Figure 3.1 highlights the number of keywords identified in each sub-corpus of the ATC, along with the number of keywords unique to each sub-corpus.

This graph points to a number of observations. First, there is a relatively small number of keywords present in most of the sub-corpora. This reflects the consistency across the ATC as a whole that was highlighted in the NOW-AU comparison, which showed a large number of keywords common to all or many

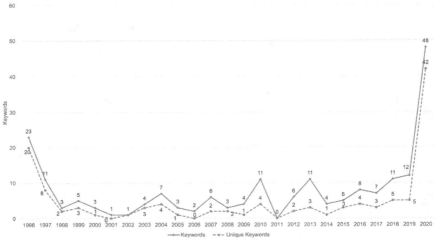

Figure 3.1 Number of lexical keywords and unique keywords by annual sub-corpora.

of the sub-corpora. Second, for most of the annual sub-corpora, there was a mixture of keywords common to other sub-corpora and unique keywords, with unique keywords comprising somewhere around half of the keywords in most years. This suggests a mixture of more and less transient keywords, not only based upon news events particular to one year but also relating to longer 'story arcs' that extend beyond one or two years. The first year of the Covid-19 pandemic, 2020, which had significant effects for schools and teachers and generated a great deal of discussion about the role of teachers in remote learning during lockdown, was by far the year with the largest number of keywords, forty-nine in total with forty-one of those unique. The unique keywords for 2020 include *covid*, *lockdown*, *distancing* and so on: words that were scarcely part of common lexicon prior to the pandemic. The years 1996 and 2018 were the two years with the next highest number of both keywords and unique keywords. The year 1996 was a year of significant industrial action on the part of teachers in NSW and elsewhere in Australia, and the vast majority of keywords in 1996 related to this. Marriage equality was passed into law in Australia in December 2017, as part of the Marriage Amendment (Definitions and Religious Freedoms) Act, and 2018 was a year consumed with public discussions around freedom of religion. The majority of 2018 keywords related to this debate, linked as it was in the media to schools, teachers and their work (a topic for further exploration below). These three examples, one from within the world of education and two very different ones from outside, serve to illustrate the way in which media reporting of issues to do with teachers is reflective of both broader social events and discussions,

Change Over Time

and more local and specific ones. Discussions of teachers in the print media are both distinct from and also influenced by broader social policy shifts and social movements.

Initially, the group of keywords identified was divided into unique and diachronic keywords (i.e. those key in more than one of the annual sub-corpora), and close concordance analysis was performed for all keywords in all years in which they were key. Table 3.5 includes keywords that were unique in each year of the ATC, organized by year, with adjacent notes about key events referenced by the keywords, as identified through concordance analysis. The keyword *Scott* is included in the table twice, once in 2016 where it referred predominantly to Mark Scott, who was appointed as Secretary of the NSW Department of Education in that year, and once in 2020 where it referred predominantly to Prime Minister Scott Morrison.

The unique keywords displayed in Table 3.5 reflect issues and events bounded within a single year, and on occasion issues that crossed years in the corpus but were represented slightly differently in different years. For example, 1996 and 1997 were characterized by widespread industrial action on the part of teachers' unions in different states and territories. The unique keywords of 1996 reflect the industrial action in NSW (*Denis, Fitzgerald*) and South Australia (*Giles, Lucas, SAIT*),[1] while the unique keywords of 1997 reflect ongoing industrial action in Queensland (*Mackie, Quinn*). Unique keywords are linked on occasion to federal elections and changes in government at the Commonwealth level (2004 *Latham*, 2013 *Coalition*, 2016 *Malcolm*).

At different points of the twenty-five years of the ATC, unique keywords reflect particular moments of debate around issues related to teachers and schooling. A national debate, reflected in the unique keyword *values*, erupted in 2004 around 'Australian *values*' and how far public schools and public school teachers promoted or withheld support for such values.

> In a weekend interview with The Age, [then Prime Minister] Mr Howard said parents were deserting the state school system because they felt it was 'too politically correct and too values-neutral'. (Guerrera, Leung and Crabb 2004)

Part of the broader culture wars stoked in many different ways by Howard over the course of his prime ministership, this ongoing debate was spurred

---

[1] *SAIT* refers to the South Australian Institute of Teachers, the legacy name of the teachers' union in South Australia, which in 1993 had become the South Australian branch of the Australian Education Union (AEU).

Constructing Teacher Identities

Table 3.5 Unique Keywords by Year (with Associated Events Noted)

	Unique Keywords (ordered by LR)	Associated Events
1996	SAIT, Lucas, Giles, offs, Fitzgerald, dispute, Denis, strikes, Janet, rolling, industrial, strike, resolve, negotiate, claim, rise, wage, hit, productivity, trade	End of the Accord; Industrial action and salary negotiations in many states and territories
1997	percent, Kemp, Mackie, Quinn, Boston, Royal, Commission, allegations	Continuing industrial action and salary negotiations; Wood Royal Commission into Paedophilia and government response (NSW); National Child Protection strategy
1998	computers, unit	NSW Department of Education Computers in Schools Program; *Computers in the Classroom* series of articles in *The Australian*; Changes proposed to the NSW HSC, including related to 2- and 3-unit studies
1999	Simpson, web, HSC	'Web page' and 'web site' used commonly
2000	Delahunty	Ongoing wage negotiations and settlements
2001		
2002	Watkins	
2003	Refshauge, Iraq	Australian involvement in second Iraq war
2004	Latham, values, discrimination, male	Federal election; national debate about 'values' in public schools
2005	pleaded	A number of high-profile child protection cases
2006		
2007	McGowan, summer	
2008	Rudd's, revolution	Start of the Rudd–Gillard 'education revolution'
2009	Anna	Queensland students identified as strongly underperforming in the second year of NAPLAN
2010	boycott, Gillard's, website, tests	First year of My School website; AEU boycott; League Table discussion
2011		
2012	Adrian, Baillieu	

Table 3.5 Continued

	Unique Keywords (ordered by LR)	Associated Events
2013	autonomy, reforms, Coalition	Defeat of Rudd-Gillard government by Liberal–National Coalition
2014	Facebook	
2015	headmaster, abuse, abused	Royal Commission into Institutional Responses to Child Sexual Abuse (Federal)
2016	STEM, Malcolm, gender, Scott (Mark), Simon	Safe Schools controversy; First full year of Malcolm Turnbull's prime ministership
2017	digital, marriage, engagement	Marriage Equality postal vote; New Digital Technologies Australian Curriculum
2018	religious, freedom, Chris, faith, gay	Teacher's Pet podcast about teacher Chris Dawson; Ruddock Religious Freedom Review
2019	PISA, ATAR, climate, OECD, degrees	New ATAR requirement for teaching degrees; School Climate Change Strikes; PISA 2018 results released
2020	covid, coronavirus, pandemic, distancing, lockdown, virus, transmission, remotely, reopen, infection, restrictions, closures, Andrews, isolation, vulnerable, cancelled, remote, online, cabinet, spread, safe, return, Mitchell, advice, amid, closed, health, anxiety, shut, crisis, Scott (Morrison), medical, transition, face, returning, home, attendance, Daniel, tested, normal, specialist, risk, cases	Covid-19 global pandemic forces widespread school shutdowns in Australia and elsewhere

along in 2004 by \$30 billion of pre-election funding contributed by the Commonwealth to values education. The funding came with conditions, however, among them:

> Every school must also have a functioning flag-pole, fly the Australian flag and display the values framework in a prominent place in the school, as a condition of funding. (Howard and Nelson 2004)

72   *Constructing Teacher Identities*

This was not by any means the first time that a Commonwealth government had sought to interfere with schools and school systems for which they have no constitutional responsibility: Prime Minister Menzies's funding of science laboratories for secondary schools in the 1960s; the three-fold increase in federal funding to schools that took place in the two years after the Whitlam government-commissioned Karmel Report in the 1970s (Campbell and Proctor 2014); and education minister in the Howard government from 1996 to 2001 David Kemp's forays into obtaining state and territory agreement for standardized literacy testing (Lingard 2000) spring to mind. In his use of teachers and schools in the fight against 'political correctness' and the overt promotion of Australian nationalism, however, Howard politicized the teaching profession in a new way, which, as I shall argue below, has become the modus operandi of subsequent prime ministers and Commonwealth governments.

The unique keywords for 2010 provide another significant example of this. While NAPLAN (the National Assessment Program – Literacy and Numeracy) testing began in 2008, as previous research has highlighted, NAPLAN-related media coverage was minimal until the launch of the My School website by the Commonwealth government in 2010. In 2008 and 2009, respectively, there were 34 and 174 articles published in the twelve national and capital city daily newspapers on NAPLAN, as opposed to 924 in 2010 (Mockler 2020a). *NAPLAN* itself is not a unique keyword in any year of the ATC, appearing as a diachronic keyword in 2010, 2013, 2018 and 2019; however, the unique 2010 keywords relate strongly to the NAPLAN/My School policy ensemble: the January 2010 publication of results from NAPLAN *tests* on the *website* strongly identified as Julia *Gillard's* brainchild, led to a proposed *boycott* of the 2010 NAPLAN tests by teachers' unions. Debates surrounding the creation of *league tables* from NAPLAN data as published on MySchool are similarly reflected in the 2010 keywords, although both are also keywords in the 2009 sub-corpus, when the debate first surfaced. In NSW, this debate was particularly potent as an amendment to the legislation was introduced by the NSW Greens and supported by the Liberal–National coalition in 2009 to ban the publication of school league tables in newspapers, opening newspapers to the possibility of legal action should they do so. The *Sydney Morning Herald* (2010) responded with not only a league table published the day after the launch of the website but also a lengthy editorial explaining that newspaper-generated league tables were a basic tenet of democracy and part of the newspaper's historical commitment to 'quality education':

Change Over Time

> Today, consistent with [our] historic support for quality education, the Herald publishes a league table of NSW schools. We do so fully aware of the controversy it is likely to raise – and in full knowledge that what we do contravenes the absurd, inconsistent and oppressive law of this state. (2010)

While the moratorium was lifted days prior to the 2010 tests, much of the reporting about teachers in 2010 related to their location within the debate around My School and whether or not they would boycott NAPLAN, all of which are clearly reflected in the 2010 keywords, both unique and diachronic.

The final set of unique keywords to be highlighted here crosses three of the sub-corpora of the ATC, and relates to somewhat connected debates around gender and sexuality education, marriage equality and religious freedom which took place in Australia in 2016, 2017 and 2018, respectively. Public discussion around school education and teachers' work in Australia in 2016 was shaped to a significant extent around the *Safe Schools Program*, a programme designed to 'help school leadership, teachers and communities create safer and more inclusive environments for same sex attracted, intersex and gender diverse students, school staff and families' (Safe Schools Coalition Australia 2021). The programme was first implemented in Victoria in 2010 and received federal funding from the outgoing Labor government in 2013. It had been formally launched by newly elected Liberal prime minister Tony Abbott in June 2013. In February 2016, *The Australian* broke an 'exclusive' front-page story about the programme, entitled 'Activists Push Taxpayer-Funded Gay Manual in Schools'. It began:

> Eleven-year-old children are being taught about sexual orientation and transgender issues at school in a taxpayer-funded program written by gay activists.
>
> The Safe Schools Coalition teaching manual says that asking parents if their baby is a boy or a girl reinforces a 'heteronormative world view'.
>
> Religious groups yesterday criticised the 'age-inappropriate' manual, which suggests that sexuality be raised in every subject area. 'Whatever the subject, try to work out ways to integrate gender diversity and sexual diversity across your curriculum,' the manual says. (Bita 2016)

The 10 February story formed the basis for a speech in the House of Representatives later that day by Liberal MP Graham Perrett (Commonwealth of Australia 2016); was followed up by an editorial in *The Australian* the following day and 'would set the political agenda for months to come' (Law 2017: 27). The concordance lines presented in Table 3.6, randomly selected occurrences

74   *Constructing Teacher Identities*

Table 3.6 Concordance Lines for *Gender* from the 2016 Sub-corpus

issues such as same-sex marriage and	**gender** and sexual fluidity. One girl wrote to
gender studies, including the contentious idea that -	**gender** and sexuality are socially constructed and change
its promotion of the contested idea that	**gender** and sexuality is fluid. It sparked a
existence has relied on rigid concepts of	**gender** - are grappling with. For the first time,
there is a need for a closer	**gender** balance. 'It wouldn't hurt to have
I don't like this thing called	**gender**-based violence'. 'She says the key has
and gender diversity'. 'Many students may believe	**gender** can only be either male or female
of new secondary school programmes that address	**gender** conflict and related bullying. While I agree
bloke quotas'" in schools and hospitals. Workforce	**Gender** Equality Agency, the federal government agency se
like a benign social trend towards more	**gender** fluidity is actually a feminist revolution toward
who suspected Jeremy was struggling with his	**gender** identity emailed him a link to a
binary stereotype – which doesn't exist because	**gender** is fluid and limitless,'" he said. 'I
ho threpsas, the one who raised him. The	**gender** of the participle tells us that it
spokeswoman said where a student may have	**gender**-questioning issues, 'the school would expect its
university undergraduate choosing to enrol in	**gender** studies units and studying these ideas to

of *gender* in the 2016 sub-corpus, highlight the flavour of the discussion around gender and sexuality in relation to teachers and their work in 2016.

The year 2017 saw the advent of a postal vote on marriage equality in Australia, which eventually, after protracted 'Yes' and 'No' campaigns, led to the passing of the Marriage Amendment (Definition and Religious Freedoms) Act (2017). That *marriage* emerged as a keyword in the 2017 corpus is reflective of the way that schools and teachers were drawn into the public debate around marriage equality, generally by proponents of the 'no' campaign, who were often also church leaders. One such example comes from an op-ed penned by the then Moderator General of the Presbyterian Church of Australia shortly after the postal vote was announced:

> Marriage, as defined today between a man and a woman, is the best way for Australian society to flourish. It has been the foundation of stable societies since time immemorial and is central to the raising of the next generation. … If same-sex marriage becomes law this will have a significant and disturbing impact on our schools. There is no doubt that teachers will be required to teach pupils about the validity of same-sex marriage. (Wilson 2017)

The potential damage to be done to children and young people by the introduction of marriage equality was a key focus of the 'no' campaign throughout the debate, and Safe Schools was often invoked as an example of this potential damage, as *Daily Telegraph* columnist Miranda Devine wrote in October 2017:

> One of the crucial issues swaying voters appears to be the link to Safe Schools and gender issues, which the No campaign has been highlighting in its ads featuring young mums. (Devine 2017)

Devine goes on in the same article to invoke tales of the Canadian experience where, post-marriage-equality legislation, teachers' unions had used legal pathways to promote the idea that the 'LGBTIQ lifestyle' should be 'celebrated' in the classroom:

> The Elementary Teachers' Federation of Ontario argued in court that since gay marriage is now the law, teachers are legally obliged to teach children not just to 'tolerate' the LGBTIQ lifestyle but to 'celebrate' it. (Devine 2017)

Table 3.7 highlights randomly selected concordance lines for *marriage* in the 2017 sub-corpus, highlighting the frequency with which this keyword was used in relation to same-sex marriage or marriage equality in this sub-corpus, providing some insight into the juxtaposition of *marriage* with young people and the work of schools and teachers.

As a concession to the hard-right faction of the conservative government, which had been advocating for an extension of religious freedom protections in the Act that legislated for marriage equality, then prime minister Malcolm Turnbull commissioned a review into the protection of religious freedom, ahead of the vote in the House of Representatives. Led by ex-Attorney General Philip Ruddock, the 'Ruddock Report' was handed down to the government in May 2018 and released to the public in December of that year, two months after the recommendations had been leaked to the press. While the review 'did not accept the argument, put by some, that religious freedom is in imminent peril' (Ruddock et al.: 8), it did recommend the amendment of the Commonwealth Sex Discrimination Act 1984 to allow exemptions for religious schools to discriminate in their employment of staff and in relation to students on the

Table 3.7 Concordance Lines for *Marriage* from the 2017 Sub-corpus

whether to support a motion to make gay	**marriage** binding ALP policy. With no resolution in sight,
wife, Adele, he enjoyed a long and happy	**marriage**, blessed by twins Sarah and Michael. It was
people who are not in a same-sex	**marriage**. But kids are being exposed to inappropriate mate
5 million Australians who voted for traditional	**marriage**. But the majority want same-sex marriage, they
what legislative provisions are dreamed up in the	**marriage** equality debate, and no matter what sophistry or
many compelling reasons for Australia to adopt	**marriage** equality, including the fact that doing so is
we go in dismantling our language. The phrase	**marriage** equality used in regard to same-sex relationships
campaigning. Was there a wrong way to support	**marriage** equality? 'We need to ensure there are many
a public denunciation of church teachings on	**marriage**. Father Frank Brennan, chief executive of Catholic
we are calling it now - is not about	**marriage**. It's about much more than that. Only
down the path of changing [the] law on	**marriage**, it's very hard to say no to
In affirming conservative views regarding	**marriage**, Margaret Court is only upholding our existing la
ought to be protected. Behind the same-sex	**marriage** movement is a superficial view of marriage that
love for the vulnerable student and spoke of	**marriage** plans in the texts, Queensland Civil and -
time was forced to surrender her position on	**marriage**. She also had to repay her teacher's

76 · Constructing Teacher Identities

Table 3.8 Concordance Lines for *Gay* from the 2018 Sub-corpus

fitted with unnecessary and flashy 'contemporary'	**gay** and Indigenous messaging - there's no evidence
schools ask a student whether they are	**gay** and then prevent them from enrolling? Best
would discriminate against someone for being born	**gay**, but intelligent people can still disagree on
freedom to kick out kids who are	**gay**. Long live freedom of faith. So the
from a man who abstained from the	**gay**-marriage vote, declaring his electorate knew his
the law change. 'In the old days,	**gay** people kept quiet. That's over. 'My
he was in a same-sex relationship.	**Gay** rights advocates have since been pushing for
it would swiftly pass legislation to protect	**gay** students against discrimination, it failed to rea
of religious freedom to being mean to	**gay** students? Not with my taxes, they don'
vows to end similar rights to expel	**gay** students. Parliament resumes today with the
the ACT, NSW and WA to reject	**gay** students'. The committee was proposing schools
right to discriminate ('Top schools split on	**gay** teachers as alumni revolt', November 3–4). As a
ban religious schools from discriminating against	**gay** teachers as the government prepares to introduce
Australia's most senior Catholics has suggested	**gay** teachers would be more acceptable at religious
in Victoria to target students for being	**gay**. The Greens sought in 2016 to strip Victoria

basis of sexual orientation, gender identity or relationship status. What seems to have been little known within the community at the time was that broad-based exemptions to the sex discrimination act already existed for schools across Australia on the basis of sexual orientation, relationship status and so on.

Public outcry against the proposed changes was strong, despite an ongoing campaign on the part of the Christian schools lobby and others to maintain the right to discriminate against gay teachers and students. Four of the six unique keywords in 2018, *faith*, *freedom*, *gay* and *religious*, reflect this debate and the centrality of teachers and schools to discussions of religious freedom and faith-based discrimination in Australia. The randomly selected concordance lines for *gay* and *faith* highlighted in Tables 3.8 and 3.9 reflect the flavour of this public discussion.

Public debates around values, gender identity, marriage equality, faith and so on in Australia are not exclusively about the issues on which they focus. As Poulos has shown, over the course of the period covered by the ATC, and in the face of low levels of party differentiation brought about by the embrace of neoliberalism on both sides of politics,

> One of the few locations for vigorous partisan distinction became the 'culture wars'. Fought on values and in public policy debates on issues including history, racism, education (funding and curriculum), and social inclusion and exclusion (especially LGBTIQ rights), 'ambiguous (and necessarily vague) Christian rhetoric' (Maddox 2011: 288) was deliberately used to mark the battlelines. (Poulos 2020: 14–15)

What this analysis shows is that teachers and their work have also been implicated in the culture wars, through a focus variously on the values they do or do not

Change Over Time

Table 3.9 Concordance Lines for *Faith* from the 2018 Sub-corpus

which they regard as attacking their Catholic	**faith** and the autonomy of their families. The
exemptions in the Sex Discrimination Act for	**faith**-based educators. The group of 34 includes the
allowed him to reduce the right of	**faith**-based organisations to discriminate against
any religious activities were an add-on.	**Faith**-based schools did not discriminate against any
of its conduct'. The panel also agreed	**faith**-based schools should have some discretion to
Freedom of religion laws should allow	**faith**-based schools to sack or exclude practising
Act. Instead of upholding the ability of	**faith**-based schools to promote their own ethos
Sundays. He did not speak of his	**faith**, but it sustained him throughout. He was
for meaningful action to protect people of	**faith** in Australia following the damaging leak of
even when we have placed great	**faith** in our own opinions. We shouldn't
his abuse. It has also destroyed their	**faith**. 'It was', says one of his Sydney
run rather than walk towards the desired	**faith** on offer and to not identify with
going to be certain elements of that	**faith** that are taught,' Mr Coe said. 'By
treatment of charities that are founded on	**faith**. The St Vincent de Paul Society is
discretion to ensure the ethos of their	**faith**, they differ on how this principle should

teach to their students; on the curriculum they promote in their classrooms and on their sexuality, relationship status and fidelity to the moral code of the 'faith-based schools' in which many of them teach.

The diachronic keywords across the twenty-five years of the corpus highlight the interplay between teachers' work and politics in public discussions about education. Table 3.10 presents the twenty-eight keywords that were key in more than one year between 1996 and 2020, organized according to the overarching three topics of politics, education policy and teachers and schooling, identified through the concordance analysis process described above.

Twenty of the twenty-eight diachronic keywords relate to politics, and here some interesting insights are raised. First, despite the constitutional responsibility for schooling in Australia residing with the states and territories, and thus states and territory governments and ministers being typically more 'hands on' with schooling and teachers than their Commonwealth counterparts, Commonwealth ministers and prime ministers' names are far more prominent on the keyword lists. Where state and territory ministers for education or premiers do appear on keyword lists, they tend to do so in only one sub-corpus, rather than over the duration of their tenure. The two exceptions to this are John *Aquilina*, NSW minister for education from 1995 to 2001, whose last name was a keyword in the 1996, 1997, 1999 and 2000 sub-corpora; and *QNP* (Queensland National Party), which governed Queensland from 1995 to 1998 and was a keyword in the 1996, 1997 and 1998 sub-corpora. All other state and territory politicians whose names were

Table 3.10 Diachronic Keywords by Year

		1996	1997	1998	1999	2000	2001	2002	2003	2004	2005	2006	2007	2008	2009	2010	2011	2012	2013	2014	2015	2016	2017	2018	2019	2020
Politics	Aquilina	•	•		•	•																				
	QNP	•	•	•	•																					
	Carr		•							•																
	Howard									•		•														
	Brendan									•	•															
	Nelson									•	•															
	Julie											•	•													
	Bishop											•	•													
	Rudd												•	•	•	•										
	Gillard															•		•	•							
	Julia															•		•	•							
	Garrett																	•	•							
	Abbott															•			•	•						
	Pyne																		•	•	•					
	Christopher																		•	•	•					
	Turnbull																					•	•	•		
	Birmingham																					•	•	•		
	Morrison																								•	•
	Dan																								•	•
	Tehan																								•	•
Education policy	Gonski																	•	•			•	•	•		
	NAPLAN															•			•					•	•	
	league														•	•										
	tables														•	•										
Teachers and Schooling	mathematics																							•	•	
	mental																								•	•
	wellbeing																						•		•	•
	Federation	•				•																				

keywords in any of the sub-corpora appeared as such in only one year. They were as follows:

- State ministers for education: Rob *Lucas*, SA, 1993–7 (1996); Bob *Quinn*, Qld, 1996–8 (1997); Mary *Delahunty*, Vic, 1999–2002 (2000); John *Watkins*, NSW, 2001–3 (2002); Andrew *Refshauge*, NSW, 2003–5 (2003); Mark *McGowan*, WA, 2006–8 (2007); *Adrian* Piccoli NSW, 2011–17 (2012) and Sarah *Mitchell*, NSW, 2019–21 (2020).
- State premiers: *Anna* Bligh, Qld, 2007–2012 (2009); Ted *Baillieu*, Vic, 2010–13 (2012); Daniel *Andrews*, Vic, 2014–21 (2020).

Leaders from five of the eight states and territories are represented on this list, reflecting the way in which the coverage included in the ATC is not limited to the more populous east-coast jurisdictions.

At a Commonwealth level, the picture is quite different. Up to 2005, Commonwealth politicians appear as keywords very sparsely in the ATC annual sub-corpora. Federal Minister for Education David *Kemp* (1996–2001) appears as a keyword in 1997; then Leader of the Opposition Mark *Latham* in 2004, the year he was defeated in a federal election; and John *Howard*, prime minister from 1996 to 2007, in the year in which he won his last election (2004) and the year of his defeat (2007). Conversely, until 2005, the name of no federal politician appeared as a keyword in more than one year. *Brendan Nelson*, minister for education from 2001 to 2005 appeared as a keyword in the 2004 and 2005 sub-corpora, beginning with the Australian values debate discussed above. From 2005 onwards, every Commonwealth minister for education and prime minister's name appears on the keyword list for the majority of years of their tenure, as follows:

- Commonwealth ministers for education: *Julie Bishop* (2006–7, keywords 2006 and 2007); Peter *Garrett* (2010–13, keyword 2012 and 2013); Simon *Birmingham* (2015–18, keyword 2016, 2017 and 2018); *Christopher Pyne* (2013–15, keywords 2013, 2014 and 2015) and *Dan Tehan* (2018–20, keywords 2019 and 2020).
- Prime ministers: Kevin *Rudd* (2007–10; 2013, keyword 2007, 2008, 2009 and 2010); *Julia Gillard* (2010–13, keywords 2010, 2012 and 2013); Tony *Abbott* (2013–15, keyword 2010, 2013 and 2015); Malcolm *Turnbull* (2015–18, keyword 2016, 2017 and 2018) and *Scott Morrison* (2018–21, keyword 2018, 2019 and 2010).

The one exception to this was Julia Gillard's tenure as minister for education (2007 to 2010), during which time she and Prime Minister Kevin Rudd took joint public responsibility for the enactment of the 'Education Revolution' as a core Commonwealth government priority post the 2007 election. In 2010, *Julia*, *Gillard* and *Gillard's* are all keywords, reflecting a sense within the print media of her ownership of the My School website, in the same way as *Rudd's*, keyword in 2008, reflected the way in which the 'Education Revolution' was ascribed by the print media to the prime minister.

Essentially, via these keywords we can track the rise of Commonwealth influence in school education since the mid-2000s. While Howard was prime minister for the first eleven years of the ATC, he makes it only onto the list of keywords in this collection of articles about teachers in only two years of his prime ministership, both election years where the media coverage was ostensibly about the alternative offered by the opposition in terms of education policy. All subsequent prime ministers and ministers are key to media coverage about teachers, highlighting the growing importance of the national in public discourses about education in Australia. This shift has been well documented in the field of critical policy sociology using a policy analysis lens (see e.g. Savage and Lewis 2018; Savage and Lingard 2018; Savage and O'Connor 2015) and reflecting on the evolution of the national reform agenda in education, but here we have strong evidence not just for education but also for teachers and their work becoming and remaining a touchstone for public discussions about politics. Concurrently, looking at the diachronic keywords in the ATC sub-corpora related to education policy itself (*Gonski, NAPLAN, league, tables*), we see growing attention since the Rudd–Gillard years to this national reform agenda and in particular to mechanisms of accountability and to questions of school funding. In the final four years of the corpus, we see an emerging and sustained focus on issues related to *wellbeing* and *mental* health, along with attention to *mathematics* (often related to national and international standardized testing results) and *specialist* teachers, also connected to the national reform agenda through the national push for more specialist teachers in primary schools (particularly those skilled and qualified in STEM areas).

The keywords for the annual sub-corpora thus show not only the strong interplay of the politics and education in public discussions of teachers and their work, but also the prominence of teachers in discussions of broader social issues. Finally, the various waves of education reform, particularly over the final decade of the ATC, are reflected in the unique and diachronic keywords.

Diachronic collocates of *teacher* and *teachers*

The diachronic keyword analysis provides an insight into the changing 'aboutness' of the ATC over the twenty-five-year period; however, in order to examine changing representations of teachers over time, a diachronic collocation analysis was conducted. The parameters discussed in Chapter 2 were once again employed, and collocates were generated for both *teacher* and *teachers*, for each year of the ATC. Collocates were divided into two groups, the first constituting what Gabrielatos and Baker have referred to as 'consistent collocates' (Gabrielatos and Baker 2008), 'words that stably collocate with the node in multiple datasets and are to be viewed as indicating

Change Over Time

Table 3.11 Consistent Collocates of *Teacher* and *Teachers*, Ordered Alphabetically

Teacher	Lexical	classroom, education, English, every, former, good, high, one, parent, primary, said, school, student, training, year
	Grammatical	been, had, has, her, his, was, who
Teachers	Lexical	all, Federation, high, many, more, most, need, new, NSW, other, parents, pay, per cent, president, primary, principals, Queensland, said, school, schools, some, state, students, support, union, work
	Grammatical	also, and, are, being, for, from, have, our, should, than, their, were, who, will, with, would

core elements of meaning, semantic associations and semantic prosodies' (Germond, McEnery and Marchi 2016: 141). The consistent collocates of *teacher* and *teachers*, defined here as those collocating with the node word in at least 25 per cent (nineteen) of the annual sub-corpora, are presented in Table 3.11.

Similar to the lockwords discussed above, the consistent collocates provide a point of comparison between the 'top level' analysis of the whole ATC and the year-by-year collocation analysis, allowing this closer look to either confirm or raise questions about the conclusions drawn on the basis of the whole corpus. Each of the consistent collocates of both node words included in Table 3.11 were also identified as collocates of the relevant node word (i.e. either *teacher* or *teachers*) in the ATC as a whole in Chapter 2 (see Table 2.8). The observations made in relation to these collocates in Chapter 2, then, might be thought of as representative not only of the corpus as a whole, but also of each of the twenty-five years within the ATC. The consistent collocates relate primarily to teachers' work (e.g. classroom, parent, secondary, school), but also include those that designate particular groups of teachers (e.g. former, new, English). Qualitative (e.g. *good*) and quantitative (e.g. *one, many, most, some*) markers also are consistent collocates, as are words relating to teacher education (*training*) and teachers' industrial involvement (*Federation, President*). On balance, the consistent collocates point to a similar analysis as that presented in Chapter 2 in relation to the collocates of *teacher* and *teachers* across the ATC as a whole.

Having attended to the similarities across the twenty-five sub-corpora via the consistent collocates, change over time is explored by focusing on the top ten lexical collocates of both *teacher* and *teachers* for each year. The decision to focus on ten (rather than, say five or twenty) collocates for each year was a result of some trial and error, trying to strike a balance between an analysis

82 *Constructing Teacher Identities*

that highlighted the most important changes over time while at the same time not drawing attention to *every* change over time. Using this method, fifty-eight collocates were identified for *teacher* and fifty for *teachers*, with most collocates straddling more than one sub-corpus. Collocates were then grouped according to the categorization used in Chapter 2, and Tables 3.12 and 3.13 present the diachronic collocates for *teacher* and *teachers*, respectively. Note that consistent collocates also appear on these lists, in cases where they were amongst the top ten collocates in any given year.

In relation to *teacher*, the consistent prominence of *former* teachers as both sources for stories and the focus of stories is evident in this analysis, as is a consistent focus on some types of teachers over the duration of the ATC: *English* teachers, *primary* teachers and *head* teachers are key examples here. Other adjectives, such as *male* appear more frequently in one half of the corpus than the other, while others still (*drama*, *female*, and *science* teachers, for example), are prominent collocates in a small number of sub-corpora. Teacher education, or the *training* of teachers, is an ongoing concern within the ATC, with *training* appearing as a collocate of *teacher* in all twenty-five sub-corpora. In relation to teachers' work, *student* and *parent* are, unsurprisingly, also frequent top ten collocates of *teacher*, pointing to the centrality of these key groups in reporting on teachers and their work. Perhaps the most interesting collocate of *teachers* when viewed diachronically is that of *quality*, which appears as a top ten collocate only sporadically until 2007, and remains until 2019.

This prevalence of *quality* as a collocate of *teacher*, raised also in the analysis presented in Chapter 2, points to the growing importance of the discourse of teacher quality in discussions and debates about teachers and teaching over the past decade in particular (Mockler 2020b). Further analysis of the 'quality issue' is the focus of Chapter 5.

With respect to *teachers*, the diachronic collocates presented in Table 3.13 reveal a consistent industrial edge on reporting about *teachers* collectively, as demonstrated in the ongoing prominence of *union*, *Federation*, *president*, and *pay* as top ten collocates of *teachers* for almost all twenty-five of the annual sub-corpora. Consistent collocates of *teachers* are less common outside of the 'industrial' category. *Male* is a collocate of *teachers* in eight of the twenty-five sub-corpora, over the period from 1997 to 2017, suggesting a relatively frequent return to discussions of male teachers over this period. Consistent with the discussion in Chapter 2, *female* does not appear as a top ten collocate of *teachers* in any of the sub-corpora, indicating that *male teachers* are more often referred to collectively than *female teachers*. *Principals* is a collocate of

Table 3.12 Diachronic Collocates of *Teacher* (Top Ten per Year)

		1996	1997	1998	1999	2000	2001	2002	2003	2004	2005	2006	2007	2008	2009	2010	2011	2012	2013	2014	2015	2016	2017	2018	2019	2020
Types of teachers	former	●		●	●	●	●	●	●	●	●	●	●	●	●	●	●	●	●	●		●	●	●	●	●
	English	●		●	●	●	●	●	●	●	●				●	●	●	●	●	●	●	●				
	primary				●	●	●		●		●			●	●		●	●	●	●	●	●	●		●	●
	head	●			●	●	●			●		●	●				●						●	●		
	music			●		●					●				●							●	●	●	●		●
	male		●				●	●	●		●					●										
	secondary								●		●							●		●		●			●	●
	maths			●							●				●		●	●				●				
	aides			●							●					●										●
	aide									●		●	●													
	high																			●				●		●
	science	●													●											
	female								●		●															
	physical								●	●																
	drama											●									●					
	piano						●																			
	dance									●																
	librarian															●										
	librarians															●										
	yoga																					●				
	sports																					●				
Teachers' work	training	●	●	●	●	●	●	●	●	●	●	●	●	●	●	●	●	●	●	●	●	●	●	●	●	●
	parent	●	●	●	●	●	●	●	●	●	●	●	●	●	●					●			●	●	●	●
	student	●	●	●	●			●		●		●	●	●				●							●	
	registration			●	●			●															●			
	become																	●		●		●				
	courses	●			●																					
	board			●																			●			
	qualified														●										●	
	college																	●								●
	becoming							●																		
	standards																		●							
	review																			●						
	advisory																				●					
	group																				●					
	ministerial																				●					
	initial																								●	
	child's																									●
Qualitative Markers	quality					●			●			●	●	●	●	●	●		●		●	●	●	●	●	●
	bad														●											
	performance															●										
Industrial	unions					●				●			●	●		●										
	salaries										●															
Professional	professional																					●				

Table 3.12 Continued

		1996	1997	1998	1999	2000	2001	2002	2003	2004	2005	2006	2007	2008	2009	2010	2011	2012	2013	2014	2015	2016	2017	2018	2019	2020
Quantitative markers	shortage	•	•	•	•	•	•	•	•				•	•												
	numbers	•					•	•											•							
	every			•														•								
	shortages								•					•												
	ratios																		•							•
	another				•	•																				
	ratio																									•
Voice	told															•		•								

Table 3.13 Diachronic Collocates of *Teachers* (Top Ten per Year)

		1996	1997	1998	1999	2000	2001	2002	2003	2004	2005	2006	2007	2008	2009	2010	2011	2012	2013	2014	2015	2016	2017	2018	2019	2020
Industrial	union	•	•	•	•	•	•	•	•	•	•	•	•	•	•	•	•	•	•	•	•	•		•	•	•
	Federation	•	•	•	•	•	•	•	•	•	•	•	•	•	•	•	•	•	•					•	•	•
	president	•	•	•	•	•			•	•	•	•	•	•	•	•		•	•	•	•					•
	pay			•		•					•	•	•	•	•	•		•	•	•					•	•
	association				•				•			•	•	•			•				•					
	strike	•				•				•					•				•							
	paid											•	•				•	•	•							
	shortage						•	•	•																	
	Denis	•																								
	Fitzgerald	•																								
	Simpson				•																					
	Sue				•																					
	unions														•											
Types of teachers	male			•				•	•	•	•									•	•		•			
	primary						•				•										•	•	•			
	secondary						•		•										•		•	•				
	maths											•				•				•	•					
	classroom													•	•						•					
	qualified																			•	•		•			
	specialist							•											•							
	Catholic	•																								
	TAFE	•																								
	casual				•																					
	kindergarten					•																				
	teach									•																
	English									•																
	gay																								•	

Change Over Time

Table 3.13 Continued

		1996	1997	1998	1999	2000	2001	2002	2003	2004	2005	2006	2007	2008	2009	2010	2011	2012	2013	2014	2015	2016	2017	2018	2019	2020
Geographical markers	Queensland		●	●						●	●	●				●	●			●	●	●	●		●	●
	NSW	●	●	●	●	●	●			●	●	●	●		●		●									●
	Victorian													●	●			●								
	ACT																	●								
Teachers' work	principals		●	●	●	●	●	●	●	●	●	●	●	●	●	●	●	●	●	●	●	●	●	●	●	●
	professional			●			●	●	●	●		●	●							●		●		●		●
	parents		●	●							●	●	●								●	●	●			●
	support															●		●			●	●	●	●		●
	college															●	●	●			●	●	●			
	training															●			●	●		●	●		●	
	institute	●																								
	trained							●																		
	become																								●	
	staff																									●
Qualitative markers	quality													●					●						●	
	performance												●													
	best																	●								
Other collocates	against		●																					●		
	extra							●	●																	
	sexual		●																							
	must																					●				

teachers in twenty-four of the twenty-five sub-corpora, highlighting the frequent use of phrases, such as 'principals and teachers' and 'teachers and principals' in discussing teachers as an occupational group. *Professional* is a collocate of *teachers* in eleven of the twenty-five sub-corpora, in seven of the ten years from 1998 to 2007 when teaching standards and accreditation processes were commonly commented on in the media, and in four years since 2010.

In terms of changing representations over time, this analysis primarily draws attention to the increasing prominence of *teacher quality* in the ATC over time, and the decreasing emphasis on *male teachers* and the *teacher shortage* over the same period, the latter somewhat ironic given the recent acknowledgement that Australia faces a critical teacher shortage (Baker 2021). In terms of discourse prosody, the analysis suggests a level of consistency, with the important exception of the increased attention to *quality*, which will be explored in greater depth in Chapter 5.

Conclusion

Diachronic analysis of both keywords and the collocates of *teacher* and *teachers* in the ATC highlights a number of things. First, that there is an underlying level of consistency in both the 'aboutness' of the corpus and the way in which teachers are represented in the corpus over time. These underlying consistencies co-exist with changing patterns that reflect both external factors, such as political and policy changes and broader social movements, and factors internal to the profession, such as changing industrial and professional conditions. Furthermore, these changes manifest both as 'one off' variations where a word will become key or strongly collocated for a short moment in time such as *ministerial, advisory, group*, which are all collocates of *teacher* in the 2015 sub-corpus, the year of the *Teacher Education Ministerial Advisory Group* report (Craven et al. 2015), or the attention reflected in keyword analysis to issues around *marriage* equality and *religious freedom* in 2017 and 2018 or as patterns that signal more enduring shifts in the discourse, such as the embrace of teacher *quality* since 2007. While this analysis of change over time has highlighted some of the broad discursive shifts in reporting on teachers over the past twenty-five years, in the next chapter we will explore a different aspect of the discursive construction of the Australian teacher, through considering the similarities and differences of representations in different types of newspapers.

4

The 'Newspaper Effect' in the Australian Teacher Corpus

Having explored the shape of the Australian Teacher Corpus (ATC) and changing constructions of teachers and education over time, in this chapter attention turns to the newspapers themselves, and specifically to the similarities and differences in their representations of teachers and their work. As noted in Chapter 2, the print media landscape in Australia is one characterized by concentration of ownership, with seven of the twelve newspapers in the ATC owned by News Corp Australia; four by the Nine Entertainment Company (until 2018 Fairfax Media), which also owns one of the three national commercial free-to-air television stations and a host of radio stations nationally; and the remaining one by Seven West Media, which owns another of the free-to-air commercial television stations. Despite this concentration of ownership, it would be simplistic to assume that the readership of co-owned newspapers is similar. The combination within and across of tabloid and broadsheet newspapers, left- and right-leaning ones, national and state/territory based ones, suggest that there are likely to be differences in what is considered newsworthy by different newspapers, and thus that the focus and shape of reporting might be different.

A variety of strategies will be used to explore such questions, and the ways in which the discursive construction of teachers is similar and/or different across the newspapers in the ATC. First, consonant with Chapters 2 and 3, keyword analysis will be used as a starting point, exploring the similarities and differences between sub-corpora of articles published in each newspaper in terms of their general 'aboutness'. Here we will push beyond the more obvious differences (related to location, for example), to identify some of the 'pet issues' and ongoing interests evident in the sub-corpora. Second, and again consonant with Chapters 2 and 3, collocation analysis will be used to compare 'the company teacher/s keep' across the different newspapers, and again to observe similarities and

88   *Constructing Teacher Identities*

differences. Finally, a 'problem frame' analysis of a small number of prototypical texts from each of the sub-corpora, identified using keywords, will be presented. This analysis will map the dominant frames and news values in use in relation to teachers in the newspaper sub-corpora and explore how far these can be accounted for using the attributes and characteristics of the publications and their parent companies.

Keyword analysis: A starting point for understanding the differences between newspapers

Keyword analysis was employed as a way in to understanding the differences and similarities between the twelve newspapers in terms of their stories about teachers. To conduct this analysis, similar to the process used in the diachronic analysis presented in Chapter 3, the ATC was divided into twelve newspaper sub-corpora, and each was compared to the other eleven combined. As with previous keyword analysis presented in this book, Bayesian Information Criterion (BIC) values were used as an indicator of statistical significance, and Hardie's Log Ratio statistic was used as an indicator of effect size, with a Log Ratio of 1.5 set as the threshold, and all keyword analysis was conducted using WordSmith Tools 8 (Scott 2020b). Additionally, in order to attend to dispersion and ensure that words were not identified as key as a consequence of having been used many times in a small number of articles, only words appearing in at least 5 per cent of the texts within the sub-corpus under investigation were included in the analysis.

Table 4.1 presents the keywords for each newspaper sub-corpus, ordered according to Log Ratio values. The number of keywords identified in each sub-corpora ranges from seven (in the *Herald Sun* and the *Sydney Morning Herald*) to forty-nine in the *Australian Financial Review* (AFR). The large number of keywords in the AFR is largely a consequence of its explicit economic and financial focus, as opposed to the general news coverage provided in the other eleven publications in the ATC. This means that the 'go to' focus of stories and also the chosen vocabulary tends to be different from the AFR to the other newspapers.

The state and territory capital city newspapers in particular exhibit strong geographic markers in their keyword lists, in most cases with both the name of the state or territory, for example *ACT, Queensland, NT*, and the capital city both appearing as keywords, for example *Canberra, Brisbane, Darwin*.

The 'Newspaper Effect' in the Australian Teacher Corpus

Table 4.1 Keywords for Newspaper Sub-corpora within the ATC, Ordered According to Log Ratio

The Australian	Qld, Vic, universities, Australian's, Indigenous, Rudd, instruction, academics
The Australian Financial Review	Gonski, billion, business, market, financial, universities, STEM, investment, growth, reform, sector, economic, PISA, fund, investors, bank, productivity, economy, spending, China, Grattan, companies, capital, reforms, infrastructure, OECD, wages, finance, corporate, Singapore, credit, labour, increases, markets, equity, autonomy, innovation, Labor's, Asian, boom, rises, socio, chairman, revenue, CEO, founder, country's, relative, chancellor
The Advertiser	SA, Adelaide, South, Giles, Lucas, Flinders, Port, Janet, dispute, AEU
The Age	Victorian, Melbourne, VCE, Victoria, offers, Bracks, Bluett, Victoria's, Kennett, Monash, Melbourne's, university's
The Canberra Times	ACT, Canberra, service, Belconnen, Barr, ANU, Canberra's, Queanbeyan, dance, Haggar, ACT's, particularly, club, Clive, reporter, branch, assembly
The Courier-Mail	Queensland, Brisbane, QNP, percent, QTU, Bligh, Queensland's, Quinn, programme, Brisbane's, prep, coast, Anna, license, gold, reproduce, Ryan, dated, sunshine, Ann
The Daily Telegraph	NSW, Federation, Sydney, dunce, dux, Aquilina, Maralyn, HSC, Carr, Sydney's, Parker, hills
The Herald Sun	any, English, Victorian, maths, VCE, Bluett, Victoria's,
The Hobart Mercury	Tasmanian, Tasmania, Hobart, Tasmania's, Bartlett, Wriedt, Tasmanians, Launceston, AEU, Bay, Paula, Sandy, colleges, Kingston, grade, Greens, tomorrow, essential, interstate, reforms, resource, island, district
Northern Territory News	NT, Darwin, Territory, Palmerston, Northern, Springs, Nightcliff, Alice, Katherine, CLP, Territorians, remote, Casuarina, Stirling, Doo, Syd, Tennant, Indigenous, Creek, Territory's, Darwin's, request, middle, awards, Stuart, excellence, thank, interstate, bush
The Sydney Morning Herald	HSC, NSW, Federation, syllabus, Aquilina, Carr, Macquarie
The West Australian	WA, OBE, Perth, McGowan, Gisborne, Ravlich, WA's, Keely, Collier, Carpenter, department, Ljiljanna, courses, SSTU, Constable, West, council, Sharyn, shadow, O'Neill, delay, implementation, Anne, outcomes, Edith, Cowan, Mike, shortage, Liz, district, department's, Alan, refused, controversial, Rob

Newspapers based in smaller and/or more isolated capital cities often have keywords that relate to localities in their sub-corpus: this is the case for *The Advertiser* (*Port (Adelaide, Augusta)*), the *Canberra Times* (*Belconnen, Queanbeyan*), the *Hobart Mercury* (*Launceston, Sandy Bay, Kingston*) and *Northern Territory News* (*Palmerston, Alice Springs, Nightcliff, Katherine, Casuarina,* (Humpty)

90   *Constructing Teacher Identities*

Doo, Tennant Creek). Concordance analysis suggests that this phenomenon is reflective of newspapers in smaller states and territories relying on the news value of proximity (often coupled with personalization) in stories about teachers and schools. In general, news with a strong local edge is more readily reported in the major newspapers in these smaller states and territories.

Second, across most of the state and territory newspaper sub-corpora, the keyword analysis suggests a strong focus on industrial issues. That this focus is largely absent from the national newspapers is unsurprising, given the state-based nature of industrial action in education in Australia; however, as noted in Chapter 3, national attention on industrial action or proposed industrial action is evident across the ATC at different points in time. In the state and territory newspaper sub-corpora, reporting of industrial negotiations between state-based teachers' unions is localized via reference to the key players in the negotiations, most commonly union leaders. Examples of this include *Janet Giles*, president of the South Australian teachers' union from 1992 to 2001 (*The Advertiser*); Mary *Bluett*, president of the Victorian branch of the Australian Education Union (AEU) from 1995 to 2012 (*The Age*, the *Herald Sun*) and *Clive Haggar* – secretary of the Australian Capital Territory (ACT) Branch of the AEU 1995 to 2008 (the *Canberra Times*). Other keywords relating to industrial negotiations or action include *dispute* (*The Advertiser*), *AEU* (*The Advertiser*, the *Hobart Mercury*), *QTU* (Queensland Teachers' Union) (*The Courier-Mail*), (NSW Teachers') *Federation* (*Daily Telegraph*, *Sydney Morning Herald*), *SSTU* (State School Teachers' Union WA) (the *West Australian*) and *branch* (the *Canberra Times*). These references to teachers as industrial actors within the ATC often exhibit the news value of negativity, with strong overtones of self-interest on the part of the teaching profession with respect to pay and conditions, and a suggestion of negative consequences for students, schools and school systems.

Special interest issues: Outcomes-based education and the *West Australian*

Some of the keywords for some state and territory-based newspapers reflect connection with curriculum-related issues, for example, those surrounding the HSC,[1] and *syllabus* in the *Sydney Morning Herald* sub-corpus, and VCE[2] in *The Age*. For the most part these keywords are dispersed throughout the sub-corpus

---

[1] The Higher School Certificate, or HSC is the leaving credential in NSW.
[2] The Victorian Certificate, or VCE is the leaving credential in Victoria.

The 'Newspaper Effect' in the Australian Teacher Corpus 91

and either related to annual examinations or results (on the part of VCE and HSC) or to New South Wales (NSW) syllabus revisions, which take place every five to ten years and are a central focus of education discussions in NSW (Riordan 2011). The emergence of *OBE*, or outcomes-based education, as a keyword in the the the *West Australian* sub-corpus is of particular interest as it reflects a specific moment of highly focused and concentrated media attention, in this case to outcomes-based education in Western Australia (WA), and the proposed expansion of Outcome-Based Education (OBE) in the mid-2000s to the upper years of secondary schooling. In their study of the *West Australian's* coverage of teachers from 1987 to 2007, Shine and O'Donoghue note that the newspaper's attention to outcomes-based education began in April 2005 and 'became the source of significant, almost daily, coverage in the newspaper in 2006 and 2007' (Shine 2012: 171; Shine and O'Donoghue 2013a: 169). The *West Australian* sub-corpus of the ATC certainly reflects this intensity of coverage, and along with *OBE*, the keywords *Ravlich*, *Ljiljanna* (both names of then WA education minister) and *controversial* are largely linked to the OBE debate led by the newspaper over this time.

As Shine and O'Donoghue (2013) note, OBE had been introduced in the late 1990s in Western Australian primary and lower secondary schools to positive coverage in the *West Australian*, which lauded the then new curriculum framework for its enhanced focus on values. By 2006, OBE had become what a senior columnist referred to as an 'ongoing campaign' for the newspaper, an issue 'pursued so relentlessly and with such passion', positioned as a fight for 'the fundamentals of the education of WA's children' (Murray 2006). It is difficult to say what had changed between the positive coverage in the newspaper of the initial implementation of OBE in the late 1990s and the crisis of education represented in OBE in the mid-2000s, although the West Australian government had changed during this time frame, from the Liberal government led by Richard Court to the Carpenter Labor government. While probably not a purely partisan move on the part of the *West Australian*, the argument around OBE had a number of key ingredients that sustained its coverage over the period from 2005 to 2007: a Labor government and education minister (Ljiljanna Ravlich), the natural opponents of the right-leaning newspaper, aiming to introduce a set of educational reforms described by the conservative prime minister of the day as 'gobbledegook' (King 2007), against a backdrop of grassroots opposition in the form of the People Lobbying Against Teaching Outcomes (PLATO) group. There are 356 articles in the *West Australian* sub-corpus that reference outcomes, comprising 14 per cent of the sub-corpus as a whole, and 53 per cent of the articles published in 2006, at the height of the OBE coverage.

92   *Constructing Teacher Identities*

As a group, these articles exhibit the full range of news values, which over the rise and demise of outcomes-based education in Western Australia (closely paralleling the rise and demise of Education Minister Ravlich) means that reporting on OBE became almost a self-sustaining ecosystem. *Consonance* is reflected in the invoking of policymakers' adherence to 'faddish' approaches to education; *eliteness* in the soliciting of views from high-ranking politicians and professors, *impact* in the repeated invocation of falling education standards; *negativity* in the negative assessment of both the educational approach constituted by OBE and its proponents; *personalization* in the involvement of People Lobbying Against Teaching Outcomes (PLATO) and its founders, ordinary teachers and 'concerned citizens'; *proximity* in the ongoing reiteration of OBE as a uniquely Western Australian approach at this time; *superlativeness* linked to the novelty and scale of the reforms; *timeliness* produced over an extended period through tracking the minutiae of developments in the reforms on an almost-daily basis and *unexpectedness* in the portrayal of the reforms as contentious, controversial or broadly discredited elsewhere.

Table 4.2 displays fifteen randomly selected concordance lines for the keyword *controversial* (listed alphabetically according to the word directly to the right), highlighting the frequency with which *controversial* is used as a descriptor of outcomes-based education within *The West Australian* sub-corpus of the ATC. While *controversial* is used in four cases here in relation to things other than OBE (e.g. school vouchers and 'performance pay' for teachers), concordance analysis of all 172 instances of *controversial* within the sub-corpus highlights that in 131 of these instances it was used to describe outcomes-based education. While *controversial* is the top collocate of *outcomes-based* in the *West Australian* sub-corpus, most of the collocates in the top twenty (ordered by Mutual Information (MI), see Table 4.3) contribute to the negative discourse prosody of *outcomes* and speak to the news values of negativity, superlativeness or unexpectedness.

Together, the collocates work as a constant reminder over this period to readers of the *West Australian* that OBE is not only *controversial*, but also *contentious, discredited, disastrous* and a *debacle*. They reference the *furore* in which the *critics* and *opponents* of OBE and the *architects* of the *system* participated. Teachers are simultaneously implicated in and removed from the OBE debacle, which is positioned as a consequence of the blunt-force will of the state government, inflicted on all teachers but openly opposed by some.

The most recent article in the sub-corpus on outcomes-based education was published in 2018, a full decade after the idea was abandoned in Western

Table 4.2 Concordance Lines for *Controversial* in the *West Australian* Sub-corpus

Rob Martin Involved in the	**controversial** Anchorage Development at North Fremantle.
Education options remain	**controversial** and varied with some parents choosing home schooling
was forced to ditch some of the more	**controversial** aspects of OBE, some teachers warn that the result is a
that left out the more	**controversial** bits and did not follow evidence-based lesson plans
The committee inquiring into the	**controversial** introduction of OBE to Years 11 and 12 recommended
effort and behaviour criteria as part of the	**controversial** move to an outcomes-based education system. But Ms
bleak assessment of their first year under the	**controversial** new scheme. Three teachers from Kent Street and
in over the next three years for the	**controversial** OBE system at upper school level. In a submission to
Teachers of	**controversial** outcomes-based education courses scheduled to start
that it is rolling back big chunks of the	**controversial** outcomes-based education system as smoke and
State government's attempts to impose the	**controversial** outcomes-based education system on Year 11 and 12
Applications have opened for the	**controversial** scheme, which from next year will reward top teachers
and they were confident about how the	**controversial** scheme would be taught and assessed. But Premier
Wants to expand	**controversial** school voucher system to help primary students bring
Yesterday Ms Ravlich said she would not delay	**controversial** system because she did not want to deny students

Table 4.3 Top Twenty Collocates for *Outcomes-Based* in the *West Australian*, Ordered by MI

controversial, architects, contentious, discredited, disastrous, readiness, furore, introduction, debacle, opponents, system, implementation, delay, education, approach, critics, framework, upper, implementing, engineering

Australia. Headlined 'Expert Fears Failed School Policy is Back' (Hiatt 2018), the article uses 'WA's failed experiment with outcomes-based education' as a touchstone, invoking the University of Western Australia academic 'whose review of OBE contributed to its demise' and quoting his speculation about the then upcoming 'Gonski 2.0' review: 'The concern is a potential revisiting of what we had in WA during the OBE period.' It appears that given that the *West Australian* has not published an article that includes the term *outcomes-based* since, this 'potential revisiting' did not come to pass; however, this most recent example illustrates the 'watchdog' role assumed by the newspaper on this issue and vigilance with which they pursue it. It also illustrates the way that 'outcomes-based education' had become something of a 'signature' (Gamson and Lasch 1983), or shorthand in the West Australian context, for 'contentious' or 'disastrous' ideas about education that threaten the status quo.

Enduring interests in *The Australian*

While the outcomes-based education debate in the *West Australian* is a single, if protracted, instance of a newspaper focusing on a singular issue related to

94 *Constructing Teacher Identities*

teachers and teaching, it is by no means the only one identifiable within the ATC. Another evident in the keyword analysis of the newspaper sub-corpora is that of *The Australian's* advocacy for particular forms of *instruction* over the years. These include 'direct *instruction*' and 'explicit *instruction*' in the mid-2010s, sometimes equated in *The Australian* (most often by contributor Noel Pearson) with 'effective *instruction*' (see e.g. Pearson 2011, 2018). Closely related to this is the newspaper's ongoing stoking of 'the literacy wars' (Snyder 2008), which can be observed to have occurred at a number of different points within the past twenty-five years, and manifests in advocacy for phonics *instruction*, often presented as 'evidence-based reading *instruction*', to the exclusion of all other methods of teaching reading. Windle (2015) has written of the literacy 'debate', encompassing reporting on both direct instruction and phonics as an example of 'coercive neoliberalism' (127), noting that *The Australian* has played an aggressive role in their promotion. Indeed, a glance across the ATC at the occurrence of *direct instruction*, *explicit instruction* and *phonics* highlights that *The Australian* contains a disproportionate representation of all three: almost 48 per cent of all occurrences of *direct instruction* in the ATC are in *The Australian*, 41 per cent of *explicit instruction* and over 31 per cent of *phonics*.

The flavour of *The Australian's* reporting on *instruction* can be gleaned in Table 4.4, which includes fifteen randomly selected concordance lines for *instruction*. Approximately a third of the instances of *instruction* in *The Australian* sub-corpus are accompanied by the descriptor *direct* or *explicit*, but regardless of the descriptors used, the concordance highlights a consistent perspective on *instruction* on the part of *The Australian*. This perspective assumes that learning comprises the transmission of knowledge from teacher to student, and is the by-product of teacher-directed instruction alone. Perceived threats to 'effective instruction' constitute any teaching, learning and assessment strategies that suggest any level of student agency in their learning. As case in point, frequent contributor Kevin Donnelly's take on formative assessment after the publication of the Mparntwe Education Declaration (Education Council 2019) in 2019 is instructive:

> schools are being forced to embrace what is known as formative assessment, a situation where students are not ranked one against the other or against year level standards but instead the focus is on personal growth, progression points and developmental continuums.
>
> Even though it is not evidence-based, it has not been successfully implemented anywhere else in the world and it is costly and impossible [sic]

Table 4.4 Concordance Lines for *Instruction* in *The Australian* Sub-corpus

they are doing before you give an	**instruction**. * Praise your child immediately if they do
learning by doing than rote learning and	**instruction**. At the same time, across the
sometimes openly, during my attempts at	**instruction**. At recess one day the principal asks
Explicit teaching, sometimes known as direct	**instruction**, is one approach where teachers are in
guidance or encouragement - and even less direct	**instruction** - to pursue the courses that truly keep
is an example of explicit or direct	**instruction**, in which the skill is demonstrated
awarded $22m in 2014 to roll out direct	**instruction** nationally. Ms Jones said she would also
mostly used techniques associated with direct	**instruction**, such as explicitly stating the goal of
shoulder and repeats her question, and her	**instruction**. Slowly the words form in my mind,
be the basis of all early literacy	**instruction**,' she said. 'Learning via whole words, sight
was showing teachers effective methods of	**instruction**, informed by feedback and data tracking students'
, even in big classes, such as peer	**instruction**, where a lecturer pauses so nearby students
some were openly disparaging of explicit phonics	**instruction**, describing it as a 'prescriptive approach' and '
sort of learning, by osmosis and self-	**instruction**, became almost impossible after World War II,
approach based on knowledge and direct teacher	**instruction**. This is 'especially concerning' because the OECD

apply in the classroom, the Alice Springs declaration embodies this new-age, faddish approach to assessment. Teachers are told they must 'effectively identify learners' progress and growth, and design individualised and adaptive learning programs' and that students should be allowed to 'reflect on and monitor their own progress to inform their future learning goals'. (Donnelly 2019)

There are factual inaccuracies of Donnelly's statement about formative assessment, which is far from being a 'new-age fad' but has instead been part of the educational repertoires of teachers and schooling systems since the 1970s, and for which robust evidence has existed since at least the 1990s (see e.g. Black and Wiliam 1998; Black et al. 2004). Quite aside from this, here Donnelly also highlights a perceived absurdity, assumed to be shared by readers of *The Australian*, of the possibility of young people reflecting on and monitoring their own learning.

Donnelly's education-focused contributions to *The Australian* from 1996 to 2020 amount to over 270,000 words (approximately half of these articles are included in the ATC), ranging across teaching instruction, national testing and of course the national curriculum, of which Donnelly was appointed to co-chair a review in 2014 by newly elected Prime Minister Tony Abbott and Education Minister Christopher Pyne. Donnelly is a former teacher, ex-chief of staff to Minister Kevin Andrews in the Howard government, and since 2009 director of the 'Education Standards Institute', defined as a 'conservative minded, internet-based think tank' (Donnelly 2009). Donnelly has thus been both a commentator on and a player in the education culture wars since the mid-2000s: in 2006 the

96   *Constructing Teacher Identities*

self-defined 'cultural warrior' (Donnelly 2021) had forty-six commentaries published in *The Australian* alone.[3]

Donnelly's commentaries typify *The Australian*'s perspective on teachers' work, often coordinating with editorials and news stories to draw out educational crises or panics over a period of days, weeks or months. His work has been part of ongoing conversations in *The Australian* about the devaluing of Judaeo-Christian traditions and 'national' values in the curriculum: 'Our core values as a nation are being lost in the educational shuffle' (Donnelly 2013); backlash against references to gender within curricula or classrooms as other than biologically determined: 'Classrooms are for teaching maths and English, not for enforcing politically correct ideologies' (Donnelly 2012); and 'progressive' educational 'fads', defined as anything other than 'traditional', 'chalk and talk' teaching: 'Effective classrooms are those where teachers actually teach, instead of "facilitating", and where more time is spent on whole class work instead of students working individually or in groups' (Donnelly 2005). While Donnelly is by no means the only commentator or journalist in *The Australian* employing this approach, he has been one of the most consistent voices in this newspaper as represented in the ATC, with his work appearing in eighteen years of the sub-corpus, spread from 1996 to 2020 inclusive.

That *Indigenous* appears as a keyword in the *The Australian* sub-corpus is broadly reflective of the newspaper's long-term commitment to influencing policy around Indigenous affairs over the past decade (Waller and McCallum 2016). This position was elaborated in 2014 by the then Editor at Large Paul Kelly:

> We have been very committed to moving away from what we feel was the commitment to progressive and unsuccessful policies in Indigenous affairs. We have worked with a number of Indigenous leaders in particular, Noel Pearson, to try to change the agenda and put a much greater emphasis on individual responsibility. (Kelly 2014)

Pearson, director of the Cape York Institute and a key proponent of direct and explicit instruction for Aboriginal children in remote communities, was indeed prominent in *The Australian* over the years covered by the ATC, with 255 articles authored by him over this time and a further 2,690

---

[3] Donnelly is a widely published commentator in the Australian print media, with over 650 articles published in ten newspapers (all except *The West Australian* and *Northern Territory News*) between 1996 and 2020. His work most regularly appears in *The Australian*, however, which published almost 50 per cent of his articles over this time frame.

referencing him and his work. That *The Australian* makes no pretence of the responsibilization of First Nations Australians is resonant with the deficit discourses that surrounded its support of the Howard government's 'Northern Territory Emergency Response' in mid-2007 and to the ongoing rhetoric around 'Closing the Gap'.

The *Australian Financial Review*: Growing attention to markets and autonomy

Finally, to the *Australian Financial Review*. While this sub-corpus is the smallest in the ATC, it is particularly interesting because of the newspaper's (a) national scope and (b) economics and finance focus. Unlike other newspapers in the ATC, the AFR's interest in matters related to teaching was not consistent over the twenty-five years of the ATC, and neither does it correspond with the distribution of all articles across the twenty-five-year span. Figure 4.1 shows the distribution of articles in the AFR and the ATC, expressed as percentages of the whole, for purposes of comparison. While a far smaller proportion of articles was published in the AFR and the ATC in the years between 1996 and 2003, in 2004 there was a peak of articles in the AFR that corresponded with that of the ATC and was related to the strong education focus of the federal election, held in October of that year. A further peak, also mirroring the ATC more broadly, occurred in 2007/8 with the

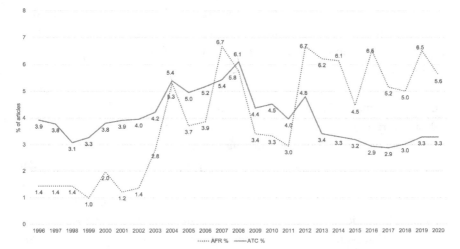

Figure 4.1 Percentage of articles in the ATC and AFR sub-corpus published by year.

lead-up and then early years of the 'Education Revolution' of the Rudd–Gillard government. Following a relative slump in articles from 2009 to 2011, since 2012 a higher proportion of articles focused on teachers has been published in the AFR than in the ATC comparatively. This heightened interest in the years from 2012 to 2020 means that over half of the articles in the AFR sub-corpus were published in these years.

Keywords from the AFR sub-corpus reflect the economic and financial focus of the newspaper, although they additionally highlight the constitution of education in human capital terms. The keywords reflect ongoing discussions of school funding (*Gonski, billions, financial, investment, sector, fund, spending, capital, infrastructure, equity, socio-economic*), industrial negotiations (*wages, increases, labour, rises*) and the role of education in building human capital (*STEM, growth, productivity, economy, innovation, boom, country's*). A focus on the performance of Australian education systems in international standardized tests is evident from the keyword list and concordancing (*STEM, PISA, OECD*), complete with the use of *Singapore* as a 'reference society' (Sellar and Lingard 2013). While *market* and *reform* might on the surface be seen to be related, concordance analysis revealed that *market* was used within the AFR sub-corpus to refer to education or schooling markets only infrequently, with other markets commonly referenced including the housing market and the labour market. *Reform*, on the other hand, was most frequently used to refer to school or education reform generally, or funding *reform*.

Autonomy, a focus in the AFR particularly from 2012 onwards, is used predominantly in the context of school and principal autonomy, as highlighted in Table 4.5, and generally in presenting an argument for or rationale for increased autonomy and decentralization. Often within the sub-corpus, this argument is presented with comment from the Centre for Independent Studies, a pro-market reform conservative think tank which is an AFR go-to for comment on matters educational. Finally, a number of keywords point to voices of authority in the AFR sub-corpus, including *productivity* (commission), *Grattan, chairman, CEO, founder* and (vice-)*chancellor*. Resonating with the news value of eliteness, these keywords point to the typically high-status people and organizations sought after for comment on education issues within the AFR. While across the board, the voices of those other than school (or even system) personnel tend to be privileged in stories about education, the *Australian Financial Review* is not a publication that typically seeks comment on educational matters from teachers or school principals.

Table 4.5 Concordance Lines for *Autonomy* in the *Australian Financial Review* Sub-corpus

key to building good schools is not	**autonomy** alone, but also investing in school leadership. '
Britain, league tables of 'value-add' measures.	**Autonomy** and accountability: Governments have given self
at addresses teacher practice and quality, school	**autonomy** and leadership'. Before we start a new
school principals, agrees. Not only will more	**autonomy** enable these schools to meet the wishes
, progress should be made now on greater	**autonomy** for principals and schools, a focus on
ion to equip students for vocational education. *	**Autonomy** for principals to make decisions, appoint teacher
mpler budgeting and resources allocation and more	**autonomy** in decision making. 'Opposition education spokesm
while Victoria led the way on school	**autonomy** in the 1990s, NSW, which has one
the 1990s the push for greater school	**autonomy**, led by Victoria, changed the principal's
. In part because they have not achieved	**autonomy**, neither profession is treated with as much
In WA, the education department recently limited	**autonomy** on hiring teachers after it emerged that
. If the system gives teachers the pedagogical	**autonomy**, that's sure to make a difference,
Liberal Party rhetoric about states' rights and	**autonomy**. This is a formula for inertia, for
in Western Australia, which gives state schools	**autonomy** to hire and fire staff as a
and parents that the new flexibility and	**autonomy** will be reined in by state education

Similarities and differences in collocates of teacher/s in the ATC newspaper sub-corpora

Using the same settings as in Chapter 3, collocates were identified for both *teacher* and *teachers* in each of the twelve newspaper sub-corpora (see Table 4.6). Some of the collocates clearly resonate with the keyword analysis, with geographical and cultural markers (mostly in the form of proper nouns) scattered across most of the sub-corpora and reflecting the local nature of many stories about teachers and schools. Only 57 of the 600 collocates in Table 4.6 (across *teachers* and *teacher*) are unique to one newspaper, indicating that despite these local differences, there are many similarities in the way teachers are positioned and reported across the newspaper sub-corpora, and thus many similarities between this list and the collocates within the ATC as a whole, as reported in Chapter 2. In particular, many words used to designate 'types' of teachers are common collocates across a majority of sub-corpora including *former, primary, English, support, high* [school], *science, male, maths* and *music*. Further, *student/s* and *principal/s* are collocated with *teacher* and/or *teachers* in all twelve sub-corpora, while *parent/s* are collocated with *teacher/s* in all sub-corpora except that of the AFR. Again, these are largely consistent with the broad findings presented in Chapter 2 in relation to the ATC as a whole, suggesting that despite local differences, there is a level of commonality across the twelve publications that resonates with the 'top level' findings.

Across all newspaper sub-corpora, a range of collocates was identified related to teachers as professionals and teachers as workers, or industrial actors, and a closer look was taken at the spread of these collocates across the sub-corpora.

100   *Constructing Teacher Identities*

Table 4.6 Top Twenty-Five Collocates of *Teacher/s*, Organized by Newspaper Subcorpora and Ordered by MI (Unique Words in Bold)

	Teachers	Teacher
The Australian	federation, qualified, unions, principals, association, union, pay, professional, primary, president, maths, training, best, teach, parents, classroom, support, Queensland, NSW, better, good, science, need, many, English	initial, training, quality, unions, former, courses, student, **programs**, primary, professional, English, maths, education, every, high, classroom, who, good, science, school, one, year, was, her, had
The Australian Financial Review	**Ontario**, federation, qualified, **nurses**, **credit**, salaries, union, unions, paid, professional, principals, pay, primary, classroom, best, NSW, quality, teach, maths, training, better, performance, who, science, good	**ratio**, initial, training, quality, salaries, unions, **improving**, former, courses, English, student, **improve**, **development**, performance, **standards**, classroom, primary, education, maths, good, class, school, **program**, who, pay
The Advertiser	principals, **Australian**, students, schools, primary, parents, school, student, male, union, college, science, pay, education, **south**, support, training, cent, public, state, per, need, help, high, **said**	**Adelaide**, maths, shortage, primary, student, school, parent, secondary, students, former, college, science, training, male, education, music, **teachers**, high, English, quality, class, **says**, year, become, every
The Age	qualified, male, paid, principals, professional, pay, Victorian, parents, primary, training, union, secondary, best, classroom, support, many, science, are, new, were, who, cent, need, per, other	shortage, unions, former, training, parent, quality, English, courses, maths, primary, student, secondary, music, classroom, science, who, college, every, another, high, class, good, one, school, education
The Canberra Times	male, principals, pay, professional, parents, NSW, classroom, support, best, union, public, primary, science, **ACT**, were, are, who, students, need, work, our, many, cent, school, other	**librarians**, **librarian**, former, salaries, training, quality, parent, maths, English, student, college, primary, classroom, music, **dance**, become, performance, high, science, who, every, class, school, pay, her
The Courier-Mail	union, **Steve**, **Ryan**, president, male, principals, Queensland, college, pay, primary, parents, support, classroom, were, are, many, need, students, who, cent, have, more, schools, work, good	aide, aides, registration, former, parent, board, training, male, primary, music, student, English, high, **full**, another, told, who, every, school, classroom, one, **time**, had, good, **Brisbane**
The Daily Telegraph	are, casual, cent, federation, have, male, many, more, **most**, need, NSW, parents, pay, president, primary, principals, public, strike, students, support, union, were, who, **will**, **yesterday**	another, casual, class, classroom, English, every, female, former, good, head, high, male, maths, old, one, parent, primary, quality, school, student, TAFE, told, training, was, who
The Herald Sun	male, principals, paid, pay, support, Victorian, union, secondary, parents, primary, are, staff, best, were, many, per, cent, students, should, other, who, help, state, more, have	**awards**, former, parent, female, primary, secondary, training, college, student, year, music, who, high, another, told, your, **principal**, school, had, was, **Melbourne**, **his**, Victorian, **has**, one

The 'Newspaper Effect' in the Australian Teacher Corpus   101

Table 4.6 Continued

	Teachers	Teacher
The Hobart Mercury	male, principals, professional, parents, pay, **Tasmanian**, support, science, **Tasmania's**, training, were, staff, who, are, many, college, classroom, help, union, students, more, work, primary, should, cent	**assistants**, aide, aides, shortage, registration, former, **numbers**, training, music, English, science, student, primary, who, every, high, class, classroom, college, school, one, support, pay, was, had
Northern Territory News	principals, strike, paid, **world**, support, **remote**, parents, **working**, pay, **Territory**, union, are, many, best, **day**, staff, were, need, new, more, our, work, schools, who, have	ratios, registration, former, parent, board, **asked**, student, senior, music, English, secondary, primary, told, **award**, **middle**, high, who, every, old, class, year, her, school, was, one
The Sydney Morning Herald	federation, president, association, NSW, principals, professional, pay, support, primary, parents, training, many, were, best, are, who, English, students, need, have, other, should, good, more, new	head, parent, former, training, quality, English, maths, science, primary, music, high, student, classroom, become, every, another, who, school, good, one, class, education, your, her, was
The West Australian	**Mike**, **Anne**, union, **Keely**, president, **Gisborne**, state, pay, English, **group**, association, **concerns**, principals, many, **against**, science, support, school, were, college, who, parents, have, are, **would**	shortage, **shortages**, **relief**, former, quality, training, music, primary, senior, another, who, classroom, high, every, science, student, college, English, old, school, told, one, her, **after**, was

Tables 4.7 and 4.8 highlight collocates of *teacher* and *teachers* that relate to teacher professionalism and teacher industrialism, respectively. In both cases collocates for *teacher* and *teachers* are presented separately. I acknowledge that this is a somewhat arbitrary divide: it is not the case that teachers are either professional *or* industrial in their orientation, and indeed for many years now Australian teachers' unions have fulfilled both industrial and professional mandates (Sachs 1997). My attention here in drawing this divide has been on how the collocates position teachers within the articles, based not only on the words themselves but on their use in context, as explored via concordance analysis.

With respect to teacher professionalism, collocates here are related to issues around teacher education, professional development and registration and issues of 'performance'. Two words, namely *training* and *quality* were collocated with *teacher*, and one, *best*, with *teachers* in a majority of the sub-corpora. *Good* was collocated with *teacher*, and *professional* and *training* with *teachers* in half of the sub-corpora. Thirteen of the 'teacher professionalism' collocates, however, were collocates in only three of the sub-corpora or less, suggesting some variation in the way teachers are represented as professionals across the newspapers. In

Table 4.7 Collocates Relating to Teacher Professionalism for Both *Teacher* and *Teachers*

		The Age	Syd. Morn. Herald	Canberra Times	Courier Mail	Daily Telegraph	Herald Sun	Hobart Mercury	Ad. Advertiser	NT News	West Australian	Australian Fin. Rev.	The Australian
Teacher	Training	•	•	•	•	•	•	•	•		•	•	•
	Quality	•	•	•		•			•		•	•	•
	Good	•	•		•	•						•	•
	Registration				•			•		•			
	Courses	•										•	•
	Initial											•	•
	Performance			•								•	
	Improve											•	
	Improving											•	
	Standards											•	
	Program											•	
	Programs												•
	Professional												•
Teachers	Best	•	•	•			•			•		•	•
	Professional	•	•	•				•				•	•
	Training	•	•					•	•			•	•
	Good		•		•							•	•
	Qualified	•										•	•
	Performance											•	
	Quality											•	
'Teacher Professionalism' collocates		8	7	5	4	3	2	4	3	2	2	17	12

examining these differences by attending to the collocations in each newspaper, it becomes apparent that the two national newspapers, *The Australian* and the *Australian Financial Review*, have the most sustained focus in this area, with twelve and seventeen of the twenty collocates, respectively. The Fairfax/Nine Media broadsheets (*The Age*, the *Sydney Morning Herald* and the *Canberra Times*) demonstrate the next most sustained focus, while the tabloid newspapers, both those of News Corp Australia and Seven West Media, have *teacher/s* collocated less with words related to teacher professionalism, beyond *training* and *quality*. Most interestingly, a raft of words related to teacher performance, including not only

Table 4.8 Collocates Relating to Teacher Industrialism for Both *Teacher* and *Teachers*

		The Age	Syd. Morn. Herald	Canberra Times	Courier Mail	Daily Telegraph	Herald Sun	Hobart Mercury	Ad. Advertiser	NT News	West Australian	Australian Fin. Rev.	The Australian
Teacher	Shortage	•						•	•		•		
	Pay			•				•				•	
	Unions	•										•	•
	Salaries			•								•	
	Numbers							•					
	Ratio											•	
	Ratios									•			
	Shortages											•	
Teachers	Pay	•	•	•	•	•	•	•	•	•	•	•	•
	Union	•		•	•	•	•	•	•	•	•	•	•
	President		•		•	•					•		•
	Federation		•			•						•	•
	Paid	•					•			•	•		
	Strike					•				•			
	Unions											•	•
	Salaries											•	
Teacher Industrialism collocates		5	3	4	3	5	3	5	3	5	5	10	6

performance itself, but also *improve, improving, standards* and *qualified* are not collocates of either *teacher* or *teachers* in any of the tabloid newspapers. It seems that a focus on issues related to teacher performance, at least as far as it consistently employs these particular words to describe teachers themselves, is largely limited to the broadsheets and concentrated in particular within the national broadsheets.

A slightly different pattern is evident with the sixteen collocates categorized as related to 'teacher industrialism'. While *pay* is a collocate of *teachers* in all twelve sub-corpora and *union* in eleven (all except the *Sydney Morning Herald*), very few others appear as collocates in more than a few of the sub-corpora. Again, the national newspapers seem to demonstrate the most sustained interest in teacher industrialism as indicated by the collocates (and once again, the AFR more so than *The Australian*), but the interest here is more with respect to *pay* and *union* interaction than in *strike/s* or *shortage/s*, which tend to be more the province of the tabloid newspapers. On the whole, the collocates suggest a more variable discourse prosody for *teacher/s* with respect to teacher professional issues across the twelve sub-corpora than industrial issues, and particularly a more prominent focus on issues related to performance and to a lesser extent quality in the broadsheet newspapers than the tabloids. Across both professional and industrial domains, the *Australian Financial Review* produced more significant collocates for both *teacher* and *teachers* than any other newspaper sub-corpus, suggesting a focus not only on teacher quality, performance and professionalism but also on industrial issues such as salaries, generally more closely related to the AFR's economic and financial orientation.

Prototypical texts

Given the nuances of the different newspaper sub-corpora, as highlighted in keyword and collocation analysis, I was keen to take a 'deeper dive' into each sub-corpus, by 'downsampling' Baker 2019; Baker and Levon 2015) a selection of prototypical texts from each for closer analysis. This analysis of prototypical texts was undertaken with a specific focus on the representations of teachers in the texts, and with particular attention to what David Altheide (e.g. 2013) refers to as 'the problem frame'. Drawing on Goffman (1974) and Iyengar's (1991) work on media framing, Altheide argues that the problem frame 'promotes a discourse of fear that may be defined as the pervasive communication, symbolic awareness and expectation that danger and risk are a central feature of the effective environment' (Altheide 1997: 648). He outlines the problem frame as 'an important innovation that satisfies the entertainment dimension of news. It is an organizational solution to a practical problem: how can we make real problems seem interesting? Or, more to the practical side of news, how can we produce reports compatible with entertainment formats?' (1997: 653). Altheide posits that the problem frame implies that

- something exists that is undesirable,
- many people are affected by this problem (it is relevant),
- unambiguous aspects or parts are easily identified,
- it can be changed or 'fixed',
- there is a mechanism or procedure for fixing the problem and
- the change or repair agent and process is known (usually government).
  (1997: 655)

The software package ProtAnt 1.2.1, developed by Laurence Anthony and Paul Baker (2017), was used to identify a selection of texts within each sub-corpus for closer analysis. ProtAnt provides what Anthony and Baker (2015) describe as a 'principled' method for identifying texts in a large corpus to focus on for further analysis, using keyword analysis to identify the texts that are most representative of the 'aboutness' of the corpus. Three other decisions were important, however, in alighting on this particular group of texts, and I settled each of these through a process of trial and error, until I was confident that the texts identified were an accurate representation of each sub-corpus.

First, mindful of Anthony and Baker's observation that 'the choice of reference corpus plays an important role in determining which texts are selected as typical or not' (Anthony and Baker 2015: 286), I experimented with the best reference corpus to use, and here I alighted on the NOW-AU corpus rather than comparing each sub-corpus to the remainder of the ATC. The reason for this was the need to find a way of exploring the subtle differences in the representations of teachers across the sub-corpora, and my early experimentation with ProtAnt and the ATC produced a set of prototypical texts focused more on the nuances of state and territory politics than on this. The second decision related to which measure of prototypicality to utilize in the selection of texts: while the raw number of keywords in each text privileged longer articles, normalized keyword frequency (i.e. the number of keywords per 1,000 words) privileged short articles which may have used only one or two keywords. In an attempt to alight on the most 'typical' texts in the corpus, and in view of the radically differing word length of texts across each of the sub-corpora, I made the decision to filter out of the selection articles that were overly short or overly long in comparison with other articles in the sub-corpus. In order to do this, I initially calculated means and standard deviations for word length in each sub-corpus, with a view to selecting only from articles within one standard deviation of the mean; however, the prevalence of 'outliers', articles with an extremely large or small word count in most of the sub-corpora, meant that the median and interquartile range were preferable measures to use. I thus calculated these statistics for each of the twelve sub-corpora and used the interquartile range (i.e. the word length of articles in the 'middle two' quartiles) as a filter for selection, effectively focusing the selection on articles that were neither overly short nor overly long. My extended reading of randomly selected articles from each of the sub-corpora suggested that the identified articles were a good representation of each. The headlines of the sixty prototypical texts selected (five from each of the newspaper sub-corpora) are provided in Table 4.9.

The two questions guiding the analysis, which was conducted over successive readings of the sixty prototypical articles selected were (a) what representation/s

106 *Constructing Teacher Identities*

Table 4.9 Top Five Prototypical Texts for Each Newspaper Sub-corpus

The Australian	1. More Funds for Primary Schools (2008) 2. Testing Revival Spotlights The three Rs (1997) 3. Make Kids Learn: Uni Trainers on Notice (2015) 4. Prove Teaching Skills in Classroom or Fail Course (2017) 5. Numeracy Skills Crisis Grows (2007)
The Australian Financial Review	1. Falling Class Sizes Raise Education Bill (2017) 2. Learning Tops Funding (2012) 3. Labor'sMaths Teaching Vow a Fail: Expert (2016) 4. Small Class-Size Change for $1.5b Result (2016) 5. Are Primary Teachers Ready to Give Coding Lessons?: Ian Chubb Says No (2015)
The Advertiser	1. Lucas Plea Ignored as Teachers Stop Work (1996) 2. Cap Class Sizes at 18; Principals Call for New Limit (2004) 3. Specialist Teacher Shortage Undermines Curriculums (2004) 4. Extra Teachers, Smaller Classes the Primary Goal (2003) 5. Basic Skills Tests a Winner: Lucas (1997)
The Age	1. State's Primary Class Sizes at Lowest Level (2006) 2. Warning on Maths Teacher Shortage (2019) 3. For Teachers, Challenge is to Never Stop Learning (2007) 4. Catholics Attack Over Class Sizes (1998) 5. Parents Push for Increased Catholic School Funds (2008)
The Canberra Times	1. Education Safe Schools Row Kikkert on Attack over Program (2017) 2. Liberals Pledge Boost Catholic Funding and Take Curriculum Back to Basics (2020) 3. Worth of Private Schools Queried (2007) 4. Radford College Should Lose ACT Govt Funding, Union Says (2020) 5. Kindergarten Pupils Exempt from New Assessment Rules (2006)
The Courier-Mail	1. Parents' Pressure Forces School Asbestos Removal (2005) 2. Primary Kids Show their True Class (2015) 3. Millions Spent on Wealthy Schools (2005) 4. Three Rs or State Teachers Are Out (2009) 5. School War over Funding (2004)
The Daily Telegraph	1. Beach Lesson Learnt - Teachers Turn Backs on Tougher Schools (2005) 2. 1840 Classes Need a Teacher (2010) 3. Schools 'Rated Like Fast Food' (1996) 4. Education Torn by Religious Pay Divide (2004) 5. Battler Kids in Class Awe-Fare (2020)
The Herald Sun	1. Labor Claims Class Size Win (2001) 2. School Literacy Threat (2003) 3. Search for a Teacher (2003) 4. Never Stop Learning (2010) 5. All Class on Winners' Roll Call (2008)
The Hobart Mercury	1. Schools Face Row Fallout (1996) 2. trike Savings Will Go Back to Schools (1996) 3. Libs Rip into Teachers for Joining Rally (2004) 4. Teacher Ratio Mismatch (2015) 5. Teachers Tackle Science Bartlett Considers Retraining Scheme (2006)

Table 4.9 Continued

Northern Territory News	1. Partnerships in Learning (2008) 2. Awards Pay Tribute to Those Who Inspire (2015) 3. Darwin Teachers Rebel (2001) 4. Numbers Stress Out Teachers (2002) 5. You Just Don't Get It: Teachers Slam Minister (2013)
The Sydney Morning Herald	1. Catholic and State Schools Add to HSC All-rounders (2010) 2. Happy Learners in a Class of Their Own; Top of the State (2010) 3. Primary Classes Bulge In Breach of Guidelines (2002) 4. No Yearning for the Past from Long-Serving Teachers (1997) 5. Teaching Degrees Cost Thousands More than Limit (2006)
The West Australian	1. Results Add Weight to Year 7 Claim (2010) 2. Legal Threat against Teachers (2010) 3. Unions Hit Back at OBE 'Slurs' (2006) 4. Opposition Wants More Year 10 Tests (2007) 5. Teachers Unqualified: Survey (2006)

of school teachers are explicit and/or implicit in this rendering and (b) what use is made of the problem frame, either explicitly or implicitly in this article? This analysis gave rise to three discrete although interrelated expressions of 'the problem' within the prototypical texts, each of which will be explored at some length here.

The problem of quality and quantity

Almost half of the sixty prototypical articles worked with the multifaceted problem of teacher quality and teacher quantity. While some articles were focused explicitly on teacher quality itself as a problem, others, through their focus on teacher shortages, raised issues related to the consequences of teacher supply problems, including the issue of 'unqualified' teachers teaching outside of their areas of expertise. Additionally, a range of articles focused not explicitly on the *problem* of teacher quality as on its flipside, the *celebration* of teacher quality in the form of narratives around heroic teachers, and these too will be considered within this problem framing.

Teacher quality

The problem of 'teacher quality' is primarily the province of prototypical articles from *The Australian* and the *Australian Financial Review*: in both cases all five prototypical articles reflected this problem framing, along with one prototypical article from each of *The Age* and *The Courier-Mail*. Articles that work with this

108 Constructing Teacher Identities

problem frame tend to focus on 'improving teacher quality' (Ferrari 2008), often with emphasis on getting 'the best quality teachers in classrooms' (Balogh 2017) as a means of achieving this improvement:

> Ms Gillard said the national partnership on teacher quality would target critical points in a teacher's career, aiming to attract, train, develop and retain quality teachers in the classrooms. (Ferrari 2008)

The focus on the problem of poor teacher quality often swiftly turns to the issue of initial teacher education and the notion that reform of university-based initial teacher education programmes is the solution to this particular problem, including the regulation of entry into initial teacher education. The importance of attracting not only the right people into the teaching profession but also ensuring that the 'wrong people' do not get into, let alone out of, initial teacher education, is an ongoing point of discussion, and one on which even the teachers' unions are seen to take a more hard-lined position:

> The Australian Education Union yesterday criticised the government's failure to impose higher Australian Tertiary Admission Rank scores for entry to university teaching degrees. 'An ATAR score is not the only thing that makes a good teacher, but we need to recognise that a teacher's academic ability is important, and that we need some minimum requirements,' AEU federal president Correna Haythorpe said yesterday. (Bita and Ferrari 2015)
>
> Australian Education Union federal president Correna Haythorpe said ... 'We support the professional standards. We do think it is important that graduate teachers can meet the standards and are proficient when they enter the classroom. However, we're very concerned that the government's focus is at what happens at the end of initial teacher education programs and they don't focus on the beginning,' Ms Haythorpe said. (Balogh 2017)

This argument, often reported in the print media, that a potential teacher's achievement at the point of entry to a four-year initial teacher education degree should be just as significant as their level of attainment at the end of their professional education in designating whether they are or will become an excellent teacher is illogical, but used to great effect not only by union officials but also by policymakers. Discourses around attracting the 'best and brightest' into teaching, whether judged via Australian Tertiary Admission Rank (ATAR) or another measure, allow their proponents to maintain an aura of 'high standards' and 'rigour' in making noise about teacher quality, while at the same time not directly criticizing *current* teachers. This is of particular use to politicians with an investment in education as their 'signature' (such as Gillard) and to teachers' unions commonly criticized for protecting rather than critiquing teachers, both of whom benefit from openly taking a hard line on teacher quality in the public space without alienating their constituents by engaging in 'teacher bashing'.

Beyond admission of candidates, teacher education is also linked to the problem of teacher quality through a relatively strong focus on the issue of *classroom readiness*, emboldened by the publication of the Teacher Education Ministerial Advisory Group (TEMAG) report *Action Now: Classroom Ready Teachers* in 2015 (Craven et al.). As an example, in one of the prototypical articles published in *The Australian* around the same time, the chair of the Australian Institute for Teaching and School Leadership (AITSL), described as 'teaching guru John Hattie', is quoted in the following way:

> 'When you look at teachers in their first two years out of university, the common complaint by the profession and by the new teachers is they don't know if they're having an impact. That's criminal', Professor Hattie told The Weekend Australian.
>
> 'Show me your graduates can affect kids' learning. That's the main focus.' Professor Hattie said universities would have to 'worry about' how well their student teachers performed in classrooms. (Bita and Ferrari 2015)

Leaving aside the issue of how far 'knowing if they're having an impact' was indeed a common and significant concern on the part of beginning and experienced teachers at the time, the article proceeds from a supposedly agreed assumption that universities have previously not been concerned with 'how well their student teachers performed in classrooms', elsewhere expressed as 'hands-on competence in the classroom' (Balogh 2017), a claim for which there is neither evidence nor foundation provided.

The problem of teacher quality is expressed in the prototypical texts in terms of poor literacy and numeracy, both of teachers themselves (Chester and Chilcott 2009) and consequently their students (Maiden 2007), of teachers being 'not up to the task' of leading improved learning in STEM in primary schools (according to then chief scientist Ian Chubb) (Dodd 2015) and of teachers lacking accountability and attention to what constitutes good teaching (Lebihan 2012). Three of the prototypical articles from the *Australian Financial Review* focus on the cost of strategies designed to create greater equity, such as attempts to constrain class sizes (Dodd 2017) and reforming school funding formulae (Lebihan 2012). On the latter, one article uses evidence from The Grattan Institute, a public policy think tank whose school education programme is generally – although not exclusively – aligned with neoliberal ideas, to argue stridently that there are alternatives to improving education other than redistributing funding. These include:

> that classrooms are continually observed and teachers are told how to improve teaching and learning; teachers conduct research about what works and what doesn't and measure outcomes, and; teacher education and professional learning focus on how to improve student learning rather than teacher qualifications [sic]. (Lebihan 2012)

This largely impoverished view of 'teaching quality', complete not only with a sense of good education as that which can be neatly quantified, measured and scaled up and with a sense of good teaching able to be imparted via a (presumably) external expert, is instructive and broadly representative of representations within these prototypical texts. It resonates with a view of education, subscribed to by the two national newspapers in particular, but more broadly also, as a tool for economic development, preparing citizens to 'contribute to production rather than relying on the welfare state' (Tan 2014: 429). Articulations of the 'teacher quality' issue in the ATC broadly will be taken up further in Chapter 5.

Teacher shortages

The discussion of the shortage of teachers, particularly in the areas of mathematics and science, permeates the prototypical texts, generally in tandem with a level of panic about 'unqualified' teachers stepping in to take classes in these areas:

> Too many Australian secondary school teachers are forced to teach maths despite being unqualified to do so ... (Carey 2019)

> More than a third of WA schools have unqualified teachers taking up to five classes a day in subjects such as maths, science and English, a survey of 25 per cent of Australian public high schools shows. (Hiatt 2006b)

Teacher shortages are sometimes connected in the prototypical articles with other consequences, such as changes or cuts to the curriculum, 'forcing principals to drop subjects' (Chapman 2004) or the need for different approaches to retraining to be adopted, such as one proposed in Tasmania in the mid-2000s to 'turn existing non-science teachers into science teachers through retraining' (Grube 2006). The consistent element across prototypical articles reporting on teacher shortages, however, is a low-level panic about children being taught by *unqualified* teachers and the possible consequences of this, linked on occasion to declining performance on international testing in critical areas such as mathematics and science (Carey 2019).

The counter-narrative of the good or heroic teacher

Finally, in relation to the problem of teacher quality and quantity, there is a small but strong counter-narrative running through the prototypical articles around the 'good' or heroic teacher. Often utilized in the prototypical articles in discussions of awards for teachers, either prospective or just awarded, this narrative frequently draws on nostalgic ideas about inspirational teachers, for example:

> When you think of your favourite teacher, what qualities come to mind? Their enthusiasm and passion for learning? Or the way they kept encouraging you to succeed?
>
> All adults probably have a memory of an exceptional teacher, someone who taught them things they have never forgotten or made them feel more confident.
>
> But how many people got around to telling those teachers that they had made such a significant contribution to their lives?
>
> Every year the Herald Sun searches for these types of teacher to honour them [sic]. (Matthews 2003)

While awards, often run by newspapers themselves, generally seek to acknowledge excellence in teaching and to 'create awareness and appreciation of educators among the general public' (2015), they are in essence focused on the achievements of individuals, whose accomplishments are often implicitly contrasted with the collective of the teaching profession more broadly. Further, these good news stories often work with stereotypes about teachers, such as the observation of one award winner that 'the holidays are attractive, but that's not enough to sustain you day to day if you're not doing something you love' (Clark 2010).

Narratives of good teachers are sometimes embedded in the prototypical texts in stories of teachers whose students have achieved well on high-stakes assessment, such as the National Assessment Program – Literacy and Numeracy (NAPLAN) testing or leaving credentials. These articles often also employ comparisons between schools and school systems, such as one prototypical article entitled 'Catholic and State Schools Add to HSC All-rounders' (Patty 2010), published in the *Sydney Morning Herald* in 2010, which somewhat curiously works from the premise that high achievers in the NSW Higher School Certificate will be drawn from the 28 per cent of secondary schools located within the independent school sector at the time (Australian Bureau of

Statistics 2021), as opposed to the remaining 72 per cent constituted by public and Catholic systemic schools. The article included a quote from the president of the NSW Secondary Principals Council noting:

> 'Where a student has ability and commitment to studies and works with teachers who are similarly committed, this achievement is possible in all schools.' (Patty 2010)

A similar level of surprise is evident, both on the part of the journalist and the principal in question who was said to be 'astounded' in another article reporting on a systemic Catholic school that had 'topped the state' in NAPLAN in 2010. The school's success is attributed primarily to 'first-class teaching', with 'excellent teacher and quality programs [that] focus on the achievement of all students in our school to achieve their personal best' (Lewis 2010).

While there is nothing intrinsically wrong with these good news stories of committed and successful teachers, or indeed with seeking to acknowledge and pay tribute to good teaching, this counter-narrative essentially serves to reinforce rather than provide a serious alternative to the problem of teacher quality as established in the prototypical articles. The 'exception that proves the rule' rarely provides a counter to discourses that suggest that poor teacher quality is the province of the teaching profession as a whole, punctuated by pockets of excellence, where teachers make a lasting contribution, know and demonstrate their extraordinary impact and achieve excellent and measurable results along the way.

The problem of overloaded and overwhelmed teachers

The second problem frame is that of overloaded and overwhelmed teachers, evident not only as a primary frame in a third of the prototypical texts but also as a touchstone in many others. Of the prototypical articles that foreground the problem of overloaded and overwhelmed teachers, six (drawn from five of the newspaper sub-corpora) focus on the issue of class sizes and the consequences, either explicit or implied, for teachers' work. Interestingly, these articles are limited to the years between 1998 and 2004: in the mid-2010s when class size discussion is revived in the *Australian Financial Review*, small class sizes are construed as not cost effective, backed up by the view of John Hattie that 'Australia had wasted billions of dollars reducing class sizes, which didn't work because teachers didn't change the way they taught' (Dodd 2017). Leaving aside the issue of whether class sizes *alone* might be expected to 'work' in improving student learning or whether in fact they 'work' as an enabler of other strategies which do improve student learning and are more possible in the context of smaller class sizes, in the mid-2000s, discussions around class sizes tended to focus on the idea that smaller classes would enable teachers to provide more one-on-one and small group support to students, which was seen as important in supporting student learning. These articles generally run the line that 'our teachers do a great job with what they've got' (Jones 1998), in the view of one principal, or, from another article quoting a teacher, 'You have more time, there are more resources, the relationship you develop is better' (Goodfellow 2003). An article in *Northern Territory News* from 2003 entitled 'Numbers Stress Out Teachers' expressed the problem of overloaded teachers in the context of class sizes in this way:

> Territory teachers were facing high stress levels as class sizes were increasing beyond control, it was revealed yesterday.

and later, via a quote from a union official:

> It is a stress factor because of the frustration of teachers who feel they are unable to ensure an educational outcome. (Baxter 2002)

Class sizes are not regarded in the prototypical articles as the only source of overloaded and overwhelmed teachers. Less than optimal school funding is another, sometimes but not always construed in terms of the disparity in funding between public and private schools. The need for greater funding for literacy to 'help take the burden off teachers' (Webber 2000) is one aspect of this, with the same article quoting the president of the Victorian Secondary Principals Association as saying 'They [the government] are relying on the goodwill of teachers, and that is wearing thin.' (Webber 2000). In a similar vein, a 2005 article from *The Courier-Mail* argues for increased funding to remove asbestos from public schools in the interests of keeping teachers (along with their students) safe in their workplaces (Allen and Odgers 2005). The article makes this case, however, arguing that parents and teachers themselves had been instrumental in forcing the government's hand in the funding decision, noting that they had 'bowed to public pressure'.

This technique, of presenting the overworked or 'put upon' teacher as part of a broader argument about government (or prospective government) ineffectiveness is a common one within the prototypical articles. While only one of the prototypical articles from the *West Australian* sub-corpus relates to the outcomes-based education debate, it provides a good example of this, in its lead paragraph taking the high moral ground against the government in support of beleaguered and misrepresented teachers:

> State and private school teachers unions have condemned Alan Carpenter and Education Minister Ljiljanna Ravlich for publicly criticising opponents of new outcomes-based education courses as being resistant to change and not interested in the welfare of students. (Hiatt 2006a)

A similar strategy is used in a prototypical text from the *Canberra Times* in 2006, lauding the ACT (Labor) government for winning a concession from the Federal (Liberal–National Coalition) government with respect to the introduction of 'A to E' report cards for Kindergarten students, noting that 'the requirements would add to teachers' already heavy workloads'. A further example can be found in a *Northern Territory News* article about proposed changes to teacher–student ratios, where:

> Teachers wanted to go on strike and picket outside the Education Minister's office after he said they had a lot of 'down time' and could afford to look after more students. (Mills 2013)

While this strategy is not the only way in which the problem of the overwhelmed and overloaded teacher is employed – even in 'pure' good news articles about teachers, the problem of 'reform fatigued' (Vonow 2015) teachers wrangling a 'system which has generated increasing amounts of paperwork' such that 'teacher workload has increased "100-fold"' (Raethel 1997) makes the cut – it is not uncommon for teacher workload to be invoked in articles critical of government policy, lending weight to the view that such policy is ill-advised and detrimental.

The problem of bumptious teachers

Finally, the problem frame of 'bumptious' teachers is one employed as a primary frame by about 25 per cent of the prototypical articles, and also subscribed to in a number of others. The bumptious teacher shares some overlap with the problem of teacher quality, in that teachers who are unnecessarily assertive and/or perceived as self-interested do not comfortably fit the definition of the 'good teacher', and these articles often work from the assumption that good teachers would not engage in the activities or hold the perspectives being reported.

Bumptious teachers are often either on strike or threatening to strike, endangering their students' learning and inconveniencing parents. Teachers are said to have drawn up a 'hit list' (Margaretta 1996) of schools to be affected by strike action, with a strong connotation that their interest in maximizing pay and conditions is inappropriate if it gets in the way of being in the classroom. In instances where teachers are pursuing industrial action in response to policy shifts (such as those around state and national standardized testing), they are portrayed as unnecessarily contrary:

> Teachers have been at war with Federal Education Minister Julia Gillard over the My School website, launched in January, which compares student performance in the National Assessment Program Literacy and Numeracy tests for every public and private school in Australia. They argue the website stigmatises schools that achieve low scores and have demanded the Government outlaw the media from creating league tables with the data. (The West Australian 2010)

In this case, referring to the Australian Education Union boycott of NAPLAN in 2010, the absurdity of the teachers' request that 'the Government *outlaw* the media' belies the assumption built into the coverage that both the tests and the website are inherently beneficial. Bumptious teachers are similarly found either threatening industrial action or expressing their disagreement with policy moves such as the NSW minister for education's decision to release a list of 'top performing' primary schools on the NSW Basic Skills test in 1996 (Beikoff 1996), or allegedly encouraging students to attend union rallies in Tasmania in 2004 to protest inadequate school funding (Rose 2004). They can also be found just generally 'taking the easy way out':

> The state's most experienced teachers prefer a casual beach lifestyle if given a chance – leaving tough schools in Sydney's outer suburbs to the newcomers. (Bissett and McDougall 2005)

The problem of the bumptious teacher is linked to the problem of teacher quality via the vague sense in many of these articles that good teachers would not behave in such ways. The connotation is often that teachers' actions are laced with self-interest, where striking over pay and conditions is construed as a selfish act that stands in contrast to the selflessness of the good teacher. Similarly, opposing standardized testing or the publication and comparison of school

116 Constructing Teacher Identities

results is positioned as a lack of accountability. Bumptious teachers are also unnecessarily and dangerously political in their actions, and open this to their students, whether through teaching about gender theory or climate change, or performing as industrial actors, against the apolitical and neutral stance that the 'good teacher' is required to take.

Patterns and resonances across the problem frames

Looking at the problem frames in use in the prototypical texts across the twelve sub-corpora, some interesting patterns are seen to emerge. Table 4.10 highlights the primary problem frame/s in use, with the problem of quality and quantity broken down into the three sub-frames discussed earlier.

The first is that the problem of teacher quality is the only problem frame employed in both of the right-leaning broadsheet newspapers, *The Australian* and the *Australian Financial Review*. In both cases, all five prototypical texts utilized this framing of teachers and their work regardless of whether the focus of the article was school funding, class sizes, teacher education, STEM education or so on. The other two newspapers whose prototypical articles used the teacher quality problem frame, *The Age* and *The Courier-Mail*, tempered this framing with that of the overloaded/overwhelmed teacher. The only other newspaper to employ only a single problem frame in the set of prototypical articles was the left-leaning broadsheet the *Canberra Times*, where the problem of the overloaded/ overwhelmed teacher dominated.

Table 4.10 Problem Frames in Use in the Prototypical Texts

	The Age (L, B)	Syd. Morn. Herald (L, B)	Canberra Times (L, B)	Courier-Mail (R, T)	Daily Telegraph (R, T)	Herald Sun (R, T)	Hobart Mercury (R, T)	Ad. Advertiser (R, T)	NT News (R, T)	West Australian (R, T)	Aust. Fin. Rev. (R, B)	The Australian (R, B)
The problem of quality and quantity												
The problem of teacher quality	●			●							●	●
The problem of teacher shortage			●			●		●	●	●		
The problem(atic) of heroic teachers	●	●				●	●			●	●	
The problem of bumptious teachers	●					●		●		●	●	
The problem of overloaded/overwhelmed teachers	●	●	●	●			●	●	●	●	●	

Indeed, most newspapers, based on this analysis of prototypical texts, appear to vary their framing of teachers and their work. Even arguably the most right-leaning tabloid, the *West Australian* had prototypical articles drawing on the problem of overloaded/overwhelmed teachers alongside those drawing on the problem of bumptious teachers. The problem frame adopted by the largest number of newspapers was that relating to overloaded/overwhelmed teachers, evident in all except the two right-leaning broadsheets and the *Daily Telegraph*, a right-leaning tabloid.

Conclusion

On balance, there are some resonances across this keyword, collocation and prototypical text analysis of the twelve newspaper sub-corpora. First, it highlights that the key and consistent differences between the sub-corpora relate to the scope of their focus, with state and territory-based newspapers focusing on local issues and local politics (and indeed, the smaller the state/territory context, the more 'local' the focus) in reporting on teachers and education, as opposed to a more broad, national focus in the national newspapers. It has also highlighted that 'pet topics', generally consistent with the newspapers' political leanings and other interests, can be the subject of reporting and broader discussions on teachers and education over a period of months or years, and that these discussions can become more or less self-sustaining. It has highlighted that teachers are positioned as both professional and industrial actors, and that this positioning is not even or balanced across newspapers or types of newspapers. Indeed, professional and industrial representations of teachers are themselves nuanced.

Most importantly, what's clear from this analysis is that representations of teachers largely transcend simplistic understandings of newspaper 'type', or distinctions such as tabloid/broadsheet, News Corp/Nine or even left leaning/right leaning. Furthermore, the representations reflect the many faces of what Larsen (2010) has named the cultural myth of 'teacher centrality' – the phenomenon by which teachers are simultaneously seen as critical and indispensable but also regulated and rendered increasingly accountable in attempts to shore up standards and quality. The discourse of teacher centrality is evident in the ATC as much in the hero narratives and tales of overwork and exhaustion as in the panicked and troubled representations of bad or inadequate teachers.

In previous work (Mockler 2014), I have argued that in a context of largely shared views around issues, such as accountability, standards and quality in education on the part of news outlets (and indeed major political parties), much media framing of education news is lifted straight from the press releases of policymakers. Indeed we generally see news values, particularly those that relate to crisis, urgency and potential solutions 'amped up' in the press releases and policy announcements of politicians. The print media did not invent discourses around poor teacher quality or poorly behaved teachers – while these discourses are strong across most of the twelve newspapers in the ATC, they are actually both part and product of waves of policy reform that have been implemented by successive state and territory governments over the past twenty-five years. Among other things, these reforms have sought to 'fix' Australia's position in world rankings through standardizing teachers' work and professional identities but in reality they have achieved little other than creating a veneer of action that 'sticks' for an electoral cycle or two but fails to make a real difference. As the analysis in the past three chapters has highlighted, the issue of 'teacher quality' is a significant one in the ATC, and it is to a closer examination of the emergence and shape of this discourse that we now turn.

5

The Significance and Evolution of 'Quality' in the Australian Teacher Corpus

This chapter zeroes in on the issue of quality and specifically discourses of quality around teachers within the Australian Teacher Corpus (ATC). The significance of *quality* in representations of teachers in the ATC has been the subject of some attention already, from the broad view of the whole corpus presented in Chapter 2, through diachronic analysis in Chapter 3 and into analysis of the different newspaper sub-corpora in Chapter 4. Indeed, in Chapter 6, *quality* will once more emerge as a particular focus in comparisons across media texts generated in different national contexts.

'Quality' is something of a recurring theme in the texts within the Australian Teacher Corpus. One of the most frequent words in the ATC – within the top 1.5 per cent of words within the ATC by frequency – *quality* appears 16,265 times, or 360 times per 1,000,000 words. Chapter 2 explored the strong collocation between *quality* and *teacher/s* across the ATC, and the nature of this relationship, noting that of the 2,019 collocations of *quality* with *teacher* in the ATC, 1,359 (67.3 per cent) are as part of the phrase *teacher quality*, while a further 161 appear in *quality teacher* and a further 95 in *quality of the teacher*. With respect to *teachers*, the phrase *quality teachers* appears 812 times, or in 44 per cent of the 1,838 collocations of *quality* with *teachers*, and *quality of teachers* 314 times. Other frequent collocations of *quality* relate to *quality* [of] *teaching, quality* [of] *education, quality of life* and, to a lesser extent, the *quality* [of] *teacher education* and *professional development, quality* of initial teacher education *graduates, candidates* or *students* and the *quality* of *schools* and *schooling*. Across the ATC, *lifting* or *improving quality* is frequently expressed as an aim, as is a desire to move away from *low* or *poor quality* and towards *good, better, best, high, higher* or *highest quality*. The discourse of teacher quality, highlighted in the strength of the association between *quality* and *teacher/s*, was observed in Chapter 2 to discursively position teachers as either of – or not of – quality, where the attention to teachers themselves as opposed to their practices (e.g. their *teaching*) positions them as a problem requiring attention while at the same time feeding into the ongoing stereotypes of 'good' and 'bad' teachers. The analysis presented in Chapters 3 and 4 highlighted the prevalence of this discourse particularly in the two national broadsheet newspapers, *The Australian* and the *Australian Financial Review*, and the emergence of *quality* as a top collocate of *teacher* in 2007, a position sustained in the ATC until 2020, when the Covid-19 pandemic saw the discussion of teachers 'pivot' to a different direction.

This chapter builds on this analysis to consider the shape of quality, and specifically discourses around teacher quality, as represented in the ATC. I came to this research with a sustained interest in the way that *quality* is used discursively in the public space both by politicians and policymakers (Mockler 2014) and in print media (Mockler 2020a), as well as its relationship to the language of improvement and reform in education (Mockler and Groundwater-Smith 2018). Indeed, the pilot study for this larger corpus-assisted project explored the construction of *teacher quality* (against that of *teaching quality*) in print media texts, and one of my aims in this research was to explore how far the findings of the pilot study, which argued that the discourse of *teacher quality* had become a significant and relatively stable force in reporting on education, held true with respect to a much larger and more general corpus.

This chapter will be structured slightly differently to the preceding three data chapters. Given that it takes as its starting point a concept rather than being entirely corpus-led, it will begin by locating this discussion within the literature on discourses of *quality* in education, particularly as it relates to policy and media texts. From there it will move to explore the rise of *quality* over time in the ATC, including the presentation of some collocation and concordance analysis, exploring changing patterns over time. Finally, a 'deeper dive' into a small number of texts, identified due to their focus on *quality* and loosely guided by Carol Bacchi's 'What's the problem represented to be?' approach (Bacchi 2009; Bacchi and Goodwin 2016), will explore the changing problematization of *quality* within the ATC over time, tracing not only shifts but also continuities and recurring themes, in the context of education policy manoeuvres over this time.

Why quality matters

The significant presence of *quality* in the ATC, and particularly as it relates to teachers, needs to be understood in the context of growing international attention over the past twenty-five years to issues of teacher and teaching quality, and indeed

The Significance and Evolution of 'Quality' in the Australian Teacher Corpus   121

the oft-repeated claim that 'the broad consensus is that "teacher quality" is the single most important school variable influencing student achievement' (Organisation for Economic Co-operation and Development 2005: 26). Marianne Larsen (2010) has traced this attention historically, arguing that what she has referred to as 'the discourse of teacher centrality' was preceded historically, and enabled by a discourse of blame and derision about teachers which together construct teachers 'as being deficient and simultaneously shouldered with the responsibility of fixing societal and school problems' (2010: 208). Larsen argues that the discursive effects of teacher centrality have included tightened control over teachers through mechanisms of performative accountability, the increased technicization of teachers' work as a consequence of the burgeoning school effectiveness movement, the de-contextualization of teachers' work, the standardization of teacher education and the individualization and responsibilization of teachers.

A number of difficulties emerge in attempts to bring a critical eye to discourses of quality in education. One relates to the impossibility of arguing against 'quality' in the first place: as Clarke (2014: 588) has queried, 'who is going to stand up and oppose "quality education"?' There is also an implied binary that sits just beneath the surface of this discourse, equating 'quality' with 'desirable' and, equally, 'not quality' with 'undesirable'. Researchers exploring the emergence of 'quality' as a driver for education reform across school and teacher education have pointed to the ineffable nature of 'quality', which simultaneously, both in education policy – even those policies where 'quality' is a central concern – and in the public imaginary around education, is both ill-defined and simultaneously almost universally and sagely accepted as a worthy goal (see e.g. Berliner 2005; Bourke, Ryan and Lloyd 2016; Kipnis 2013). Elsewhere, I have argued that 'quality', a '[tool] of the neoliberal trade in education, is [simultaneously] slippery to define, and hard to argue against' (Mockler 2017: 335).

Alexander discusses not only the fuzziness of the notion of quality, arguing that quality is 'a mantra in need of definition' (2015: 251), but also the imprecision with which the word itself is used, and the problems this manifests:

> Though 'quality' is often used quasi-adjectively, as in 'quality healthcare', 'quality teaching', 'quality learning' and so on, it is actually a noun. The adjectival use of 'quality', as in 'quality education', is no more than a slogan, offering limited purchase on what quality actually entails. But even when used as a noun, 'quality' is multi-faceted, for it can mean an attribute – as in 'the qualities we look for in a teacher' – or a degree of excellence, as when we say teaching is of outstanding quality, in which case 'outstanding' needs to be defined. So 'quality' – as in Teaching and Learning: quality for all – can describe, prescribe or evaluate. (Alexander 2015: 251–2)

Whilst I agree with Alexander's claim that expressions such as 'quality education', which recur frequently in the ATC, are often sloganistic, the use of *quality* as a noun (e.g. as in *teacher quality* and *teaching quality*) can also have a sloganistic slant, particularly when employed as a shorthand for something else. Furthermore, as I, along with others, have argued elsewhere (Gore, Ladwig and King 2004; Mockler 2020a), *teacher quality* has its own problematic edge, assuming good teaching to be embodied rather than practised and positioning teachers themselves as either *good* or *poor*. *Teaching quality* foregrounds teaching practices rather than the hearts, minds and bodies of teachers themselves, and there is a large discursive difference, with flow-on effects, between an argument in the public space around improving *teaching* and one around improving *teachers*. The ongoing elision of *teaching quality* and *teacher quality* in policy and media spaces, where they are often used as synonyms for each other, is part of the problem, for, as Larsen has argued, 'in the intersection between good teaching and good teachers, we witness the discursive contradictions between holistic notions of the good teacher and technicist assumptions about good teaching' (Larsen 2010: 210).

This discursive contradiction simultaneously places teachers on a pedestal as the 'single most important factor in student achievement' while increasingly subjecting them and their work to impoverished, technicist assumptions about what good teaching is, and mandating evermore arduous mechanisms of accountability and control to shore up *teaching* and thus *teacher quality*. The contradiction is enabled not only by policymakers eager to argue that 'throwing money at the problem [of teaching quality] has not worked' (NSW Productivity Commission 2021: 51), and consequently to create cheaper, 'more effective' education systems, but also by supporters of the teaching profession, who often use the 'single most important' discourse by way of arguing for the critical work teachers do and the need for their work to be accorded greater status within society.

The discourse of teacher quality might be seen as a form of paternalistic chivalry, similar to 'benevolent sexism', a notion developed by Glick and Fiske (1996, 2001) in the 1990s to further and empirically explain pedestal/gutter (or Madonna-whore) syndrome, first identified by Tavris and Wade in their 1977 book, *The Longest War: Sex Differences in Perspective*. Glick and Fiske wrote about benevolent sexism in the following way:

> Although *benevolent sexism* may sound oxymoronic, this term recognizes that some forms of sexism are, for the perpetrator, subjectively benevolent, characterizing women as pure creatures who ought to be protected, supported, and adored and whose love is necessary to make a man complete. This idealization of women simultaneously implies that they are weak and best suited

The Significance and Evolution of 'Quality' in the Australian Teacher Corpus   123

> for conventional gender roles; being put on a pedestal is confining, yet the man who places a woman there is likely to interpret this as cherishing, rather than restricting her (and many women may agree). (Glick and Fiske 2001: 109)

Research has highlighted that benevolent sexism 'reduces women's negative affective and dissonance reactions to their unequal status and treatment' (Hopkins-Doyle et al. 2019: 168), and as such is representative of a kind of 'false consciousness' that 'portray[s] the interests of dominant and subordinated groups as bound together' (Hopkins-Doyle et al. 2019: 168). The discourse of teacher quality is not unlike benevolent sexism, in that it simultaneously places teachers on a pedestal where they are not only revered as 'the most important factor' but also distrusted, regulated and made accountable to standards defined elsewhere and measured arbitrarily and unwisely. Similar to benevolent sexism, the complimentary and status-referencing dimensions of the discourse of teacher quality 'obscures its ideological functions and disarms efforts to challenge it' (Hopkins-Doyle et al. 2019: 168).

As Larsen notes in the conclusion of her paper, what is required is a critical reading of discourses, such as that of teacher quality, that de-couples the pedestal from concerns about the status of the teaching profession:

> By critically 'reading' the discourses that influence teachers and their work, we can begin the task of reclaiming teaching. We need to take teaching off its pedestal without worrying about the potential loss of professional status. (Larsen 2010: 226)

This chapter is one attempt to provide such a critical reading, and to explore the discursive construction of *quality*, and particularly *teacher quality* and its variants, in the press. While much has been written about the emergence of discourses of *quality* in education (see e.g. Barnes 2021a, 2021b; Churchward and Willis 2019; Lampert et al. 2018; Rowe and Skourdoumbis 2019; Scholes et al. 2017) and the contested nature of these discourses, here I seek to explore the discourse of *quality* empirically through close attention to its place in the ATC over time.

Quality in the ATC: Clusters and collocates

As noted in Chapter 3, *quality* appears as a collocate of *teacher* for the first time in 2007, and then in each year of the ATC up to and including 2019. In Chapter 3, I suggested that this was reflective of an increased focus on the so-called issue of 'teacher quality' over the years since the election of the Rudd–Gillard government in 2007, on the back of their electoral platform commitment to the 'Education Revolution'. While 'teacher quality' does indeed emerge as significant at this point in the corpus, a systematic analysis of *quality* highlighted that the rise of *quality* in the corpus was broader than this focus on teachers and teaching.

Two strategies were used to explore the use of quality in context. The first used the 'cluster' function in WordSmith Tools 8 (Scott 2020b) to generate the top two-, three-, four- and five-word clusters including *quality*. Clusters that did not include at least two lexical words (e.g. *the quality, quality of, quality of the*) were disregarded for the purposes of this analysis. Looking at the ATC overall, the twenty most frequent clusters including *quality* (Table 5.1) highlight two key forms of usage, both employed in roughly equal measures. As Alexander

Table 5.1 Most Frequent Two- and Three-Word Clusters Including *Quality*

Cluster	#
High quality	1,649
Teacher quality	1,359
Quality teaching	993
Quality of teaching	919
Quality education	903
Quality teachers	812
Quality of education	508
Improve the quality	434
Quality of teachers	314
Teaching quality	312
Quality of life	305
Good quality	225
Improving the quality	190
Poor quality	177
Improve teacher quality	163
Quality assurance	193
Quality teacher	161
High quality education	149
Improving teacher quality	148
Better quality	125

The Significance and Evolution of 'Quality' in the Australian Teacher Corpus 125

Table 5.2 Five Most Frequent Word Clusters Including *Quality* in Each Annual Sub-corpus

	1996	1997	1998	1999	2000	2001	2002	2003	2004	2005	2006	2007	2008	2009	2010	2011	2012	2013	2014	2015	2016	2017	2018	2019	2020
High quality	•	•	•	•	•	•	•	•	•	•	•	•	•	•	•	•	•	•	•	•	•	•	•	•	•
Quality education	•	•	•	•	•	•	•	•	•	•	•		•	•	•	•	•	•	•	•	•	•	•	•	•
Quality of teaching	•	•	•	•	•	•	•	•	•	•	•		•	•	•	•	•	•	•	•	•	•	•		
Quality teachers				•				•	•	•	•		•	•	•				•			•	•	•	•
Teacher quality					•						•		•		•	•	•	•	•	•	•	•	•		•
Quality teaching						•	•	•	•	•	•	•	•	•	•	•	•	•	•		•	•	•	•	•
Quality of education	•	•	•	•	•	•						•													
Quality of life			•																						
Quality assurance	•	•																							

observed in the quotation above, quality is often used quasi-adjectivally, as in *quality teaching* and *quality education*, where it is generally used to emphasize the importance of its object. Second, *quality* is used as a noun, with this usage split into two groups of phrases, namely where it is used to signify the quality of something else (*teacher quality, teaching quality*), or where it is modified by an adjective which applies an evaluation (*high quality, good quality, poor quality*).

Taking a closer look at the ATC by year, Table 5.2 highlights the five most frequent word clusters (using the same criteria as described above) for each year of the corpus. *High quality* and *quality of education* appear consistently in the sub-corpora, along with *quality of teaching*, which was amongst the five most frequent word clusters in almost every year up to 2018. *Teacher quality* and *quality teaching* both appear in the top five clusters in the early 2000s and remain consistent thereafter, whereas *quality of education*, consistently in the top five word clusters in the first six years of the ATC, has less consistently appeared since the early 2000s. *Quality assurance* was a mid-1990s focus, driven mostly by reporting on the politics of the NSW Department of Education Quality Assurance Unit, or 'quality control flying squad' (Raethel 1996), while *quality of life* appeared in the top five clusters in only one sub-corpus, in 1998. Concordance analysis showed that *quality of life* is most usually used in observing the relationship between education and education outcomes to quality of life.

Together, these two lists highlight a focus in the ATC on quality as it relates to teaching, teachers and education more broadly. Furthermore, the focus on the level of quality (*high, good, poor, better, highest*) and an intention to *improve* quality (particularly of teachers but also more generally) can be seen in these simple frequency lists.

Taking the three interrelated concepts of teacher quality, teaching quality and education quality (as represented not only in these three two-word clusters but other two-, three- and four- word clusters, e.g. *quality education, quality of teaching, quality of the teaching*), the most frequent clusters were used to chart chronologically the prevalence of each in the ATC over time. Figure 5.1 shows each, normalized as per 1,000,000 words in each of the annual sub-corpora. Discussions of all three were at their most prevalent around 2012/2013, with teacher quality outstripping the other two, particularly in these years. Some further discussion of this will be presented later in this chapter, but suffice to say here that this analysis supports an argument that the *quality* agenda, present to some extent in the early years of the ATC, attained particular prominence in the print media in the Rudd–Gillard Labor years from 2007 to 2013.

The second strategy for exploring *quality* in context in the ATC was a focus on collocation. Here, collocates of *quality* were generated for each of the annual sub-corpora of the ATC, and consistent collocates were identified, characterized here as words that appeared as a collocate of *quality* in at least 75 per cent of the sub-corpora (i.e. nineteen or more of the annual sub-corpora). Table 5.3 highlights the eighteen consistent collocates of *quality*. These include seven nouns, namely *education, learning, life, programs, teacher, teachers* and *teaching*. For each of these, either the noun itself or *quality* was used as a descriptor: *teaching quality, quality [of] teaching* and so on. As a collocate of *quality* in the ATC, *student* is most often used as a modifier of *learning*, and *public* as a modifier of *education*. *Better, good, high* and *poor* are all most often used as modifiers of *quality*. *Access* is generally used in constructions such as *access to [high] quality X*, while the three verbs *ensure, improve* and *provide* are representative of the key actions associated with *quality* in the ATC. Finally, *our* as a collocate of *quality* is used to remind the reader of the local importance of *quality* (e.g. *the quality of our X*).

While substantial concordance analysis was undertaken for all consistent collocates, three main groups of collocates are of interest for further discussion here: the first relates to quality of *teacher/s* and *teaching*, the second to adjectives such as *high, good* and *poor* and the third to the verbs *improve, ensure* and *provide*.

Analysis of randomly selected concordance lines for *teacher* and *teaching* as collocates of *quality* (Tables 5.4 and 5.5) highlights the discourse of teacher centrality at work. Teachers and teaching as the 'most significant' factor in education come through here very clearly, as do concerted efforts to measure, boost or lift the quality of both teachers and teaching. Furthermore, a sense of crisis around teacher/ing quality is evident in the concordance, from the suggestion that there is not enough (or the correct) emphasis on teacher quality

The Significance and Evolution of 'Quality' in the Australian Teacher Corpus   127

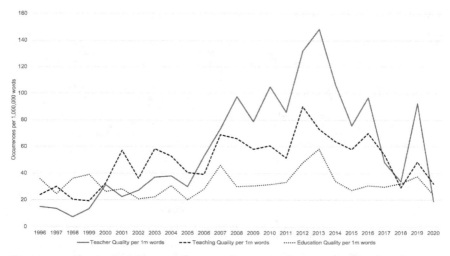

Figure 5.1 Teacher quality, teaching quality and education quality by year, per 1,000,000 words.

Table 5.3 Consistent Collocates of *Quality*, Ordered Alphabetically

---

access, better, education, ensure, good, high, improve, learning, life, our, poor, programs, provide, public, student, teacher, teachers, teaching

---

to the observation that there has been a reluctance to pursue teacher quality. A level of crisis or sense of urgency about the improvement of the quality of both teachers and teaching is evident in the concordance, along with a sense of contestability of strategies and measures to shore up quality.

In these concordance lines we see both a lauding and celebration of quality teachers and teaching as well as a denouncement of poor-quality teaching. Some of the intricacies of these representations will be explored later in this chapter through a focus on a selection of prototypical texts. Something else reflected in the concordance lines is the relatively higher occurrence of *teacher quality* when compared to *teaching quality*: nine of the fifteen concordance lines in Table 5.4 (60 per cent) include *teacher quality*, as opposed to only three (20 per cent) of Table 5.5, which include *teaching quality*, and these proportions are representative of the entire concordance. This observation is congruent with previous work, which showed that *teacher quality* was a common construction in stories focused on school teachers, while *teaching quality* was more likely to prevail in stories focused on teachers in vocational education and tertiary education (Mockler 2020a).

128 *Constructing Teacher Identities*

Table 5.4 Concordance Lines for *Teacher* as a Collocate of *Quality*

teachers. It is like having both a	**teacher** and a **quality** tutor. Therein lies the
the most important professions there is - the	**quality** of a child's **teacher** can determine their
increasing the marks required, but that the	**quality** of **teacher** was more important than the
for a good school education is the	**quality** of the **teacher**. Yet Australia faces the
of a child's education is the	**quality** of the **teacher** in the classroom,' he
of a broad set of conversations about	**teacher quality**, about improving the circumstances of
we also put too little weight on	**teacher quality**, and are reluctant to accept the
onal Development of teachers. Coalition - We view	**teacher quality** as key to the achievement of
off.' Much of the efforts on boosting	**teacher quality** concentrates on new entrants. But Greg
argue that using NAPLAN results to measure	**teacher quality** does not take into account other
from international and Australian research, that	**teacher quality** is by far the most important
only true measure of educational progress and	**teacher quality** is value-adding - in the case
the best education systems in the world -	**teacher quality**. One look at the top performing
to improve their performance. This focus on	**teacher quality** was said to be improving academic
a school teacher (many years ago) a	**quality teacher** was one who managed to keep

Table 5.5 Concordance Lines for *Teaching* as a Collocate of *Quality*

test to allow us to gauge the	**quality** of our **teaching** in those subjects. For
Age doesn't matter, it's the	**quality** of **teaching** and the communication between teacher
will also put $500 million into improving the	**quality** of **teaching** and learning at our universities,
spent on initiatives that 'genuinely improve the	**quality** of **teaching** and learning in our classrooms'.
than 72 per cent were satisfied with the	**quality** of **teaching** at their child's school.
(These awards are) a celebration of the	**quality** of **teaching** practiced every day in classrooms
most important element in education is the	**quality** of **teaching**. So the authors start with
up. There is no evidence that our	**teaching quality** is poor or decreasing but there
the curriculum and relentless efforts to lift	**teaching quality**. Research is also a focus for
was so alarmed at the impact on	**teaching quality** that it pulled 15 apprentices out of
a mentoring program works and focuses on	**quality teaching**, as Hebersham Public School shows, it
Our commitment to academic excellence and	**quality teaching** is complemented by an extensive variety
that can be rationalised and weighed. 'But	**quality teaching** isn't borne of tiered 'professional
no set of characteristics that predict high-	**quality teaching** - not state certification, not masters degrees
He said Australia's reluctance to pursue	**quality teaching** resulted in its education system falling

Concordance analysis of adjectives *high* and *poor* (as two contrasting examples), presented in Tables 5.6 and 5.7, respectively, highlights firstly that both of these adjectives is predominantly used directly to the left of the 'node word' *quality* (i.e. in the constructions *high quality* and *poor quality*). Interestingly, despite this immediate similarity between the usage of the two adjectives, they are deployed very differently with respect to the question '*poor/high quality* of what?' A wide variety of phenomena are described as *high quality* in the ATC, including resources, evidence, outcomes, schooling and student work. *High quality* is seldom used to describe teachers and teaching, and, as highlighted in Table 5.6, when it is, it is most likely to be used in relation to *attracting* high-quality teachers to the profession. *High quality* tends to refer to prospective rather than current teachers.

When it comes to *poor* as a collocate of *quality* within the ATC, the story is very different. While here a smattering of other things are deemed to be of, or potentially of, poor quality (*research, education, life, resources*), the primary discussion is about *poor quality* teachers, teaching, prospective teachers and initial teacher education programs, as highlighted in Table 5.7. In different ways, both *high* and *poor*, in their use as collocates of quality within the ATC, reflect the

The Significance and Evolution of 'Quality' in the Australian Teacher Corpus   129

Table 5.6 Concordance Lines for *High* as a Collocate of *Quality*

sociology programs. The importance of attracting	**high**-calibre applicants to **quality** teaching degrees and
think I submitted an assignment of this	**quality** in **high** school a few years back.
an effective teacher to develop into a	**high-quality** classroom practitioner could not be developed
has endorsed the cuts as necessary, saying	**high-quality** courses in all art forms will
education. I have a firm belief that	**high-quality** education comes from high-quality teaching
to cover all the costs of a	**high-quality** education, which is more than they
used in the interest of maintaining a	**High quality** education system in Australia. Schools can
employed by the school are based on	**high-quality** evidence. 'This may sound as if
There's a plethora of resources and	**high-quality** material, but we are short of
families, however, have a right to expect	**high-quality** - not minimum - numeracy outcomes from their
scholarship as an incentive, we attracted a	**high quality** pool of applicants for positions.' She
in an educated, just and open society.	**High quality** schooling is central to achieving this
to achieve the broadest possible pool of	**high-quality** suitable candidates,' Mr Grant said. '
the push will be on to attract	**high-quality** teachers who are dedicated to achieving
Give clear instructions. Provide examples of	**high-quality** work as models. Teach them to

Table 5.7 Concordance Lines for *Poor* as a Collocate of *Quality*

most of this research has been of	**poor quality**. An influential review by Stanford's
unattractive role for which you might expect	**poor-quality** applicants. She writes: 'In three days,
empowered principals are a solution for	**poor-quality** education. Labor's Better Schools plan,
concerns that some universities are producing	**poor-quality** graduates, ill-equipped for the school
revealed that they had a very	**poor quality** of life. There's also anecdotes
ongoing professional development. It is about the	**poor-quality** of teaching itself. It might be
governments are yet to tackle. In Britain,	**poor-quality** pre-service training was undermining the
courses), this leads to a growth of	**poor-quality** programs designed to attract more teacher
Teachers are urging students to beware of	**poor quality** revision material as next month's
their disruption.' Queensland school principals.	**Poor-quality** teachers are remaining in schools because
	Poor quality teachers? It is amazing, the Prime
lacking? It is called unionism and the	**poor quality** teachers unionism protects.
crash-course degree was likely to produce	**poor-quality** teachers. Would people be prepared to
The poor 1999 HSC results are due to	**poor-quality** teaching. And the person ultimately responsible
teaching profession is low-skilled teaching degrees,	**poor-quality** teaching degrees, and people are coming

news value of negativity (Bednarek and Caple 2017): anxiety about the capacity to attract *high quality* teachers and teacher education candidates, as well as about the *poor quality* of graduate and current teachers feeds into discourses of crisis and panic around education and how far the teaching profession is up to the task of supporting children and young people in their learning and achievement.

Next, we turn to the three verbs that are consistent collocates of *quality* in the ATC: *improve*, *ensure* and *provide*. It should be noted that while each of these three appears as consistent collocates in its own right, the other forms of these words (e.g. *improving*, *providing*) also appear as collocates of quality at different points in the ATC. In the fifteen randomly selected concordance lines for *improve* as a collocate of *quality* (Table 5.8), the objects of improvement relate to teaching (five), teachers (four), education (four), learning (four) and *teacher conditions* (one), said to be important for *improving teacher quality*. The prevalence of *improve* as a collocate of *quality* reflects not only the links between discussions of quality and crisis in education, but also points to an assumption of deficits when it comes to teachers and their work: improvement is seen as a remedy to *poor quality teachers* and a way of shoring up *high quality teaching*.

130   *Constructing Teacher Identities*

Table 5.8 Concordance Lines for *Improve* as a Collocate of *Quality*

and managed out of it to lift	**quality** and **improve** learning outcomes. Victoria has embarked
this? This is important in order to	**improve quality** secondary English teaching across the board.
class-size reductions combined with measures to	**improve** teacher **quality** and provide additional learning
said the government was doing plenty to	**improve** teacher **quality** following a damning new report
onal development. $120 million over four years to	**improve** teaching **quality**. Includes professional development
the value of universal education; seek to	**improve** the **quality** of teaching and learning in
ago, as part of its plan to	**improve** the **quality** of education in that state.
be part of what's necessary to	**improve** the **quality** of teaching, but it's
great challenge as a nation is to	**improve** the **quality** of Australia's education system.
by school and office based educators to	**improve** the **quality** of education in the NT.
part of what needs to happen to	**improve** the **quality** of student learning in our
a new literacy and numeracy test - to	**improve** the **quality** of teaching graduates, but their
Minister Adrian- Piccoli welcomed the pledge to	**improve** the **quality** of education across Australia, but
of a $244.6 million package of initiatives to	**improve** the **quality** of teaching and learning in
two important factors for improving teacher	**quality**. We need to **improve** teacher conditions and

Table 5.9 Concordance Lines for *Ensure* as a Collocate of *Quality*

adequately resourced and appropriately supported.	**Ensure** a **quality** teaching-learning environment in both
mechanism, as peers monitor teaching practices and	**ensure** consistency in the **quality** of teaching. CAREER
force and will work with universities to	**ensure** continuing high **quality** pre-service teacher training.
salaries had to continue to rise to	**ensure** more top **quality** young people went into
to improve the professional status and the	**quality** of teaching, and **ensure** supply of teachers.
entry standards need to be boosted to	**ensure quality** in the classroom. It would also
body in any state or territory to	**ensure quality** teaching and teacher development. A year
standard faces losing their job. To further	**ensure** teacher **quality**, the Iemma government recently
government needs to invest in additional high	**quality** teacher training to **ensure** teachers are able
five years to have the capacity to	**ensure** that **quality** education, quality research and quality
be paid significantly more than elsewhere to	**ensure** that teaching **quality** and teacher turnover is
in the ability of our principals to	**ensure** that we have **quality** staff in every
board proposes, all Queensland universities will	**ensure** the highest **quality** outcome of pre-service
would argue these conditions are necessary to	**ensure** the **quality** of the ACT's public
Coordinating professional development courses to	**ensure** they are **quality** controlled. Assisting in the

Ensure and *provide* work slightly differently in the ATC, as highlighted in Tables 5.9 and 5.10.

Ensure, which has a higher modality, more of a sense of necessity, than *provide*, is more often used within the ATC in relation to teachers and teaching, infusing quality teachers and teaching with a sense of importance and urgency. Initial teacher education is another area where quality is said to be in need of ensuring, along with teacher professional development. When it comes to *provide*, quality, or high-quality, *education* is most usually the object. This is an interesting distinction, for the subtext of the provision of quality education suggests that in relation to *education*, governments as agents, *provide*, and that given adequate resourcing, quality education ensues. Quality (of) teaching, or quality (of) teacher education, requires intervention: it cannot be expected to flow from adequate resourcing, but needs to be *ensured* through mechanisms of quality assurance or strengthening performative accountability structures for teachers (and teacher educators).

The final consistent collocate to be examined more closely here is the pronoun *our*. While not strictly speaking a lexical word, *our* has a particular discursive effect through the way it positions both the reader and the writer in relation

The Significance and Evolution of 'Quality' in the Australian Teacher Corpus   131

Table 5.10 Concordance Lines for *Provide* as a Collocate of *Quality*

be on stimulating and supporting them to	**provide** a high **quality** experience.' To that end
anti-religious, but it is determined to	**provide** a high **quality**, secular, meaningful option for
have often not had the ability to	**provide** a high-**quality** starting point for how
it was stressful for one teacher to	**provide** a **quality** education to 22 students, including five
grateful for the commitment they make to	**provide** a **quality** education for our children in
maintained 'while delivering on our promise to	**provide** a **quality** education to Queensland kids and
Schools and education authorities should	**provide** high-**quality** and appropriate professional learning for
and non-government schools could struggle to	**provide** high-**quality** education. He said the federal
want to suggest that, rather than teaching,	**quality** learning environments **provide** the key to quality
she describes as 'a mandated responsibility to	**provide** **quality** education for all Victorians', Ms Delahunty
coast, rests squarely on its ability to	**provide** **quality** education to its workers and leaders
and its dedicated teachers will continue to	**provide** **quality** education to all students, regardless of
improvements. Key objectives would be to attract	**quality** teaching candidates, **provide** incentives to develop and
of the game was no longer to	**provide** the best **quality** education to those who
work to ensure that government schools can	**provide** the same **quality** uniformly across Canberra; this

Table 5.11 Concordance Lines for *Our* as a Collocate of *Quality*

in Australia, we therefore need to increase	**quality** in **our** supply of teaching graduates, by
but what does it do for the	**quality** of education and **our** children's future?
are our parents. To ensure the highest	**quality** of education for **our** children and their
That the country recognise the importance and	**quality** of education for **our** children, and therefore
of university standards aimed at improving the	**quality** of education in **our** schools. From 2020, all
educators. Despite occasional rumblings about the	**quality** of graduates leaving **our** universities, Australian
Gillard's protestations she cares about the	**quality** of **our** educators might ring just slightly
school environment, 'We need to address the	**quality** of **our** teaching workforce', and start 'removing
two new programs designed to improve the	**quality** of teaching in **our** schools. Teacher development
teachers and other stakeholders. 'Improving the	**quality** of teaching in **our** schools is a
way have a real effect on the	**quality** of the education **our** children receive. GEOFF
it gets in research income. These become	**our** ordinary measures of **quality**, though they say
that we move into the future retaining	**our** **quality** and professional integrity as a world
way in innovative curriculum delivery, to keep	**our** **quality** teachers and develop as a community
how can it possibly hope to recruit	**quality** teachers to **our** schools. The government needs

to the subject under discussion. Table 5.11 includes fifteen randomly selected concordance lines for *our* as a collocate of *quality*, highlighting that *our* is most often used in this context linked to the news value of proximity (Bednarek and Caple 2017), and specifically as a marker of cultural proximity. The function of *our* here is to remind readers of a common, social concern around education and schooling, and particularly of the interests of *our children*. *Our* is often thus used with *quality* to remind readers of shared interests around the quality of teaching, schooling and education, and create a corresponding sense of newsworthiness around stories reporting on quality (or lack thereof) when it comes to education.

What's the problem here? Exploring *quality* through analysis of prototypical texts

In order to guide a closer analysis of a smaller group of well-selected texts, ProtAnt 1.2 (Anthony and Baker 2015) was used to select the two articles from each annual sub-corpus that were most closely focused on quality. The two articles with the highest normalized frequency of instances of *quality* were selected from each sub-corpus, with the two additional provisos that they needed to (a) include at least four instances of *quality* overall (this to exclude extremely short articles that mentioned *quality* only once or twice) and (b) be drawn from two different newspapers (this to ensure, as far as possible, a breadth of coverage). Using this criteria, fifty articles were selected and systematically examined, using the following questions, drawn loosely from Bacchi's WPR (What's the Problem Represented to Be?) framework (Bacchi 2009), as a scaffold for analysis:

- In relation to what or whom is *quality* used in this article?
- What is being problematized in this article?
- What assumptions about education are implicit in this article?
- What are the origins/contextual dimensions of this representation?

The idea here was to explore the different and possibly contrasting manifestations of *quality* over time and to identify the different discourses of quality manifest in the ATC over the twenty-five-year period. Table 5.12 provides a snapshot of the 'quality of what?' analysis, while recognizing that in many articles, *quality* was used in intertwining and overlapping ways, particularly in relation to teachers, initial teacher education and teaching. Consequently, in some articles, *quality* is used to refer to more than one 'what' or 'whom', resulting in more than two issues identified in some years.

Quality is first used in relation to teachers in the prototypical texts in 1999, and then in every subsequent year up to and including 2020, making this both the strongest and most consistent focus of *quality* amongst the prototypical

Table 5.12 *Quality* of ... in Prototypical Texts

	1996	1997	1998	1999	2000	2001	2002	2003	2004	2005	2006	2007	2008	2009	2010	2011	2012	2013	2014	2015	2016	2017	2018	2019	2020
Teachers				•	•	•	•	•	•	•	•	•	•	•	•	•	•	•	•	•	•	•	•	•	•
Initial teacher education	•	•			•					•		•							•	•	•		•		
Teaching							•		•	•	•		•	•						•		•	•		
Education			•		•	•																			
Schooling	•		•	•																					
Curriculum materials																								•	•

The Significance and Evolution of 'Quality' in the Australian Teacher Corpus   133

texts. Initial teacher education is a less consistent but more enduring focus, first appearing in the prototypical texts in 1996, and then sporadically throughout the texts through to 2018. It is important to note that particularly in the last ten years of the ATC, the conflation of *teacher quality* with issues to do with initial teacher education means that there is significant overlap here, a phenomenon which will be discussed more fully subsequently. The snapshot of *quality* teaching in the prototypical texts is similar, first appearing in the 2001 texts and then sporadically in texts through to 2018. Education, schooling and curriculum materials each appear in relation to *quality* in a small number of prototypical articles, in the case of education and schooling in the first five years of the ATC and in the case of curriculum materials in the last two.

More important than this visual longitudinal snapshot, however, is the qualitative exploration of the uses of *quality* in the prototypical texts, which needs to be understood alongside the education policy manoeuvres related to quality over the same period. Perhaps unsurprisingly, the discourse of teacher centrality is very strong in the texts that focus on *teacher quality*, although this discourse is reflected in different ways in the prototypical texts, some more subtle than others. In some articles, particularly those celebrating teachers or reporting on teaching awards, the recognition of teacher centrality is more benign:

> TEACHERS are the heart of the education system – and quality teachers are the backbone of the quality education system we have here in the Northern Territory. (Henderson 2006)

In other articles, the sustained and explicit focus on *teacher quality* by consecutive governments on both sides of the political divide is evident in the focus given to teacher centrality. In the Howard years (1996–2007), this was often expressed as a priority for the federal government:

> [Education Minister] Dr Nelson, who is on a collision course with teachers' unions over education reforms, said raising the quality, professionalism and status of teachers was the Government's top priority in schooling. (Balogh 2005)[1]

In the Rudd–Gillard years, the common parlance related not only to the importance of the teacher but also the image of a very particular type of 'good teacher':

---

[1] This sentiment is also expressed slightly differently as 'Education Minister Brendan Nelson said raising the quality and status of teachers was a priority in the area of schooling' in Milburn (2005).

The federal Minister for Education, Julia Gillard, said the research would look at 'what could work to better reward teachers for quality teaching, what could work to retain our best teachers where we want them – in front of classrooms, teaching kids'. (Patty 2008)

Ms Gillard said that nothing was more important to learning than the quality of the teacher standing in front of the classroom. (Kerr 2009)

Gillard's persistent notion that teachers perform 'in front of a class' in a simultaneous act of education and engagement, both infused and was reflected in the simplicity with which she treated complex educational problems over her time as both minister for education and prime minister. During her tenure as education minister, the National Assessment Program – Literacy and Numeracy was both launched and supercharged by the introduction of the My School website (Mockler 2016), reforms which she characterized in the following way in 2012:

When I first became Education Minister no one could even tell you which were the thousand worst-performing schools in the country. Now you can get that on your smartphone if you want . . . and have a good look. (Gillard 2012)

Ideas about simplistic comparison of schools – indeed, even simplistic identification of the 'thousand worst performing schools in the country' available to every smartphone user in Australia, are consistent with a vision of education that places the teacher 'in front of the classroom', conceives of teacher quality as something likely to be shored up by performance pay and competition and, finally, legislates that Australia will be in the 'top five by 2025', as the Australian Education Act, passed into legislation on Gillard's final day as prime minister, did (2013). Elsewhere (Mockler 2014), I have argued that the Gillard government used a pivot from a focus on equity to one on quality post the 'Gonski review' (Gonski et al.) of 2011 to alleviate the pressure of the impossible task she faced in reshaping school funding equitably, given her oft-repeated promise that 'no school would lose a dollar' (Gillard and Garrett 2012). Despite this attempt to seamlessly segue from equity to quality, pushes for more equitable funding of schools persisted, largely a product of lobbying and advocacy via grassroots movements such as the 'I give a Gonski' campaign, throughout Gillard's tenure and into Kevin Rudd's second brief prime ministership from June to September 2013. Gillard was only partially successful in her attempts to reframe the conversation, in that while *quality* became a more prominent focus during this time, equity, particularly of funding, continued on.

The bipartisanally backed notion that teachers are the 'most important factor' emerges early on in the prototypical texts, with this claim in an op-ed by a director of access economics:

> The quality of teachers is more important in education outcomes than student backgrounds, class sizes, overall education spending levels or teacher salaries. (Shann 2000)

While at different points in the prototypical articles, this claim is placed into context with the argument that 'the quality of the classroom teacher is the major in-school influence on student learning' (Dinham 2011), at other points the opposite is true with the 'most important' discourse amped up in dangerous and patently incorrect ways:

> Federal Education Minister Christopher Pyne recently said [that PISA results] showed that in Australia the No. 1 issue, in terms of the outcomes, was teacher quality. 'In fact they said eight out of 10 reasons why a student does well in Australia or badly is the classroom to which they are allocated. In other words, the teacher to whom they are allocated. One out of 10 reasons was socio-economic status background and one out of 10 were all other reasons put together.' This indicates that quality teaching is the silver bullet. (Penfold 2014)

The words attributed to the minister here were spoken by him on the Australian Broadcasting Corporation television programme *Q+A*, in September 2014 (Australian Broadcasting Corporation 2014). A commitment to improving *teacher quality* had been laid out as a priority for the Liberal-National Party (LNP) Coalition in the lead-up to the 2013 election, with then shadow education minister Christopher Pyne laying the groundwork for what would be a different pivot for the coalition government from a focus on the *amount* of funding provided to *how* funding is deployed, and how effective the funding is at 'improving quality'. The LNP government, and particularly the minister, sought to shift the conversation from funding equity to funding effectiveness, with 'quality', central to this shift, providing a benchmark for effectiveness.

So, where Gillard had failed to effectively draw attention away from equity to quality, the LNP government sought to draw it from the amount of funding to 'performance', but *quality* was still key here. The move that the LNP made here was to cast it simultaneously about the quality of teachers, teaching and teacher education – thereby effectively responsibilizing teachers and teacher educators for their *quality*, while abrogating responsibility for equitable funding or structural reconfiguration that would support systemic improvement. This shift began before the 2013 election, when, in an interview on ABC radio, Pyne expressed it in the following way:

> the first thing we would do is address issues of teacher quality in our universities. The first thing we could do is to make sure that the training of our teachers at university is of world standard. I don't believe it is.
>
> We would immediately instigate a very short term Ministerial advisory group to advise me on the best model for teaching in the world. How to bring out more practical teaching methods, based on more didactic teaching methods or more traditional methods rather than the child centred learning that has dominated the system for the last 20, 30 or 40 years, so teaching quality would be at my highest priority, followed by a robust curriculum, principal autonomy and more traditional pedagogy. So I want to make the education debate, move it on from this almost asinine debate about more money and make it about values because while money is important Fran, what we are teaching our children and how we are teaching them and who is teaching them is all much more important. (Kelly 2013, February 23)

If Gillard's vision of the 'good teacher in front of the classroom' was an impoverished and narrow one, Pyne's vision, as expressed here, was equally as impoverished but more expansive, advocating for approaches to teaching that stand in direct opposition to what evidence from decades of robust, large-scale, publicly funded, educational research has consistently indicated represents actual 'quality' in teaching (Comber 2015; Education Queensland 2001; Gore et al., 2021; Hayes et al. 2006; Ladwig et al. 2007). Already, prior to the election that would bring the LNP back to government, Pyne was laying the groundwork for a discursive shift from an 'asinine debate' about funding issues to an all-in one about the quality of teachers, teaching and teacher education.

By the time David Gonski was appointed by the LNP government in July 2017 to lead a second review, known popularly as 'Gonski 2.0', this shift had essentially taken place. The review, focused on 'achieving educational excellence', produced *Through Growth to Achievement: Report of the Review to Achieve Educational Excellence in Australian Schools* (Gonski et al. 2018) in March 2018. This report construed the issue of inequitable funding and educational disadvantage which had been the starting point for 'Gonski 1.0' as largely solved, and posed a new problem to which the recommendations of the report – largely focused on quality and improvement – aimed to provide a solution:

> The Review of Funding for Schooling in 2011 recommended a national commitment to address educational disadvantage which is now leading to the

The Significance and Evolution of 'Quality' in the Australian Teacher Corpus   137

phased implementation of a needs-based funding model to ensure adequate financial resources for all schools.

Seven years on, we need a similar national commitment to address the performance slippage that is affecting every Australian student cohort. (Gonski et al. 2018: 4–5)

This discourse of 'performance slippage', caused by poor-quality teachers and teaching and impermeable to extra funding, had well surfaced within the public space by the release of *Through Growth to Achievement* in 2018. An editorial in *The Australian*, one of the prototypical texts, published in April 2017, highlights how seamlessly the government's case was taken up in some parts of the print media:

The [PISA] report confirms what *The Australian* has argued for years: that improving teaching quality should be the focus of efforts by governments and education authorities to lift results. After a $12 billion increase in taxpayer funding since 2003–04, more money will not solve entrenched problems. Spending resources more effectively, in-service teacher training and improving education degrees so new teachers emerge with best practice classroom skills must be priorities. (Quality Teaching Must Be the Focus of School Reform 2017)

In the other prototypical text from 2017, this time from the left-leaning *Sydney Morning Herald*, the discourse of slippage and reference to misspent money is also present in reporting on a speech given by OECD Director for the Directorate of Education and Skills, Andreas Schleicher:

As policymakers have struggled to deal with Australia's slipping performance in international benchmark tests like PISA and TIMSS, the perceived quality of teachers has come under fire.

Australia has not been as good at extending its top students, and has become less effective at mitigating socio economic disadvantage in its schools. But the OECD's research suggests the problem is how our teachers are using their time.

'Australia has many ingredients of success,' Mr Schleicher said, speaking on the sidelines of the Global Education and Skills Forum in Dubai on Saturday, but our policy settings have been focusing on things that are not addressing the source of our achievement gap between students. (Munro 2017)

While the perspectives presented in these two articles are the same in essence, the (*Sydney Morning Herald*) *SMH* reference to *the perceived quality of teachers* as opposed to *The Australian*'s claim that 'improving teaching quality should be the focus of efforts' suggests that the premise of the crisis of teacher and teaching quality is at least questioned, if not rejected there.

Initial teacher education (ITE) is positioned in the prototypical texts as both a problem and a solution. As a problem it is represented as a root cause of poor teacher quality, because of both the low quality of entrants to ITE programmes and the low quality and spurious nature of ITE programmes themselves (as alluded to by Pyne in his 'world standard' comment above). A smattering of prototypical articles in the first ten years of the ATC focus on ITE, early on in relation to attracting high-quality candidates in the context of broader discussions around the status of teachers, in conjunction with a senate inquiry held between 1996 and 1998 (Commonwealth of Australia 1998). I have argued elsewhere that these discussions of teacher status, shortage and education in the late 1990s was generally not imbued with a sense of a crisis of quality (Mockler 2018), but rather a desire to make teaching a more attractive career option, and the prototypical texts focused on ITE in this period are consistent with this observation. In a 1996 article, for example, the then federal minister for Schools, Vocational Education and Training, Ross Free, is reported as saying:

> There is a need to overcome many of the myths about teaching and to inform potential students of the opportunities available in the industry in order to encourage the highest quality students to apply for teacher education. (Jones 1996)

This contrasts with crisis representations of ITE candidates in the mid-2010s, for example, 'Some of Queensland's worst-performing students have been accepted into teaching courses' (Chilcott 2014), around the time of Pyne's Teacher Education Ministerial Advisory Group (TEMAG). By this time, the entry score obtained by prospective teacher education students had come to be seen as a qualification (or otherwise) for teaching independent of the programme that ensued, and the minimum entry score for programmes a signal of their capacity to produce 'quality teachers'.

Also associated with TEMAG, whose report, *Action Now: Classroom Ready Teachers*, was released in December 2014, was the concept of 'classroom readiness' for ITE graduates, which became something of a proxy for quality of both early career teachers and ITE programmes around this time. A prototypical article from 2015 which draws on a report authored by Ben Jensen, CEO of independent think tank Learning First, and also a TEMAG member, reports on the need for greater 'hands-on experience' in ITE and

The Significance and Evolution of 'Quality' in the Australian Teacher Corpus   139

'solid quality control' of ITE programmes, using the experience of a recent graduate as a touchstone:

> Sam Nelson, who began teaching maths to high school students at Melbourne's John Paul College in 2010, found his first few weeks in the classroom 'overwhelming'.
>
> 'What's really needed is hands-on experience,' he said yesterday. 'The best lecture I had went for 15 minutes, when a great teacher came in and gave us tips on day-to-day teaching, how to manage a class, how to make notes, how to talk to students.' Mr Nelson said teaching should be more prestigious. (Bita 2015)

The notion that initial teacher education should consist of practical 'tips and tricks' designed to ensure that being a neophyte teacher is not 'overwhelming' is at the heart of the concept of 'classroom readiness', and as impoverished a vision of ITE as Pyne's vision of good teaching, encapsulated above.

Prototypical articles that focused on the quality of education and schooling broadly were confined to the first four years of the ATC, informed to some extent by the adoption of new public management principles in education in the 1990s. Quality education and schooling in these articles are said to rely variously on school autonomy (Hurrell 1997), quality assurance (Raethel 1996), heightened efficiency (Richards 1999), the quality of the leaving credential and equity of access (Image bid for state schooling 1998). Two further prototypical articles, published in 2019 and 2020, and both op-eds authored by employees of education think tank Learning First, relate to the quality of curriculum materials. These articles are of particular interest to this discussion not because of their immediate focus, but because of the conceptualization of teachers and their work embedded in their argument that teachers are somehow burdened by the need to engage in creative curriculum planning work and would be better served by pre-prepared resources.

In the 2019 article, the problem is articulated in the following way:

> In Australia, while there are differences across states, teachers are typically given much greater choice than in many other systems in the curriculum they teach. Unfortunately, the benefits of choice can, in reality, mean a lack of support and opportunity for teachers to easily access high quality curriculum materials. This increases pressure on teachers and takes up valuable time. Teachers continually ask for better support but don't receive it.
>
> No one is suggesting teachers should be forced to use specific textbooks. But other systems around the world don't ask all teachers to invest time developing their own curriculum materials. (Jensen and Magee 2019)

The idea that teachers engaging in design of classroom learning resources is somehow an optional extra on top of the job of teaching is a fundamental misunderstanding of teachers' work, as highlighted in decades of work on teachers and curriculum making (see e.g. Grundy 1998; Priestley et al. 2021; Stenhouse 1975; Yates 2009). The evidence that teachers 'continually ask for better support but don't receive it' in relation to lesson design and resource identification is absent from the article, which largely stands as an advocacy for greater standardization of teachers' work in the name of quality, despite its claim to make a case for 'putting learning at the heart of curriculum reform'. The 2020 article (Roberts-Hull 2020) names the 'problem' that 'Australian or state curriculums don't provide teachers with material for daily lessons. This work mostly falls to teachers', offering the following solution:

> Providing teachers with high-quality lesson materials is a less expensive way to improve student learning than many other initiatives.

Across the two articles, pre-prepared and standardized curriculum materials are positioned as both 'teacher's friend' and a fiscally responsible move, while the assumption that standardized teaching and learning equates with 'quality teaching and learning' is firmly embedded. In this conceptualization of teaching and learning, the good teacher has neither the time nor the tolerance for risk-taking that engaging their own creative capacities in designing resources for their classes would require.

Conclusion

In these last two prototypical articles under discussion, we see the real problem with discussions of teacher and teaching quality in the public space: while offering what are inevitably poorly defined and often highly contestable hot takes on what constitutes quality in relation to education, they almost consistently miss the point about actual threats to the quality of teaching in Australian schools. These threats lie mostly in inadequate and inequitable resourcing and in the concomitant intensification of teachers' work via a 'tsunami of paperwork' (Fitzgerald et al. 2019), which has resulted in Australian teachers having, on average, some of the longest working hours of teachers in OECD countries (Organisation for Economic Cooperation and Development 2020). High-quality teaching comes not as a consequence of standardization of teaching practice or of being 'tough on teacher education students' by imposing draconian rules about who can or cannot become a teacher, based on their own school performance. Engaging in the design of bespoke curriculum and learning resources for their students is not what's causing teachers to feel overworked and occupationally overstretched (Stacey, Wilson and McGrath-Champ 2020), any more than foisting 'technicist assumptions about good teaching' (Larsen 2010: 210), packaged as teaching standards, on teachers will shore up a mythical state known as *teacher quality*.

This chapter has shown that in print media coverage of teachers and their work, the discussion of *quality* runs deep. Anxieties about teacher quality, teaching quality and the quality of teacher education are evident across the whole of the ATC, increasing in intensity post-2000, and again in the mid-2000s. It has shown that the reputed crisis of quality in relation to teachers, their work and formation in the profession is a central concern of these media texts, but that in this they mirror the discursive embrace of quality evident in the words of policymakers and the texts they create and promote. These discussions of the quality of teachers and their work shape the broad cultural-discursive arrangements that frame teachers' practice in the many different sites within which it is enacted. They hold the capacity to influence the things that can and cannot be said about teachers' work and crowd out the capacity for teachers and school and system leaders to have genuine conversations about the quality of teaching, what constitutes good quality in teaching and what enables and constrains quality teaching. This is where a danger lies, a point I shall pick up in Chapter 7. Chapter 6, meanwhile provides a 'wider lens', a view of the ATC in context, through a comparative look at print media coverage of teachers in Canada, the United States, the UK and Australia.

6

A Comparative View of Teachers in the Print Media

In the past four chapters, the discussion has been based on the Australian Teacher Corpus, using Australian education policy as a touchstone. It is well documented, however, that transnationally, school education is subject to global education policy flows, variously described as 'policy borrowing and lending' (Lingard 2010; Steiner-Khamsi 2004), policy mobility (Ball, Junemann and Santori 2017; Gulson and Lubienski 2014) and via the metaphor of the GERM, the Global Education Reform Movement (Sahlberg 2016). Essentially, the argument, advanced over the past two decades by critical education policy sociologists and comparative education scholars, relates to the adoption of standardization and accountability regimes (manifest in, e.g. national curriculum, standardized testing, teaching standards, performance pay for teachers and so on) in multiple jurisdictions internationally. Encouraged since the 1990s in these endeavours by the Organisation for Economic Co-operation and Development (OECD) (Rizvi and Lingard 2009; Ydesen and Bomholt 2020), these different aspects of the GERM have been adopted worldwide according to 'local vernaculars' (Rizvi and Lingard 2010) which have seen them shaped, to varying degrees, to meet local needs and contexts.

In order to gain a broader view and set some of these findings in relation to teachers in the Australian print media in an international context, some comparative analysis was undertaken. It should be noted, at the outset, that this comparative work was not of a comparable scale to that undertaken with the ATC. It was not the intention to construct the equivalent of the ATC for each of the countries included in the comparative analysis (and, as the previous chapters in this book have hopefully demonstrated, neither would I have been able to have done justice to such a large amount of data in the limited space of one chapter).

144 *Constructing Teacher Identities*

Accordingly, I limited the data included in three ways. First, to four other Anglophone countries, each of which is said to bear some similarities to, and also some differences from, Australia: Canada, New Zealand, the UK and the United States. Second, in terms of time span: it was not practical to cover the same twenty-five-year period as the ATC, so I limited the time span to the final five years covered by the ATC, from January 2016 to December 2020, with the intention that this would provide an up-to-date, contemporary snapshot. Third, in terms of publications: my early investigations indicated that in most of these countries, stories about teachers tend to more regularly appear in broadsheet newspapers than tabloids, and I thus focused on broadsheets in each country. I was keen to ensure a range of political leanings in the comparative corpus, so for each country, I included the top two broadsheet newspapers (by circulation) with contrasting political leanings. Table 6.1 provides an overview of the newspapers included in the international corpus, organized by country.

The same parameters used for the ATC were used in the construction of the international corpus: to be selected, articles needed to have three or more mentions of *teacher* and/or *teachers*. Articles in all newspapers were identified via the Nexis database, with the exception of those in the *Wall Street Journal*, which were identified via the Factiva database (this because Nexis does not provide access to the *Wall Street Journal*). A similar process to the one described in Chapter 2 was used for most articles, whereby articles were

Table 6.1 Newspapers and Articles in the International Corpus

Country	Publication	Orientation	Articles	Total
Australia	*The Age*	Left-leaning	1,201	2,309
	The Australian	Right-leaning	1,108	
Canada	The *National Post*	Right-leaning	1,109	2,642
	The *Toronto Star*	Left-leaning	1,533	
New Zealand	*Dominion Post*	Left-leaning	697	2,446
	The New Zealand Herald	Right-leaning	1,749	
The UK	*The Guardian*	Left-leaning	3,317	4,848
	The Telegraph	Right-leaning	1,531	
The United States	*New York Times*	Left-leaning	3,545	4,353
	Wall Street Journal	Right-leaning	808	

converted into appropriate formats for analysis via AntConc 3.5.8 (Anthony 2019) and WordSmith Tools 8 (Scott 2020a). *Wall Street Journal* articles were additionally processed via Download Parser (Scott 2020b) software, which allowed splitting and tagging of these files. Many duplicates were removed by Nexis and Factiva in the search process, and further duplicates were removed manually via inspections of headlines and concordance lines. The number of articles shown in Table 6.1 is the final number used for the analysis after the removal of duplicates.

In order to explore the similarities and differences between the national sub-corpora, keyword analysis and collocation analysis were conducted, with concordance analysis conducted concurrently on all keywords and collocates, using the processes and parameters laid out in previous chapters. While keywords (obviously and intentionally) reflect the differences between sub-corpora, by way of attending not only to difference but also to similarities (Taylor 2018) between the representations of teachers in the different national contexts, particular attention has once again been paid here to the 'consistent collocates' (Gabrielatos and Baker 2008), defined as 'words that stably collocate with the node in multiple datasets and are to be viewed as indicating core elements of meaning, semantic associations and semantic prosodies' (Germond, McEnery and Marchi 2016: 141).

Differences and similarities in the 'aboutness' of the international sub-corpora

As a starting point, keywords were generated for each of the international sub-corpora, which resulted in the identification of 537 keywords across the five countries. As a way of making the analysis more manageable for the purpose of this chapter, the top fifty lexical keywords (according to Log Ratio values) were selected for further analysis. A concordance was generated for each of these 250 keywords, and based on concordance analysis, each keyword was allocated to a thematic group. The thematic groups emerged from the concordance analysis itself, and as Table 6.2 highlights, not all sub-corpora generated keywords related to all thematic groups.

Unsurprisingly, all five of the national sub-corpora contained a relatively large number of keywords related to locations, in all cases on a national, state/provincial and more local level. While a number of the newspapers included in this analysis, including *The Australian*, the *New Zealand Herald*, the

Table 6.2 Top Fifty Keywords for Each International Sub-corpus, Organized by Thematic Group, Ordered by Log Ratio

	Australia	Canada	New Zealand	The UK	The United States
Locations and other local markers	Melbourne's, Sydney's, Victorian, NSW, Victoria's, Australian, Melbourne, Australia's, Queensland, Sydney, Australia, ABC, Victoria, Australians	Ont, Ontario's, Toronto's, Ontario, Toronto, Province's, Ottawa, Peel, Alberta, Provincial, Quebec, Canada's, Canadian, Canadians, Montreal, Canada, Province, Queen's	Reo, Rotorua, Te, Kiwi, Nz, Auckland, Wellington, Christchurch, Zealand, Zealanders, Zealand's, Bay, Pacific	GMT, Scotland's, UK's, Transcontinental, England's, EU, Scottish, UK, Scotland, Yorkshire, Wales, Manchester, BBC, England, Ireland, Britain's, London	city's, Bronx, Calif, neighborhood, neighborhoods, Brooklyn, Fla, nation's, state's, Queens, Manhattan, Connecticut, York, Massachusetts, Boston, statewide, country's, Angeles, Jersey, Los
Politics	Merlino, Turnbull, Labor's, Malcolm, Andrews, Coalition	NDP, Lecce, Ford's, Ford, Doug, liberals, Thompson, Premier, Stephen, progressive	Hipkins, Kaye, Nikki, Ardern, Jacinda, ministry	Boris, Commons, Williamson, Tory, Nicola, PM, MPs, Jeremy, Johnson, Gavin, Ministers	Blasio
Teachers' work and other school-related	VCE, Aboriginal, mathematics, learnt, maths, Indigenous, skills, teacher's, engineering, disadvantaged, Catholic, knowledge, wellbeing, assessment, technology	sizes, elementary, Catholic, math, Indigenous, kindergarten, teens, ed	intermediate, Māori, tertiary, programmes, childhood, centres, overseas, childcare	Autumn, pupils	school's, enrollment, nonprofit, children's, graders, grader, Color, behavior, Hispanic, Latino, eighth, charter, longtime, sept

Governance/ Accountability/ Performance	NAPLAN, Gonski, numeracy, literacy, outcomes, cent, grammar, achieving	TDSB, boards, board's, trustee, board	NCEA, decile, censured, tribunal, offending, Reid, trustees, registration, disciplinary, principals, cent, misconduct, principal, complaints, inappropriate, certificate	headteachers, DFE, headteacher, GCSES, GCSE, OFSTED, councils, attainment	percent, districts, center, Harvard, superintendent, organizations, administrators, standardized
Teacher education	ATAR, tertiary, graduates, degrees, score, entry				
Unions/ Teacher Industrialism/ Activism		Bischof, bargaining, federation, Harvey, hiring, representing, Hammond, positions, contract	PPTA, NZEI, Boyle, Lynda, Stuart, shortage, workload		organized
Event/factor	marriage			NHS, Brexit, infections, healthcare, deaths, lockdown, coronavirus, shops, toll, restrictions	
Other				Prof, criticised	favor, realize, honor, realized, defense, favorite

National Post, The Telegraph and the *New York Times* are positioned as national newspapers, local concerns are also reflected in this collection of keywords. This is particularly so in the case of the US newspapers, and particularly the *New York Times*, where stories related to *Los Angeles, Massachusetts,* New *Jersey*, and the *country's* or *nation's* concerns sit alongside stories that report on local news such as *Brooklyn, Queens, Bronx, neighborhood/s*. This national-local focus is one that characterizes the US sub-corpus more than it does the other four sub-corpora.

Consistent with the analysis presented in earlier chapters of the Australian Teacher Corpus (ATC), many keywords across the sub-corpora related to politicians and political parties. In the Australian sub-corpus, these included *Malcolm Turnbull*, prime minister for three of the five years covered by the sub-corpus, and Victorian Premier *Daniel Andrews* and Minister for Education James *Merlino*, both of whom have been in office since 2014 (remembering here that *The Age*, one of the two Australian newspapers included in the analysis is a Melbourne, Victoria-based newspaper). In the Canadian sub-corpus, the names of the premier and ministers for education in Ontario, *Doug Ford* (premier 2018–current), Lisa *Thompson* (minister for education, 2018–19) and *Stephen Lecce*, minister for education (2019–current) appear as keywords. In the New Zealand sub-corpus, both names of Prime Minister *Jacinda Ardern* (2017–current) appear as keywords, along with the names of Minister of Education Chris *Hipkins* (2017–current), and previous minister of education *Nikki Kaye* (2017). In the UK, the names of Prime Minister *Boris Johnson* (2019–current), Secretary of State for Education *Gavin Williamson* (2019–current), First Minister of Scotland *Nicola* Sturgeon (2014–current) and former opposition leader *Jeremy* Corbyn (2015–20) all appeared as keywords.

Juxtaposed with this, in the US sub-corpus, the name that emerges as a politics keyword is that of New York City Mayor *Bill de Blasio* (2014–current): no federal or state-level politicians names appear. A closer investigation of this revealed that while the prevalence of names of political leaders of Australia, Canada, New Zealand and the UK is largely confined to those sub-corpora, the same is not true of US political leaders. For example, while *Trump* is the most frequent proper noun in the US sub-corpus, appearing 4,162 times, or approximately 66 times per 100,000 words, it is also the most frequent proper noun in the UK sub-corpus, where it appears 9,826 times, or 88 times per 100,000 words: more frequently according to normalized frequency than in the UK sub-corpus. This dispersion of the names of US politicians across different sub-corpora accounts for the limited number of politicians' names appearing as keywords in the US sub-corpus. It is particularly interesting given the specifically educational flavour of the articles included in these international sub-corpora, as it suggests that stories about education policy in the United States are considered to be newsworthy in other parts of the Anglophone world, while it does not seem to be the case that this same rule applies for other jurisdictions. On a more general note, however, this analysis shows that the political edge of stories about teachers observed within the ATC can be seen to be not a purely Australian phenomenon: the international analysis highlights that the links between such stories and matters of politics are common, albeit differently reflected, to all of the sub-corpora.

Across all international sub-corpora there was a prevalence of keywords related to schools and teachers' work, unsurprising given the parameters used in corpus construction. Within this thematic group, however, some differences emerged, with many keywords in the Australian sub-corpus related to curriculum areas, such as *mathematics, maths, technology* and *engineering* (usually as part of discussions of STEM (Science, Technology, Engineering and Mathematics) education. While *math* appears as a keyword in the Canadian sub-corpus, this is not a common trend across the sub-corpora generally. Characteristics of schools or groups of students are common keywords in the Australian (*Aboriginal, Catholic, disadvantaged, Indigenous*), Canadian (*Catholic, elementary, Indigenous, teens*), US (*charter, Color, eighth, grader/s, Hispanic, Latino*) and NZ (*Māori*) sub-corpora. Other aspects of the work of teachers and schools are reflected in keywords that relate to teaching and learning (such as *assessment, knowledge, learnt, skills, VCE* and *wellbeing* in the Australian sub-corpus), while others, such as *overseas* in the New Zealand sub-corpus and *longtime* in the US sub-corpus reflect characteristics of teachers referred to often in news stories in those contexts. *Autumn* and *Sept*[ember] in the UK and US sub-corpora, respectively, refer to the start of the school year. Looking across the five sub-corpora we thus see a variable but still consistent focus on substantive matters related to schools and teachers' work, although the UK sub-corpus, for reasons which will be expanded upon below, is something of an exception to this.

Keywords related to the governance of schooling and regimes of accountability and performance were strongly present across all five of the international sub-corpora. In the Australian sub-corpus these were often related to tenets of the National Assessment Program – Literacy and Numeracy (NAPLAN), including *grammar, literacy* and *numeracy*. *Gonski* also relates to accountability and performance due to the focus on 'educational excellence' in the second Gonski report, published in 2018 (Gonski et al.), and to issues of school funding, which was

150   *Constructing Teacher Identities*

the focus of the first Gonski report, dating to 2011 (Gonski et al.). The keywords relating to this theme in both of the North American sub-corpora generally refer to school *boards*, *districts* and *administrators* or *trustees* (along with *standardized* in the US sub-corpus, most often used in relation to standardized testing). The accountability and performance keywords in the UK sub-corpus sit somewhere between these two positions, including words such as *attainment* and *OfSTED* (the UK Office for Standards in Education, Children's Services and Skills), which both relate to external accountability, but then also those such as *councils* and *DFE* (Department for Education) which are related to governance. The New Zealand sub-corpus is somewhat unusual in that many of the keywords in this category relate to teacher *misconduct, inappropriate* behaviour and *disciplinary* action. *Disciplinary*, for example, appears in over 10 per cent of the articles in the NZ sub-corpus, and is used most often in reporting on decisions of the Education Council or New Zealand Teachers' Disciplinary Tribunal, as highlighted in Table 6.3.

Inappropriate, which appears in 7 per cent of the articles in the NZ sub-corpus, most usually refers to teachers forging inappropriate relationships with students, as highlighted in Table 6.4. These keywords, and others like them such as *censured, offending* and *misconduct*, point to an ongoing focus on the part of the New Zealand press (or at least the two newspapers included in this sub-corpus) on instances of transgression on the part of teachers. In this respect, the NZ sub-corpus is unlike the other four national sub-corpora: while each contains a smattering of articles focused on teacher misconduct, it could not be claimed that this is a specific focus of the Australian, Canadian, UK or US newspapers, based on the articles analysed

Table 6.3 Concordance Lines for *Disciplinary* in the NZ Sub-corpus

failing to show him sufficient respect, a	**disciplinary** decision published by the Education Council today
automatic referral to the Education Council's	**Disciplinary** Tribunal. Ackroyd sought to have Back's
threw plastic cones at another. The Teachers	**Disciplinary** Tribunal censured Justin Raymond Timoti and place
2016, was inappropriate. The New Zealand Teachers	**Disciplinary** Tribunal decision suppressed the names of the
In a recently released New Zealand Teachers	**Disciplinary** Tribunal decision, the West Auckland teacher, who
misconduct in the June 2018 year, and its	**disciplinary** tribunal found that 'serious misconduct' had
the legal maximum of 250 mcg. The Teachers	**Disciplinary** Tribunal has cancelled her teaching registration,
know the man. An Education Council	**Disciplinary** Tribunal hearing in Wellington has heard about
the subject of a New Zealand Teachers'	**Disciplinary** Tribunal hearing today. The teacher, who has
four separate incidents, the New Zealand Teachers	**Disciplinary** Tribunal only upheld one complaint. There were
to pay $4733 in costs for the Teachers	**Disciplinary** Tribunal process. Complaints from students and
students has been censured by the Teachers	**Disciplinary** Tribunal. Reg Korau, who was head of
Council. In submissions to the council's	**disciplinary** tribunal, the teacher accepted she engaged in
that misconduct cases referred to the Teachers	**Disciplinary** Tribunal trebled from 51 in the year to
run', he told the Education Council's	**disciplinary** tribunal yesterday. The Education Council has all

A Comparative View of Teachers in the Print Media 151

Table 6.4 Concordance Lines for *Inappropriate* in the NZ Sub-corpus

an explanation. He admitted his actions were	**inappropriate** and resigned on January 30, 2015. In explanation,
double jeopardy if they are accused of	**inappropriate** behaviour. Not only can they lose their
Reid immediately admitted what happened was	**inappropriate**, but described the contact as more of
genitals. He was also charged with making	**inappropriate** comments about the woman's breasts during
on the computer. 'The investigation found that	**inappropriate** images were on the laptop. It was
him - and it's not the first	**inappropriate** incident at the school. In 2010 Jagindar Singh
teacher Philip Henry Kippenberger behaved in an	**inappropriate** manner that amounted to serious misconduct.
name suppression. The teacher sent numerous	**inappropriate** messages during and outside of class time,
Another student complained the teacher made	**inappropriate** physical contact with him on two occasions,
by the Education Council after an alleged	**inappropriate** relationship with a male year-11 student.
A teacher who formed an	**inappropriate** relationship with a 13-year-old student told
A teacher accused of forming an	**inappropriate** relationship with a 13-year-old pupil who
said. Alliston said it was not surprising	**inappropriate** sexual behaviour occurred at schools because
in parking lots. She was accused of '	**inappropriate** sexual relationship' with a third student,
said there were tight rules around reporting	**inappropriate** teachers. 'The Education Act clearly says that

here. The articles in the NZ sub-corpus employ the news value of negativity (Bednarek and Caple 2017) through this focus on misbehaving teachers, which is not evident in the same way in the other international sub-corpora.

In the Australian sub-corpus, a number of keywords related to initial teacher education, which concordance analysis highlighted had a particular performative accountability edge, were present on the 'Top 50' list. *ATAR, degrees, entry, graduates, score* and *tertiary* in the Australian sub-corpus all reflect the ongoing focus in both education policy and education reporting in the years from 2016 to 2020 on the quality and content of initial teacher education. As noted in previous chapters, this has been a particular policy priority of the Abbott–Turnbull–Morrison Liberal–National Coalition government elected in 2013 and currently in power. What is notable here is not so much the prevalence of this issue in the Australian sub-corpus, but rather the lack of focus on teacher education in the other sub-corpora, highlighting a major difference that resonates with the findings in relation to the ATC discussed in previous chapters.

Keywords related to unions, unionism or teacher industrialism are mostly prevalent in Canada and New Zealand. While the lack of keywords in this category in the Australian sub-corpus might come as a surprise given the presence of the industrial focus across the ATC as a whole, it is worth remembering that the diachronic analysis presented in Chapter 3 and the newspaper sub-corpora analysis in Chapter 4 highlighted both that the discussion of industrial action was somewhat concentrated in the first half of the time span of the ATC, and that it is more common in Australian tabloids than in broadsheets. The keywords related to this theme in the New Zealand and Canadian sub-corpora reflect ongoing industrial negotiations by teachers in New Zealand and particularly in Ontario over the five years covered by the international sub-corpora. *Organized*, in the US sub-corpus, relates partially to the organization of industrial action and also to the organization of other activist initiatives by teachers, including speaking out about school shootings, gun control and Black Lives Matter.

Finally, in two of the five sub-corpora, other issues and events, ostensibly peripheral to teachers and schooling but nevertheless linked by the print media in sustained ways, emerged. The most significant of these was the prevalence of keywords related to the Covid-19 pandemic in the UK sub-corpus. A consequence partly of the sheer volume of articles published in the UK newspapers in 2020 (12 per cent of the articles in all five sub-corpora were published in the UK newspapers in 2020), partly of a focus on news related to the pandemic in the British newspapers and partly of the widespread and lengthy shutdown of schools in the UK, discussions of the impact of the pandemic on schools and teachers' work was more pronounced in the UK sub-corpus than in others. *Marriage* appears as a keyword in the Australian sub-corpus, related to debates surrounding marriage equality, religious freedom and parental rights from 2017 to 2019, and consistent with the diachronic keywords identified in Chapter 3.

Representations of teachers across the national sub-corpora: Collocation analysis

By way of exploring the similarities and differences in representations of teachers across the five national sub-corpora, an extensive collocation analysis was conducted for *teacher* and *teachers*. A snapshot of these is provided in Table 6.5, which highlights the top twenty collocates of both node words.

These snapshots are largely consistent with observations of the 'aboutness' of the sub-corpora, as introduced in the keyword analysis above, particularly with respect to teacher accountability, initial teacher education and teacher industrialism. Some of the nuances of the various sub-corpora with respect to locations and other local factors (e.g. the collocation of *French* with both *teacher* and *teachers* in the Canadian sub-corpus) identified above are also visible in these lists of collocates. Across all five sub-corpora, a delineation of different types of teachers: from *primary, secondary, elementary* and *middle* school to *English, music, history* and *math/s* is evident. Regimes of

A Comparative View of Teachers in the Print Media 153

Table 6.5 Top Twenty Collocates of *Teacher* and *Teachers*, Organized by Country Sub-corpus and Ordered by MI

	Australia	Canada	New Zealand	The UK	The United States
Teacher	initial	retired	aides	retention	evaluations
	training	supply	aide	recruitment	kindergarten
	parent	unions	shortage	assessed	English
	quality	music	supply	join	parent
	former	parent	male	qualified	grade
	courses	former	female	lesson	training
	English	history	training	assessments	math
	secondary	training	former	training	former
	primary	English	who	resources	studies
	maths	kindergarten	student	English	science
	high	science	another	supply	elementary
	music	French	college	head	pay
	student	high	childhood	maths	history
	become	elementary	high	primary	high
	classroom	full	secondary	secondary	middle
	college	student	primary	former	music
	education	who	every	grades	student
	who	grade	told	history	who
	told	told	Auckland	student	school
	science	math	has	school	old
Teachers	qualified	Federation	qualified	association	Federation
	unions	representing	disciplinary	head	unions
	male	hire	trained	union	union
	principals	elementary	post	unions	administrators
	union	secondary	primary	parents	principals
	professional	Catholic	overseas	leaders	strike
	training	Ontario	association	grades	staff
	parents	association	secondary	pay	United
	primary	fewer	kindergarten	pupils	parents
	support	English	PPTA	students	pay
	quality	unions	union	primary	American
	teach	union	principals	national	students
	better	Ontario's	tribunal	many	use
	help	college	pay	support	other
	staff	province's	strike	staff	many
	maths	French	paid	working	are
	best	workers	president	schools	college
	many	strike	childhood	their	some
	classroom	president	support	want	say
	are	staff	are	school	should

accountability, manifest in collocates such as *quality* and *best* in the Australian sub-corpus, *assessed* in the UK sub-corpus and *evaluations* in the US sub-corpus, are evident across a majority of the national sub-corpora, if articulated slightly differently in each.

154   *Constructing Teacher Identities*

Table 6.6 Consistent Collocates of *Teacher* and *Teachers*, Organized Alphabetically

Teacher	education, English, every, former, had, her, high, his, one, school, student, told, training, was, who, year
Teachers	all, also, and, are, for, from, have, many, more, need, other, our, parents, school, schools, should, some, staff, students, support, than, their, union, unions, were, who, will, with, work

By way of taking a more sustained look at similarities and differences, 'consistent collocates' were identified across the sub-corpora. Taking a cue from Gabrielatos and Baker (2008), who identified consistent collocates in their study as those that collocated with the node word in seven of their ten sub-corpora, I stipulated that to be identified as a consistent collocate a word needed to be a collocate of the node work in at least four of the five sub-corpora. The consistent collocates of both *teachers* and *teacher* are presented in Table 6.6.

Of the ten lexical consistent collocates of *teacher*, six (*education, English, high, school, student, year*) relate to aspects of teachers' work common to schooling in the five Anglophone countries. The remaining four are less self-explanatory and thus require further investigation. Table 6.7 highlights randomly selected concordance lines for *former* where it appears as a collocate of *teacher*.

The concordance analysis shows that the designation of 'former teacher' is used across the sub-corpora in two key ways, both of which suggest a positive discourse prosody. The first is to contribute a sense of legitimacy to the actions or perspectives of actors, such as in the following examples from Table 6.7:

> … a former science teacher, made masks for health care workers.

> … another former teacher and Guardian education columnist …

> Scottish Labour's education spokesman and a former teacher …

> … a former Travancore School teacher who developed the program,

Here, the *former teacher* explains, contextualizes or legitimizes actions or perspectives, reflecting the news value of positivity, while in other instances, *former teacher* is juxtaposed with descriptions of actions that are either unexpected and/or constitute misconduct, such as in the following examples from Table 6.7:

> Former Calgary teacher Neil Bantleman has been released …

> … the former high school sports teacher is alleged to have …

> A former teacher found guilty of physically assaulting a student …

A Comparative View of Teachers in the Print Media
155

Table 6.7 Concordance Lines for *Former* as a Collocate of *Teacher*

to her former school. The decision to award	**former** Avondale College **teacher** Catriona Maday the substantial
	Former Calgary **teacher** Neil Bantleman has been released
murdering and defrauding Peter Farquhar, 69, a	**former** English **teacher** at Stowe, and Ann Moore-Martin, 83,
likely murder suspects never to be charged. The	**former** high school sports **teacher** is alleged to have
of them, Jose A. G. 'Senor' Ordonez, a	**former** history teacher who was by then the school'
to penetrate.' Now back in Australia, the	**former** Save The Children **teacher** is suffering post-traumatic
When the pandemic hit, Peter's mother, a	**former** science **teacher**, made masks for health care workers. '
A	**former teacher** and debate coach at one of the
Allen said. Allen and Laura McInerney, another	**former teacher** and Guardian education columnist, came up with
education. Kiran Gill, a	**former teacher** and lead author of the report, has
A	**former teacher** at an Upper Hutt school has been
A	**former teacher** found guilty of physically assaulting a student
Still, a first is a first. And the	**former teacher** has contemplated the new kind of role
Scottish Labour's education spokesman and a	**former teacher**, said its decisions were an insult to
University's Dr Lisa McKay-Brown, a	**former** Travancore School **teacher** who developed the program,

Despite the 'bad news' aspect of the tales in this second group, *former teacher* is generally invoked here to contribute an element of surprise: implied here is an assumption that these actions and events are beyond common expectations of teachers, who are more often assumed to be law-abiding and contributing members of society. They are examples of the news value of unexpectedness in action in relation to teachers alongside that of negativity that play on the dichotomy of good and bad teachers discussed previously.

Two of the consistent collocates of *teacher*, *every* and *one* represent two ends of the quantification spectrum, and concordance analysis was conducted to explore how *one* and *every* were used in relation to *teacher* across the five national sub-corpora. Tables 6.8 and 6.9 highlight randomly selected concordance lines for both, respectively. While *every* was used in a range of ways, including in relation to student–teacher ratio ('a teacher for every X student'), its most frequent use as a collocate of teacher was in the construction 'every teacher', which, as discussed in Chapter 2, regardless of the nature of the claim about every teacher, has a homogenizing effect within the texts. Whether 'every teacher' 'does a terrific job', 'is a mini leader' or experiences anxious school dreams, to use some of the examples in the concordance lines in Table 6.8, the effect is to simplify discussions of teachers, remove contextual considerations and generalize their experience and practice. While the claims made in these texts may be innocuous enough, the argument that every teacher, regardless of where or who they teach across different national contexts, does or does not do or feel a particular thing is a problematic one that makes possible the claim that every teacher, regardless of their context *should* engage in particular, decontextualized practices.

156   *Constructing Teacher Identities*

Table 6.8 Concordance Lines for *Every* as a Collocate of *Teacher*

every school is adequately resourced and so that	**every** child and every **teacher** is properly supported.
in the next year. Schools currently get one	**teacher** for **every** 29 children aged 9–10. It's lower
Classes have been split in two, with a	**teacher** for **every** 10 or 11 students while children
$117 million a year to pay for a language	**teacher** in **every** primary school - far more than the
in RSE to ensure that at least one	**teacher** in **every** school has been trained. In the
assembly, made up of representatives from	**every** local **teacher** association in B.C., rejected the
is telling every single A-Level student, and	**every** single **teacher** and headteacher that the system
But in a statement, the department said that	**every** student and **teacher** had been affected by the
performing career. It is certainly true that not	**every teacher** could hope to hold his own technically
and specialized staff," suggesting that	**every teacher** does a terrific job. The party also
I only have anxious school dreams about myself.	**Every teacher** gets them in the lead-up to
to make a change in challenging circumstances.	**Every teacher** is a mini leader, and a good
in schools is costing taxpayers about $10,000 for	**every teacher** recruited. The Ministry of Education
further education do with no first-year students?	**Every teacher** should be able to assess their students
not require it, but I do". But not	**every teacher** who wants to resign can. Gemma Vine,

Table 6.9 Concordance Lines for *One* as a Collocate of *Teacher*

teaching art through painting by numbers,' said	**one** disillusioned **teacher**. Another said it was 'a joyless
Tom Rachman. Rachman's new novel, The Italian	**Teacher**, is **one** to stir a normally austere reviewer
respectively, his long-time coach was named PGA	**teacher** of the year. **One** of many seminal moments
teachers, especially those with families. 'A	**one** or two-**teacher** school miles away . . . might not
was indistinguishable from our private schools.	**One** public school **teacher** in South Carolina
I protested but privately, I acquiesced. With	**one** sixth of **teacher** predictions wrong or over-inflated,
to have been spell-checked thoroughly,' wrote	**one teacher** about the geometry. Teachers say there was
15-pupil limit. Each group should be assigned	**one teacher**, and children should spend their break times
him as a wicketkeeper; he may have struck	**one teacher** as a blagger but another has seen
they do simple chores. 'Celebrate the first day,'	**one teacher** said. 'Celebrate that you brushed your teeth.'
70 children, but today there are 40, with	**one teacher** - the calm and collected Puti. Some children
intermediate schools is still short of at least	**one teacher**, the teachers' union says. The result is
system, is going online. Why not Berkeley?	**One teacher** wrote a parent I know that Berkeley
Waterman, who has died aged 100, was a music	**teacher** who became **one** of the most prominent personalities
huddle in a corner awaiting orders from the	**teacher**, who must select **one** of seven commands, including

At the other end of the spectrum, as highlighted in Table 6.9, while *one* is also used in relation to *teacher* in a variety of ways, the most common usage relates to citing *one teacher* either as a source or an example of (or counter example to) an issue under discussion. *One teacher*, when providing the sole perspective on an issue, can have the same essentializing and simplifying effect as *every teacher*, however *one teacher* also, on occasion, is a gateway to acknowledging and celebrating outstanding or 'hero' teachers.

Finally, *training* emerged as a consistent collocate of *teacher* across the five sub-corpora. Concordance analysis, randomly selected lines of which

A Comparative View of Teachers in the Print Media

Table 6.10 Concordance Lines for *Training* as a Collocate of *Teacher*

that there is room for employment-based	**teacher training** and the Government will continue
they don't properly prepare you for during	**teacher training**. And yet, the way a teacher responds
and the occasional educators' conference. As	**teacher training** changed, the once-autonomous teachers'
then won a place to St Mary's	**teacher training** college, in Fenham, Newcastle upon
to describe herself as 'a dwarf' during her	**teacher training** exams. "In just three days, I had
as merely the result of a bumped elbow.	**Teacher training** had prepared me, a little, for spotting
thinking. A DfE-commissioned report into	**teacher training** in 2015 highlighted the need for better
have staunchly resisted efforts to make	**teacher training** more rigorous. New York's high-performing
Department of Education's most recent initial	**teacher training** number census found almost one in five
received this knowledge as part of their initial	**teacher training**. Richards never reported what happened
Computers in Homes and the Kotahitanga	**teacher training** scheme, and developing a 30-year plan for
Cuarvan when she'd just graduated from a	**teacher training** school in rural Oaxaca. These schools
stopped and shot at the buses carrying the	**teacher-training** students. Later, they fired at others also
successful use, however, will make demands on	**teacher training** that the present system may not be
Not good enough. John Capel, Black Rock	**Teacher training** Trainee teachers should be alongside

are contained in Table 6.10, highlighted that by far the most common construction employing this collocation was the phrase *teacher training*, and that across the five sub-corpora, a number of key uses were made of this construction. First, the question of the utility and practicality of teacher training was a focus of many of the articles, including those below that touch upon *employment-based teacher training*, that note that there are important aspects of teaching *they don't properly prepare you for during teacher training* and that claim that *trainee teachers should be alongside teachers*. A second and related theme is that of the need to facilitate improvement in teacher training, which is said to have been *staunchly resisted*. While the most sustained focus in the international sub-corpora, as noted above, occurs in the Australian sub-corpus – the collocation and concordance analysis shows that these concerns about initial teacher education (and indeed, professional development, which, in the UK and US texts in particular, is sometimes also referred to as *teacher training*) are shared.

With respect to *teachers*, the consistent collocates of most interest (being lexical words not representing routine aspects of schooling) were *support* and *union/s*. Randomly selected concordance lines for *support* as a collocate of *teachers* are included in Table 6.11, and these highlight three main aspects of *support* as it relates to teachers.

The first is in the construction *support staff*, as a separate category of school staffing to teachers themselves. In most examples of this within the sub-corpora, teachers and support staff are grouped together. The other two relate to teachers providing support to students, as highlighted in the following extracts from Table 6.11:

158   *Constructing Teacher Identities*

Table 6.11 Concordance Lines for *Support* as a Collocate of *Teachers*

MORE than 200 Scottish schools have vacancies for	**teachers** and classroom **support** staff as pupils return
g to violence prevention and workplace safety for	**teachers** and **support** staff in schools. Both the CTF
and should be avoided. School leaders, governors,	**teachers** and **support** staff must work to end the
children to learn language correctly." How	**teachers** can **support** transgender students
more graduates into permanent teaching positions,	**support** experienced **teachers** back into the
at a further disadvantage, denying them the	**support** of **teachers** during the school year and
why we pulled out all the stops to	**support** pupils, parents, and **teachers** when schools
teach more students with fewer resources and less	**support**. Secondary **teachers** teach up to 180 students
really want for Christmas is real recognition and	**support**. Teachers in Australia work some of the longest
recover. She said classroom donations would give	**teachers** "the **support** they need to inspire their students
that they'll be the right complement of	**teachers** to **support** our kids." But schools continue to
in high-demand locations. "By providing further	**support** to **teachers** whose provisional certificate is nearing
"take more responsibility" for funding learning	**support** training for **teachers**, at undergraduate level
in New Zealand were unlikely to improve unless	**teachers** were given more **support** to increase their
41 languages between them, so we need supply	**teachers** who can **support** that need, but the quality

… teachers can support transgender students …

… denying them the support of teachers …

… they'll be the right complement of teachers to support our kids …

… we need supply teachers who can support that need …;

And to teachers needing support in their work:

… we pulled out all the stops to support pupils, parents, and teachers when schools closed …

… teach more students with fewer resources and less support …

… really want for Christmas is real recognition and support …

These two not incompatible discourses around *support* appear to be dispersed across each of the national sub-corpora and occur in roughly equal measure, where teachers are seen to both give support to their students (and indeed to each other) and to be in need of (sometimes additional) support to do their jobs well. Interestingly, in relation to *support*, there seems to be little evidence of deficit discourses around teachers and their work: where *support* is used in relation to teacher needs, a sense of the appropriateness of this support to ensure excellence is conveyed rather than a sense of support required to make up for shortcomings or inadequacy.

Both *union* and *unions* are consistent collocates of teachers across the national sub-corpora; however, for economy of space I have chosen to focus in this discussion on the concordance for *unions* only, which had the stronger

A Comparative View of Teachers in the Print Media   159

Table 6.12 Concordance Lines for *Unions* as a Collocate of *Teachers*

said. 'In no way is the union stopping	**teachers** from teaching. **Unions** are supportive of teachers
drivers of workload. I want to work with	**teachers**, heads, the **unions**, everybody, to bear down on
While the Times survey found broad support for	**teachers**, opinions on their **unions** were split, with 34 percent
to oppose educational innovation at home, the	**unions** representing America's **teachers** have gone abroad in
it, still very unclear. In recent weeks,	**unions** representing **teachers** have told members to use their
has proved controversial since its inception with	**teachers' unions** decrying it as an 'expensive distraction' that
at a charity gala earlier this month. But	**teachers unions** detect a nefarious purpose. This $35 million
the province, and noted Ontario's four main	**teachers' unions** have appealed to the labour board because
'go to war with premier after premier.	**Teachers' unions** have had a difficult time dealing with
charter schools and repeatedly tangled with the	**teachers unions**. He beefed up the city's police
the ultimate evil or the optimal solution? Do	**teachers' unions** protect kids or preserve entitlements? Are
spent fighting any reform aimed at relaxing the	**teachers unions'** stranglehold on the public schools would be
have voted to cut public education and attack	**teachers' unions**. 'Teachers are turning this moment into a
of politics, racial bias and the power of	**teachers' unions**, to name just a few hurdles. Mr.
tractable resistance from states, territories and	**teachers' unions**, whose objections fly in the face of

collocation of the two, and of which randomly selected lines are presented in Table 6.12. With some notable exceptions across all five sub-corpora, reference to *teachers' unions*, which is the most common phrase within the sub-corpora employing the collocation, most often has an adversarial edge. Whether unions are said to *oppose educational innovation*, noted to have a *stranglehold on public schools*, constituted as a *hurdle* to be overcome or questioned as to whether their mission is to *protect kids* or *preserve entitlements*, in subtle and not-so-subtle ways, unions are often positioned as the enemy of education and the common good.

Furthermore, teachers themselves are often separated out from teachers' unions, such as in the claim that 'I want to work with teachers, heads, the unions, everybody', made by then UK secretary of state for education Damian Hinds in 2018 (Rayner 2018) or the observation in the US context that 'While the Times survey found broad support for teachers, opinions on their unions were split …' (Goldstein and Casselman 2018). The effect of this, that teachers are sometimes, although not always, categorized as separate from their unions allows the unions to be a convenient scapegoat, positioned as comprising the more belligerent and self-interested members of the teaching profession while preserving the image of the mainstream teacher as supportive and hard-working.

Having explored the similarities in representations of teachers across the national sub-corpora, we now turn to the unique collocates for each sub-corpus, which will facilitate a focus on the differences in representations. Table 6.13 highlights the unique collocates of *teacher* and *teachers*, organized by sub-corpus. Many of the

160 *Constructing Teacher Identities*

Table 6.13 Unique Collocates of *Teacher* and *Teachers*, Organized by Country Sub-corpus and Ordered by MI

	Australia	Canada	New Zealand	The UK	The United States
Teacher	initial, quality, courses, become, good, new, being	retired, unions, French, full, Toronto, any, time, because	aide, aides, shortage, male, female, childhood, Auckland, early, him, support, the	retention, recruitment, assessed, qualified, lesson, assessments, head, grades, years, she, and, students, for	evaluations, studies, pay, middle, public, first, your
Teachers	male, professional, training, quality, teach, better, maths, best, classroom, NSW, good, well, teaching, Australian	representing, hire, elementary, Catholic, Ontario, fewer, English, Ontario's, province's, French, workers, province, Toronto, which, its, been, says, the	disciplinary, trained, post, overseas, kindergarten, PPTA, tribunal, paid, childhood, early, Zealand, three, get, because, over	head, leaders, grades, pupils, national, working, want, children, told, that, those, had, they, not,	administrators, United, American, use, state, city, out

collocates, while unique, are either very 'local' words (*French, Toronto, Auckland, middle*) in that they relate to specific locations or reflect the local organization of schooling. Others, such as *head* in the UK sub-corpus, represent local vernacular expressions, where other words are used in different contexts: *principals* is a collocate of *teachers* in the Australian, New Zealand and US sub-corpora. Despite the need to take these nuances into account when examining the unique keywords, a number of strong differences between the national sub-corpora are evident.

Initial teacher education and entry to the profession is reflected in the collocates of teacher in both the Australian and UK sub-corpora. While *training* was a consistent collocate of *teacher* across the national sub-corpora, the prevalence of initial teacher education-related collocates (*become, courses, initial, training*) in the Australian sub-corpus reflects a particular intensity of discussion of teacher education in the public space in Australia that evidently is not consistent across the other four contexts. *Qualified, recruitment* and *retention* in the UK sub-corpus, along with *new* in the Australian sub-corpus all point to a focus on early career teachers which is largely absent from the other three

A Comparative View of Teachers in the Print Media 161

sub-corpora, and are resonant with the explicit focus on entry to the profession within these jurisdictions over this time period.

Second, the very strong and sustained focus on 'teacher quality' in the Australian sub-corpus is reflected in collocates of both teacher (*good, quality*) and teachers (*best, better, good, professional, quality, well*), and this focus is largely unique to the Australian context. While *assessed* and *assessments* are collocates of *teacher* in the UK sub-corpus, concordance analysis highlighted that these were largely used in relation to the cancellation of General Certificate of Secondary Education (GCSE) examinations in 2020 due to the Covid-19 pandemic, and the application instead of teacher *assessment*, rather than *assessment* being used in relation to teachers themselves. In the US context, *evaluations* (see Table 6.14, ordered alphabetically by the word immediately to the left of *evaluations*, to highlight the focus of the evaluations in question) links with discourses of teacher quality. Concerns are demonstrated here around what teacher evaluations highlight about teachers' work, student learning and so on, along with the politics and practicalities of linking teacher evaluations with student test scores. That is to say that while the language of *teacher quality* is particularly prominent in the Australian sub-corpus, the discourse of teacher quality is not necessarily confined to Australia and, at the very least, is evident in discussions of teacher evaluation in the US context.

Finally, the unique collocates for the New Zealand and Canadian sub-corpora are consistent with points raised earlier in this chapter around the focus in New Zealand articles around *disciplinary* matters to do with teachers, and in Canada around industrial action, reflected in collocates such as *unions* (unique as a collocate of *teacher*), *representing* and *workers* (as collocates of *teachers*).

Table 6.14 Concordance Lines for *Evaluations* in the US Sub-corpus

the Lutheran Services staff, does practice CLASS	evaluations of each teacher twice a year, to
multiple indexes, including how teachers fare on	evaluations or growth in student learning, as measured
test scores be included in educators' performance	evaluations. The Connecticut Education Association
For years, Mr. Wilson had received positive	evaluations, both from superiors and subordinates,
percentapproval.com, has published 10,000 student	evaluations, but not all of them were from
the first to measure how teacher	evaluations positively affect student learning in the
children's test scores played in teacher	evaluations, Gov. Andrew M. Cuomo convened a task
the use of test scores in teacher	evaluations. If appointed, she would focus on restoring'
including special education services, teacher	evaluations and hollow requirements that "in some
limits. They are not tied to teacher	evaluations. And this year, what was a three-
Mr. Gates's foundation supported tying teacher	evaluations to student test results and backed the
an advocacy group that supports tying teacher	evaluations to state test scores, said all students
life chances. In response, many teachers'	evaluations have been tied to how their students
at DeWitt Clinton, ineffective ratings on their	evaluations; a principal contributes only part of a
said it would add more subjectivity to	evaluations for about 75,000 teachers and water down

162 *Constructing Teacher Identities*

The issue of quality

Finally, given the emergence of discourses of quality as so central to the ATC, and the observation above that that discourse is both particularly strong in the Australian sub-corpus and somewhat differently articulated elsewhere, a collocation analysis for *quality* was undertaken, along with complementary concordance analysis. Table 6.15 highlights the consistent collocates of *quality* across the five sub-corpora, again applying the rule that to appear as a consistent collocate, a word had to collocate significantly with *quality* in at least four of the five sub-corpora.

Four of the five consistent collocates are perhaps unsurprising, relating very clearly to the way we tend to discuss quality (of anything) in the public space: *high, improve*[d] and *improving* quality are almost universal aspirations regardless of the field, and *quality* and *quantity* are regular running mates. *Teaching* as a collocate of *quality* is interesting for two reasons: one that relates to the discussion of discourses of quality discussed in Chapter 5, which, as we have seen, in the ATC tends towards *teacher* rather than *teaching* quality. Second, it is notable that while it is regarded here as a consistent collocate of *quality*, *teaching* and *quality* are collocates not in the Australian sub-corpus, but rather in the remaining four national sub-corpora.

When it comes to the unique collocates of *quality* in each of the sub-corpora, represented in Table 6.16, the reverse is true: *teacher* is a unique collocate of *quality* in the Australian sub-corpus, which seems to lend weight to the argument, presented in the previous chapter, that 'teacher quality' is a particularly important and seemingly Australian vernacular thing. The unique collocates of *quality* in the five sub-corpora suggest that quality is discursively linked with instruction, accountability, standards and particular educational contexts such as early childhood education and care across all contexts. The Australian collocates, however, are consistent with the findings presented in Chapter 5, with a particular emphasis on the quality of teachers themselves and on attracting the 'best and brightest' to the teaching profession.

Table 6.15 Consistent Collocates of *Quality*, Ordered Alphabetically

high, improve, improving, quantity, teaching

A Comparative View of Teachers in the Print Media   163

Table 6.16 Unique Collocates of *Quality*, Organized by Country Sub-corpus and Ordered by MI

Australia	attracting, lifting, instructional, materials, highest, boost, measure, teacher, professional, importance, focus
Canada	accountability, EQAO, maintaining, office, affect, defend, direct, experience, impact, courses, life, care, Ontario's, good, system, learning, while
New Zealand	cards, retention, lift, sexuality, processes, confident, ECE, water, control, childhood, supply, lower
The UK	CQC, efficacy, laboratories, provision, graduates, improved, assured, complained, content, produce, monitoring, delivering, standards
The United States	alliance, council, affordable, preschool, applicants, consistent, deserve, pre, instruction, increasing, advocacy, concerns, universal

Conclusion

This chapter has sought to do something a little different from the preceding chapters, by in some ways shifting the emphasis from the representations of teachers in the Australian print media to a broader Anglophone focus, but at the same time it has sought to explore some of the findings presented in previous chapters against texts from contexts other than Australia. It has shown that while there are international resonances in discussions of teachers, highlighted in discussions of consistent collocates and shared themes across keywords, there are also distinct differences in representations across the five countries represented in this analysis. The focus across the international sub-corpora on aspects of teachers' work and also on issues of governance and accountability (despite the local differences) highlight some of the commonalities in media discussions of teachers and their work across these five national contexts globally. Some of the key differences between the sub-corpora, and particularly areas where the Australian texts stand out as unique, serve to reinforce the findings from the analysis of the ATC presented in the previous chapters, for example in relation to *quality*. As an international survey, however, this chapter has perhaps raised more questions than it is capable of answering. The sample of texts used was necessarily limited here, as was the capacity to engage in deep analysis of the nuances within and between sub-corpora. What the analysis here has shown is that a more sustained international investigation with a representative corpus from a number of different contexts would be likely to shed further light on both the local vernaculars and shared discourses around teachers and their work in this age of global educational reform.

7

Teachers in the Print Media: Conclusions, Limitations, Prospects

This final chapter draws together the findings presented across the analysis chapters; highlights some of the methodological questions, issues and limitations associated with this research; and explores some possible directions for future research both with and beyond the Australian Teacher Corpus (ATC). In the first part of the chapter, I return to the central research problem as articulated in Chapter 1, namely how teachers and their work are represented in the ATC and how these representations have changed over time, to explore the cultural-discursive arrangements suggested and reinforced by the print media discourses that surround teachers' work. At each stage within this book, I have sought to transparently present the methodological decisions I have taken in the research and to reason out these decisions, and while my hope is that this goes some way towards demonstrating the trustworthiness of this research, I am also conscious that it is not without its limits. The chapter will therefore consider these limitations and how they bound what can and cannot be said about representations of teachers by virtue of this analysis. Finally, this project was large, in many ways larger than I could have anticipated at the outset, and at every point along the way I have had to make decisions about what to 'zoom in' on and what to pay only passing attention to. The book therefore concludes by pointing to possible directions for future research, including aspects of the ATC that have not been analysed here in great detail but have emerged as potentially interesting, as well as other adjacent possibilities that have been raised by this research.

Teachers in the print media: Key observations

First, both the ATC itself and the analysis presented in the preceding chapters have highlighted the sheer volume of articles produced in the Australian print media about teachers from 1996 to 2020. As was observed in Chapter 2, this coverage appears to be denser than reporting on other occupational groups such as doctors, lawyers and nurses, with an average of fifty articles on teacher/s produced in the Australian print media for each of the 1,300 weeks included in the ATC, as opposed to twenty-one for nurse/s, for example (when assessed using equivalent measures). The upshot of this is that we talk about teachers and teaching a lot in the public space: teachers and their work are not only topics of interest and relevance to newspapers' readers, but are also linked to largely common experiences of school and related to significant public policy issues around education and schooling.

While coverage may be dense, however, it is also uneven. The ATC highlights that attention to teachers and teaching has shifted in volume over the twenty-five-year period, with the years from 2004 to 2012, and in particular the 'education revolution' years of the Rudd-Gillard government (2007 to 2013) providing a high point in coverage. Coverage is similarly uneven when it comes to publications and again there is no simple explanation for this. The six newspapers with the largest article counts in the ATC (accounting for 71 per cent of the articles overall) include three broadsheets, three tabloids, one national newspaper and capital city newspapers from four of the eight states and territories. They also include four News Corp Australia and two Nine Publishing newspapers, and furthermore on the surface these newspapers might be expected to share a sense of 'imagined preferences' (Richardson 2007: 92) of their readership with those in which far fewer articles about teachers were published over the same time frame. For instance, the Sydney-based News Corp tabloid the *Daily Telegraph* contributed 60 per cent more articles to the ATC than its Melbourne-based counterpart, the *Herald Sun*. Understanding the coverage is thus a complex matter: a confluence of local and national/international factors, orientation and ideology that cannot be simply explained through reversion to 'what tabloids do', for example.

Further, we have seen, over and over again from the first broad look at the 'aboutness' of the ATC right through to international comparisons, that these articles ostensibly about teachers and teaching have a political edge. On the whole, they are not 'feel good' human interest stories about things happening in schools for better or worse, but more often about reforms to education and to teachers' work specifically, driven by politics and policymakers. Sometimes the coverage is motivated by large-scale policy shifts and new policy solutions put forward by governments: again, the 'education revolution' years are a good example of this, as is the 'national values' campaign of the early 2000s and the 'classroom ready' era of the mid-2010s. In these instances, teachers have often

Teachers in the Print Media: Conclusions, Limitations, Prospects 167

been 'collateral damage', the key players in negative coverage brought about by the need of governments and policymakers to be seen to be doing something, regardless of how far the 'something' is, on occasion, the generation of a (policy) solution in search of a (policy) problem.

Associated with this political edge, we have observed that coverage of teachers and teaching in the print media is often linked to crisis, both real crises (such as that of teacher shortages) and imagined ones (such as the ongoing saga of 'teacher quality'). Milton Friedman, thought to be one of the 'fathers' of neoliberalism, wrote almost forty years ago that 'only a crisis – actual or perceived – produces real change. When that crisis occurs, the actions that are taken depend on the ideas that are lying around.' He continued on to argue that the role of advocates of free market reform such as himself was to 'develop alternatives to existing policies, to keep them alive and available until the politically impossible becomes politically inevitable' (1982: ix). In the ATC, we see a range of ideas about education and teachers' work kept 'alive and available' by both newspapers and politicians over time. Some of those explored in this book relate to attracting the 'best and brightest' to teaching, improving 'teacher quality' through increasing accountability and returning to traditional methods of teaching including direct and explicit instruction.

The analysis has also highlighted similarities and differences between representations of teachers in the Australian print media and in a selection of purpose-made international sub-corpora, drawn from Canada, New Zealand, the UK and the United States. Resonances here included the political edge of the coverage, but the Australian focus on 'quality', linked to a range of perceived and imagined crises of education, across teaching, performance and teacher education, was largely unique to the Australian context. The growth of discourses of quality, and particularly teacher quality over the second half of the twenty-five-year period covered by the ATC, and a level of focused concentration on these is particularly evident in the two national broadsheet newspapers, *The Australian* and the *Australian Financial Review*.

On a methodological level, the analysis has, I hope, made a contribution to reinforcing the largely consistent findings of a range of small-scale, close studies through providing a broader perspective by virtue of the size and scope of the ATC. The work also constitutes a methodological advance in studies of media and education, allowing for a level of precision and detail in broad-based analysis of large amounts of data. This is not to suggest that this approach should supplant such close studies, but rather that it makes a rich addition to the suite of methods available to researchers within the field.

So what? Some reflections on media representations and teachers' work

But what does it all mean? It is one thing to trace patterns of representations and explore shifts and nuances, but do these representations really matter and if so to whom and to what end? It was established in Chapter 1 that one of the aims of this book was to explore the implications of representations of teachers in the print media for the 'practice architectures' of teachers' work: the cultural-discursive, material-economic and social-political arrangements that enable and constrain sayings, doings and relatings within sites of practice (Kemmis and Grootenboer 2008; Kemmis et al. 2014; Mahon et al. 2017). Elsewhere (Mockler 2018), I have considered the contribution of education policy discourses to the practice architectures of teachers' work, noting that 'the capacity for arrangements to enable and constrain practice are largely contextual and locally mitigated' (275), warning against sweeping generalizations that imply that the preconditions for practice are somehow dictated by policy discourses and translate into the same arrangements in every site of practice for every practitioner. Similarly, the means by which media discourses impact practice are neither simple nor linear: the concept of 'media logic' (Altheide 2021; Altheide and Snow 1979), as discussed in Chapter 1, is useful here. It suggests that media forms and media content powerfully shape public understandings, and that 'audiences-as-actors normalize these forms and use them as reality maintenance tools' (Altheide 2013: 225). I suggested in Chapter 1 that these 'reality maintenance tools' merge with readers' internalized narratives of schooling and teachers, and join also with the ever-evolving 'cumulative cultural text of teaching and schooling':

> a multi-layered and shifting repository of popular images of teachers and students from movies, books, songs, television, the mass media, the Internet, collective memories, school pictures, yearbooks, and so forth. These images accumulate over decades and shift in the public imaginary, coexisting side by side or beneath each other in both harmony and dissonance. (Weber 2006: 72)

The cultural-discursive arrangements that frame teachers' work are impacted, on a broad social level, by dominant representations of teachers in the print media. Discourses of quality in particular offer some insight into these cultural-discursive arrangements, in that they offer a set of 'reality maintenance tools' for the general public that work from the premise that teachers are of poor quality. They make it possible to say and indeed repeat things about teachers and their

Teachers in the Print Media: Conclusions, Limitations, Prospects 169

work that are fuzzily defined and largely unsubstantiated, they invoke images of good and bad teachers that hold teachers up on a pedestal while simultaneously deriding them, and they encourage readers to generalize from these images to the profession as a whole.

On a material-economic level these discourses suggest a dichotomy of practice where some 'doings' are 'common sense' while others are unproven fads, and that the difference between the two is both self-evident to the untrained eye and uncontested. On a social-political level they set up an 'us-vs-them' relationship between the public and the teaching profession that breeds contempt on one side, and defensiveness on the other. There is an additional complexity to this relationship given that the 'general public' actually comprises not merely of disinterested citizens, but also of parents, prospective parents and 'community members' that many schools rely on as sources of support, financial and otherwise.

These discourses, of quality, crisis and so on, are not entirely responsible, of course, for circumscribing the practice architectures of teachers' work. As 'reality maintenance tools', however, they have flow-on effects to the way that education is understood by policymakers, who make decisions that impact the material-economic realities of teaching and that also shape aspects of the social-political arrangements, such as the profession's relationship with governments and the public. Regardless of how direct or indirect this influence is, the potential for pervasive and consistently presented media discourses around teachers and their work to impact not only the cultural-discursive but also the material-economic and social-political arrangements that govern the work of the profession is real.

My claim here is not that media discourses are responsible for dictating the conditions under which teachers practice, or for making some practices acceptable and others not. They do, however, both reflect and reinforce public perceptions of teachers and their work and these, through the political process, come to impact policy that governs teachers' work. Furthermore, they reflect to teachers themselves the esteem in which they are or are not held in different quarters of the community, and contribute to the shaping of teacher identities, which in turn has complex and uneven effects that impact the materiality and experiences of schooling not only for teachers but for their students as well. They convey to the profession an assessment of what it is to be a teacher, and in so doing open up and close off different possibilities for different teachers, dependent on their location within the field. For these reasons, they are worthy of the kind of examination this book has provided.

Methodological considerations and limitations

This research project was big – perhaps if I had realized the scale of it at the outset I might have been less ambitious. It became obvious very early on that there were many, many decisions to be made that would each shape the project in small but potentially important ways. Some of these decisions related to key methodological questions such as which tools to use in the analysis, which statistical tests and values and which thresholds, although these tended to be easier ones to resolve. They were variously dealt with via engaging substantially with the research literature on corpus approaches to the social sciences and methods of corpus analysis, and on occasion via conversations with generous colleagues, but in most cases if there was not a 'right' and 'wrong' option, there were 'better' and 'worse' options and a relatively clear justification to be made.

The more difficult decisions by far were those that emerged in the course of the analysis: which words and phrases were worthy of 'drilling down' on in the chapters and which ones would be moved past with a brief explanation. In the course of the analysis, I examined over a thousand concordances, some of which included thousands of lines, and mercifully for the reader, I suspect, made a very limited selection for further discussion in each chapter of the book. In these decisions I was guided not only by the concordance analysis itself but also by the questions around representations and discourses driving the inquiry and by my knowledge of the history of Australian education over the period from 1996 to 2020. In each case I strove to make rational and defensible decisions; however, I recognize that the interpretation provided as a consequence of the sum of those decisions is different from that which might have been generated by different decisions. The aim here was not to produce *the* definitive, replicable account of analysis of the ATC, but rather *an* account, based on transparent and justifiable decision-making, to produce a reliable and trustworthy overview of my analysis of the ATC.

The size and breadth of the ATC brought with it another set of limitations, for the level of variation in the concordance analysis sometimes meant I could not arrive at a justifiable conclusion in relation to a question or issue, and at other times that I had to make an 'on balance' call based on a majority of instances, while acknowledging that a range of counterexamples were also present. In presenting this analysis I have aimed to give account of this, highlighting variation and not suggesting, either explicitly or by omission, that 'all instances of X suggest Y', except in the rare case where they in fact do. This approach I have balanced with the need to resist the urge to give detailed explanations of

Teachers in the Print Media: Conclusions, Limitations, Prospects   171

exceptions and minor discrepancies at every turn, knowing that this would risk the possibility of allowing the trees to crowd out the forest, while also ensuring that the book would become a cure for (reader) insomnia.

Beyond the human dimensions of the research realized in these limitations, there are some practical limitations at play. The first of these relates to those presented in using a database such as Nexis in the construction of the corpus: while most articles are indexed in the database, some gaps do exist, particularly in the early years of the ATC, from the mid-1990s to the early 2000s. Furthermore, the filtering of identical articles was found to be not entirely accurate, and despite concerted efforts to manually identify and remove duplicates, it remains a possibility that a small number of duplicate or near-duplicate articles have remained in the ATC. Furthermore, given the historical nature of the ATC, I made the decision to limit the articles included to those which appeared in print versions of newspapers only. Expanding this to online articles, and indeed to online news publications such as *Guardian Australia* (launched in 2013) and *Brisbane Times* (a Fairfax/Nine online newspaper launched in 2007) would have provided a yet broader view, while also making comparisons between publications and over time more complex. Finally, as Caple's (Bednarek and Caple 2012a, 2017; Caple 2018) work has highlighted, there are important questions to be asked about the relationship between multimodality and discursive construction, and clearly, given the nature and focus of this research, these are not questions with which I have engaged. Caple notes that 'language-only corpora will tell us some of the story but they will not tell us the whole story' (2018: 85), and indeed, on a number of levels here I lay no claim to 'the whole story'. What I hope I have constructed is a defensible, credible and trustworthy part of the 'story', based on the corpus that I have constructed, within its parameters, boundaries and limitations. As a product of human endeavour, the corpus itself contains the certainty of error; however, to the best of my ability the errors have been identified and 'weeded out', even when doing so necessitated significant and unanticipated – sometimes eye-watering – additional work along the way.

Future prospects

The limitations noted above point to some fertile possibilities for future research. Expanding and/or refocusing the ATC to include online 'print' sources might provide a greater breadth for understanding representations of teachers in the years since the establishment of online news media, for example. Engaging with the multimodality of the articles including images and other graphics (along with captions), typography and so on via corpus-assisted multimodal discourse analysis (Bednarek and Caple 2014), might be another. Further comparative work, based on similarly constructed corpora from other national and sub-national contexts would be a further possibility, allowing for mapping of the discursive construction of the various dimensions and manifestations of the global education reform movement in different contexts, along with an exploration of different representations of teachers. Supplementing the print media focus of the ATC with broadcast media sources would allow for a more broad-based analysis, removing the limits presented by utilizing print media sources alone. Adding social media sources would be yet another possibility.

All of these possibilities, however, involve *adding* to the corpus as it stands, but at the same time I am aware that there are as-yet untapped lines of inquiry in the already very substantial ATC that this analysis has not been able to explore, given the confines of a single book. First, while 'quality' has taken a central place in the analysis, due both to its emergence as a key issue over the course of much of the twenty-five-year period of the ATC, and to my original interest in this discourse, there remain other key aspects which have not yet been subjected to the 'zoom lens'. There are at least two important lines of inquiry that remain. The first is around teacher education and 'training', which emerged as an issue of importance and a somewhat consistent focus within the ATC from the early years through to more contemporary times. While I have explored various aspects of this at different points, particularly in the light of the emphasis on 'classroom readiness' (Craven et al. 2015) over the past decade or so, given the ongoing and recurring political and other attention over the time span of the ATC to the form, duration and quality of initial teacher education (Louden 2008), a more sustained analysis of this within the corpus would be both possible and useful.

Second, and related to this first line of inquiry, commentary on early career (or 'new') teachers is frequent in the ATC and linked often to discussions of both initial teacher education and teacher shortages. As I have observed in previous work on early career teachers in both policy and media texts (Mockler 2018, 2019b), the discursive positioning of early career teachers underwent a large shift between the late 1990s, when they were largely positioned as the solution to problems of teacher shortage, and the mid-2010s, when they were largely positioned as a problem or potential problem requiring increased regulation and 'quality assurance'. This research was based on a 'snapshot' of texts from 1998/99 and 2014/15; however, the attention to early career teachers across the

Teachers in the Print Media: Conclusions, Limitations, Prospects   173

twenty-five-year period of the ATC suggests that a closer discursive tracing might be possible. Representations of early career teachers in the public space potentially influence entrants to the profession, and in times of significant teacher shortage (such as is the current situation in Australia) are particularly worthy of research attention.

Issues around teachers, gender and sexuality are clearly 'live' within the ATC, highlighted not only in the recurring emergence of *male* as a keyword and collocate, but also in the differential use of 'male' and 'female' within the corpus. Further, the emergence of gender and sexuality as a focus in the latter years of the ATC, related to the 'safe schools' debate of 2016 (Law 2017) and then to discussions of sexuality linked to the marriage equality debates of 2017 and 2018. These issues continued to be significant in the post-marriage equality era due to discussions of religious freedom and the capacity of schools to discriminate against teachers and other staff on the basis of their sexuality (Ruddock et al. 2018). From discussions of the desperate shortage of male teachers and associated need for children and young people to have specifically male role models, to the prevalence in some pockets of the ATC of stories about (mostly female but sometimes male) teachers transgressing sexually, to these broader discussions of gender and sexuality as they relate to teaching and schooling, there is much in the corpus to be explored in this area.

Another potential focus that has gone largely unexplored in this book is that of voice. While the recurring emergence of verbs such as 'said', 'says' and 'told' as keywords within the analysis has been acknowledged and discussed in brief, there is untapped potential in questions around 'who says?' This was an angle explored in the pilot research for the ATC project (Mockler 2020a), where it was found that a disproportionately small number of sources on matters related to school education came from the teaching profession, as compared to those on matters related to higher and vocational education. Politicians and other policymakers' voices were found to be dominant, while in relation to higher education the voices of vice chancellors, academics and students were more likely to be included. Furthermore, the prevalence of 'former' within the ATC (a collocate of 'teacher' in each of the twenty-five years of the corpus) raises some interesting questions about the voices and perspectives of former teachers and their role in shaping representations of the teaching profession over time, and this too could be a fruitful line of inquiry.

The analysis conducted here was very much corpus-led: it began with the ATC (which clearly had been constructed according to very particular parameters, and thus an inherent orientation) and worked backwards to education policy reforms and to other educational reforms and developments over the twenty-five-year period. It has thus worked with and paid particular attention to things *present* in the corpus, with these (keywords, collocations etc.) forming a starting point for analysis and mapping. As Duguid and Partington (2018: 38) have noted, common wisdom holds that 'a corpus can yield no information about phenomena it does not contain', a claim they argue is 'based on a failure to grasp the complexity of the notion of absences and an underestimation of the flexibility of corpus techniques'. Instead, attention to what is absent in this corpus maybe another productive future line of inquiry. While it is not true that this analysis has paid no attention to absence, working more iteratively between the education policy reforms and the ATC might have developed a slightly different analysis that paid more attention to the absences in the media discourses than the presences, raising (and answering) interesting questions about what makes it in and what doesn't, and of course, why.

Beyond these broad lines of inquiry, some further, more specific possibilities remain. There is no doubt greater potential to engage with the analysis through close attention to 'downsampled' (Anthony and Baker 2015) collections of prototypical texts. The ATC also includes a range of different types of articles, from news stories and feature articles to commentary and editorials. It has not been possible in this analysis to closely explore the nuances of different representations in these different types of articles; however, doing so, perhaps using a media framing lens, might yield some interesting insights. Potential also exists to further explore particular 'policy moments' of interest and importance in relation to teachers and their work, examining the relationship between press releases, media coverage, policy documents and so on, to identify exactly where it is that the frames that have come to dominate media coverage of teachers emanate from. While earlier work using a far smaller selection of media texts and a single policy moment (Mockler 2014) has suggested that much media framing of education emanates from policy and policymakers, the ATC has great potential for exploring how far this argument holds on a broader scale.

Finally, the last year covered by the ATC saw the onset of the Covid-19 pandemic, and, as demonstrated in the diachronic analysis presented in Chapter 3, the 2020 texts bear some significant differences to those of prior years. The impact of the pandemic on teachers and their work is not yet able to be assessed in full – as I finish this manuscript in early October 2021, Sydney is once again in lockdown, its longest to date – and schools in New South Wales (NSW) have not long concluded their first full term of online learning since the pandemic began. In other parts of the world cases are once again on the rise as a consequence of new strains of the virus and governments are imposing and releasing restrictions as required. Conventional wisdom and anecdotal evidence suggest that public attitudes towards teachers have shifted as a consequence of the pandemic, with 'home schooling' demonstrating the magnitude and level of difficulty of teachers' work to parents and generating previously unknown levels of appreciation. The ATC, possibly extended beyond 2020 in years to come, holds the potential for investigating this shift empirically over time, including during and beyond the pandemic.

Concluding thoughts

I began this research with a deep concern about how teachers and their work were represented in the media, and an adjacent question about how far my observations, both as a 'concerned citizen' and a researcher used to working with small groups of specifically chosen texts, were reflected in broader patterns of coverage. As a concerned citizen was I responding to my outrage being piqued, with a perception that outrage-piquing stories were the norm? Was it just that my own news consumption somehow leaned towards such stories while others remained 'out there' in other places unread? As a researcher was it just that the 'lightning rod' topics of interest on education policy and reform generated negative coverage while elsewhere stories reflective of the nuance and complexity of teaching lay unexamined? I have come to the conclusion of the project no less concerned, but with convincing and empirical evidence that my concerns are, at least, justified.

One of the articles in the ATC noted that 'teacher bashing is one of the few allowed sports in Australia these days' (Thorp 2020), and it's true that often when groups of teachers get together socially, the talk turns to the way 'their kind' is consistently represented in the press. It seems that despite the casual nature of these observations, they are borne out by a systematic and large-scale reading of the print media data: while not all reporting on teachers subscribes to 'teacher bashing', there is enough negative coverage of teachers and their work to make these perspectives understandable.

The media coverage, however, does not come from nowhere, and it is worth remembering that the strong political edge of the ATC is reflective of the close relationship between politics and reporting, and also between policy and media discourses. At a time when politicians and policymakers will readily acknowledge problems with attracting and retaining teachers, and happily make proclamations about attracting the 'best and brightest' to the profession, they also heartily subscribe to discourses that make the profession look less than desirable to both prospective and current teachers. This is one practical reason why these discourses are problematic. Another is that the rhetoric and discursive illusion of central concepts such as 'quality' get in the way of authentic discussions about how our education system can and should continue to develop to improve the educational opportunities of all children and young people. These are important conversations to have in the public space and they demand that we move beyond simplistic representations of 'all teachers' and dichotomies of 'good' and 'bad' teachers. Attending to 'quality' is a poor substitute for affecting changes to issues on both systemic and local levels that are much more intractable and much harder to address, but that will create greater equity and opportunities for high achievement for all students – the hallmarks of true 'high-performing' systems. It is my hope that this book has gone some way towards opening up this conversation, and that it might make a small contribution to more honest and considered discussions of teachers and their work in our public spaces.

References

Alexander, Robin J. (2012), 'Moral Panic, Miracle Cures and Educational Policy: What Can We Really Learn from International Comparison?', *Scottish Educational Review*, 44 (1): 4–21.

Alexander, Robin J. (2015), 'Teaching and Learning for All? The Quality Imperative Revisited', *International Journal of Educational Development*, 40: 250–8.

Alhamdan, Bandar, Khalid Al-Saadi, Aspa Baroutsis, Anna Du Plessis, Obaidul M. Hamid and Eileen Honan (2014), 'Media Representation of Teachers across Five Countries', *Comparative Education*, 50 (4): 490–505.

Allen, Elizabeth and Rosemary Odgers (2005), 'Parents' Pressure Forces School Asbestos Removal', *The Courier-Mail*, 26 May: 3.

Altheide, David L. (1997), 'The News Media, the Problem Frame, and the Production of Fear', *The Sociological Quarterly*, 38 (4): 647–68.

Altheide, David L. (2013), 'Media Logic, Social Control, and Fear', *Communication Theory*, 23 (3): 223–38.

Altheide, David L. (2021), 'Media Logic, Fear and the Construction of Terrorism', in vom Lehn, Dirk, Natalia Ruiz-Junco and Will Gibson, eds, *The Routledge International Handbook of Interactionism*, 277–87, London: Routledge.

Altheide, David L. and Robert P. Snow (1979), *Media Logic*, Beverley Hills: Sage.

Anthony, Laurence (2017), AntFileConverter (Version 1.2.1), Tokyo: Waseda University.

Anthony, Laurence (2019), AntConc (Version 3.5.8), Tokyo: Waseda University.

Anthony, Laurence and Paul Baker (2015), 'ProtAnt: A Tool for Analysing the Prototypicality of Texts', *International Journal of Corpus Linguistics*, 20 (3): 273–92.

Anthony, Laurence and Paul Baker (2017), ProtAnt (Version 1.2.1), Tokyo: Waseda University.

Australian Broadcasting Corporation (2014), Q+A *Education and Disadvantage*.

Australian Bureau of Statistics (2021), 'Schools, Australia 2020', retrieved from https://www.abs.gov.au/statistics/people/education/schools/latest-release (accessed 1 September 2021).

Australian Communications and Media Authority (2021), 'Media Interests Snapshot', retrieved from https://www.acma.gov.au/media-interests-snapshot (accessed 1 July 2021).

Australian Education Act (2013, 26 July).

Australian Government Department of Education, Employment, and Workplace Relations (2010), 'Digital Education Revolution –Overview', retrieved from https://web.archive.org/web/20091029142009/http://www.deewr.gov.au/Schooling/Digital EducationRevolution/Pages/default.aspx (accessed 4 August 2020).

178 *References*

Bacchi, Carol (2009), *Analysing Policy: What's the Problem Represented to Be?*, Frenchs Forest, NSW: Pearson Education.

Bacchi, Carol and Susan Goodwin (2016), *Poststructural Policy Analysis: A Guide to Practice*, New York: Springer Nature.

Baker, Jordan (2021), 'Public School Teacher Shortage Raises Fears They Will "Run Out of Teachers"', *Sydney Morning Herald*, 7 October: 1.

Baker, Paul (2006), *Using Corpora in Discourse Analysis*, London: Bloomsbury Academic.

Baker, Paul (2010), 'Representations of Islam in British Broadsheet and Tabloid Newspapers 1999–2005', *Journal of Language and Politics*, 9 (2): 310–38.

Baker, Paul (2011), 'Times May Change, but We Will Always Have Money: Diachronic Variation in Recent British English', *Journal of English Linguistics*, 39 (1): 65–88.

Baker, Paul (2019), 'Analysing Representations of Obesity in the Daily Mail via Corpus and Down-Sampling Methods', in Egbert, Jesse and Paul Baker, eds, *Using Corpus Methods to Triangulate Linguistic Analysis*, 85–108, London: Routledge.

Baker, Paul and Erez Levon (2015), 'Picking the Right Cherries? A Comparison of Corpus-Based and Qualitative Analyses of News Articles about Masculinity', *Discourse & Communication*, 9 (2): 221–36.

Baker, Paul and Erez Levon (2016), '"That's What I Call a Man": Representations of Racialised and Classed Masculinities in the UK Print Media', *Gender and Language*, 10 (1): 106–39.

Baker, Paul and Tony McEnery (2019), 'The Value of Revisiting and Extending Previous Studies: The Case of Islam in the UK Press', in Scholz, Ronny, eds, *Quantifying Approaches to Discourse for Social Scientists*, 215–49, Cham: Springer International.

Baker, Paul, Costas Gabrielatos and Tony McEnery (2013), *Discourse Analysis and Media Attitudes: The Representation of Islam in the British Press*, Cambridge: Cambridge University Press.

Ball, Stephen J., Carolina Junemann and Diego Santori (2017), *Edu.Net: Globalisation and Education Policy Mobility*, Abingdon: Routledge.

Balogh, Stephanie (2005), 'Teachers' Institute to Lead the Way', *The Courier-Mail*, 11 May: 30.

Balogh, Stephanie (2017), 'Prove Teaching Skills in Classroom or Fail Course', *The Australian*, 31 August: 4.

Barnes, Melissa (2021a), 'Framing Teacher Quality in the Australian Media: The Circulation of Key Political Messages?', *Educational Review*: 1–17.

Barnes, Melissa (2021b), 'Policy Actors or Objects of Policy? Teacher Candidates' Interpretations of "Teacher Quality" Policy Initiatives in Australia', *Teaching and Teacher Education*, 106: 1–11.

Baroutsis, Aspa (2016), 'Media Accounts of School Performance: Reinforcing Dominant Practices of Accountability', *Journal of Education Policy*, 31 (5): 567–82.

Baroutsis, Aspa (2019a), 'Mapping the Field of Education Research and Media', in Baroutsis, Aspa, Stewart Riddle and Pat Thomson, eds, *Education Research and the Media: Challenges and Possibilities*, 1–24, Abingdon, UK: Routledge.

References

Baroutsis, Aspa (2019b), 'Understanding Media Mentalities and Logics: Institutional and Journalistic Practices, and the Reporting of Teachers' Work', *Discourse: Studies in the Cultural Politics of Education*, 40 (4): 545–59.

Baroutsis, Aspa and Bob Lingard (2017), 'Counting and Comparing School Performance: An Analysis of Media Coverage of PISA in Australia, 2000–2014', *Journal of Education Policy*, 32 (4): 432–49.

Baroutsis, A. and Lingard, B. (2019), 'Headlines and Hashtags Herald New "Damaging Effects": Media and Australia's Declining PISA Performance', In A. Baroutsis, S. Riddle and P. Thomson, eds, *Education research and the media: Challenges and possibilities*, London: Routledge.

Baroutsis, A., Riddle, S. and Thomson, P., eds (2019), *Education Research and the Media: Challenges and Possibilities*, London: Routledge.

Basten, Carolyn (1997), 'A Feminised Profession: SWomen in the Teaching Profession', *Educational Studies*, 23 (1): 55–62.

Baxter, Penny (2002), 'Numbers Stress Out Teachers', *Northern Territory News*, 5 November: 6.

Bednarek, Monika. (2016), 'Inventory of Linguistic Devices Constructing Newsworthiness', retrieved from https://www.newsvaluesanalysis.com/wp-content/uploads/2017/08/Bednarek-2016-Inventory-of-linguistic-devices-constructing-newsworthiness.pdf (accessed 20 January 2021).

Bednarek, Monika (2020), 'Invisible or High-Risk: Computer-Assisted Discourse Analysis of References to Aboriginal and Torres Strait Islander People(s) and Issues in a Newspaper Corpus about Diabetes', *PLoS ONE*, 15 (6): e0234486.

Bednarek, Monika and Georgia Carr (2020), 'Diabetes Coverage in Australian Newspapers (2013–2017): A Computer-Based Linguistic Analysis', *Health Promotion Journal of Australia*, 31(3): 497–503

Bednarek, Monika and Helen Caple (2012a), ' "Value Added": Language, Image and News Values', *Discourse, Context & Media*, 1 (2): 103–13.

Bednarek, Monika and Helen Caple (2012b), *News Discourse*, London: Bloomsbury.

Bednarek, Monika and Helen Caple (2014), 'Why Do News Values Matter? Towards a New Methodological Framework for Analysing News Discourse in Critical Discourse Analysis and Beyond', *Discourse & Society*, 25 (2): 135–58.

Bednarek, Monika and Helen Caple (2017), *The Discourse of News Values: How News Organizations Create Newsworthiness*, Oxford: Oxford University Press.

Beikoff, Katrina (1996), 'Schools "Rated Like Fast Food"'. *Daily Telegraph*, 26 November: 4.

Bell, Allan (1991), *The Language of News Media*, Oxford: Blackwell.

Berliner, David C. (2005), 'The near Impossibility of Testing for Teacher Quality', *Journal of Teacher Education*, 56 (3): 205–13.

Berliner, D. and Biddle, B. (1996), *The Manufactured Crisis: Myths, Fraud, and the Attack on America's Public Schools*, New York: Basic Books.

Bissett, Kelvin and Bruce McDougall (2005), 'Beach Lesson Learnt – Teachers Turn Backs on Tougher Schools'. *Daily Telegraph*, 26 July: 12.

Bita, Natasha (2015), 'Unis "Have Incentive" to Train Bad Teachers', *The Australian*, 28 March: 2.

Bita, Natasha (2016), 'Activists Push Taxpayer-Funded Gay Manual in Schools', *The Australian*, 10 February: 1.

Bita, Natasha and Justine Ferrari (2015), 'Make Kids Learn: Uni Trainers on Notice'. *The Australian*, 14 February: 9.

Black, Paul and Dylan Wiliam (1998), 'Inside the Black Box', *Phi Delta Kappan*, 80 (2): 139–47.

Black, Paul, Christine Harrison, Clare Lee, Bethan Marshall and Dylan Wiliam (2004), 'Working inside the Black Box: Assessment for Learning in the Classroom', *Phi Delta Kappan*, 86 (1): 8.

Blackmore, Jill and Pat Thomson (2004), 'Just "Good and Bad News"? Disciplinary Imaginaries of Head Teachers in Australian and English Print Media', *Journal of Education Policy*, 19 (3): 301–20.

Blackmore, Jill and Stephen Thorpe (2003), 'Media/Ting Change: The Print Media's Role in Mediating Education Policy in a Period of Radical Reform in Victoria, Australia', *Journal of Education Policy*, 18 (6): 577–95.

Blommaert, Jan (2005), *Discourse: A Critical Introduction*, Cambridge: Cambridge University Press.

Bokhove, Christian and Sam Sims (2021), 'Demonstrating the Potential of Text Mining for Analyzing School Inspection Reports: A Sentiment Analysis of 17,000 Ofsted Documents', *International Journal of Research & Method in Education*, 44: 443–5.

Bourdieu, Pierre (1990), *The Logic of Practice*, Cambridge: Polity Press.

Bourke, Terri, Mary Ryan and Margaret Lloyd (2016), 'The Discursive Positioning of Graduating Teachers in Accreditation of Teacher Education Programs', *Teaching and Teacher Education*, 53: 1–9.

Bourke, Theresa, Reece Mills and Erin Siostrom (2020), 'Origins of Primary Specialisation in Australian Education Policy: What's the Problem Represented to Be?', *The Australian Educational Researcher*, 47 (5): 725–40.

Brezina, Vaclav (2018), 'Statistical Choices in Corpus-Based Discourse Analysis', in Taylor, C. and A. Marchi, eds, *Corpus Approaches to Discourse: A Critical Review*, 259–80, London: Routledge.

Brookes, Gavin and Paul Baker (2021), *Obesity in the News: Language and Representation in the Press*, Cambridge: Cambridge University Press.

Burch, Brent, Jesse Egbert and Doug Biber (2017), 'Measuring and Interpreting Lexical Dispersion in Corpus Linguistics', *Journal of Research Design and Statistics in Linguistics and Communication Science*, 3 (2): 189–216.

Cabalin, Cristian (2015), 'Mediatizing Higher Education Policies: Discourses about Quality Education in the Media', *Critical Studies in Education*, 56 (2): 22440.

References

Campbell, Craig and Geoffrey Sherington (2013), *The Comprehensive Public High School: Historical Perspectives*, New York: Palgrave Macmillan.

Campbell, Craig and Helen Proctor (2014), *A History of Australian Schooling*, Sydney: Allen & Unwin.

Campbell, Craig, Helen Proctor and Geoffrey Sherington (2009), *School Choice: How Parents Negotiate the New School Market in Australia*, Sydney: Allen & Unwin.

Caple, Helen (2018), 'Analysing the Multimodal Text', in Taylor, Charlotte and Anna Marchi, eds, *Corpus Approaches to Discourse: A Critical Review*, 85–109, London: Routledge.

Caple, Helen and Monika Bednarek (2013), *Delving into the Discourse: Approaches to News Values in Journalism Studies and Beyond*, retrieved from Oxford: https://ora.ox.ac.uk/objects/uuid:1f5c6d91-bb1f-4278-a160-66149ecfb36b (accessed 1 October 2021).

Carey, Adam (2019), 'Warning on Maths Teacher Shortage', *The Age*, 11 October: 6.

Chapman, Jemma (2004), 'Principals Forced to Cut Subjects', *The Advertiser*, 19 May: 3.

Chesky, Nataly X. and Rebecca A. Goldstein (2016), 'Whispers That Echo: Girls' Experiences and Voices in News Media Reports About Stem Education Reform', *Journal for Critical Education Policy Studies*, 14 (2): 130–57.

Chester, Rodney and Tanya Chilcott (2009), 'Three Rs or State Teachers Are Out', *The Courier-Mail*, 2 May: 4.

Chilcott, Tanya (2014), 'Bar Low for Teachers – Concerns as Poor Grade Students Get into Education Courses', *The Courier-Mail*, 25 January: 7.

Church, Kenneth W., William A. Gale, Patrick Hanks, Donald Hindle and Rosamund Moon (1994), 'Lexical Substitutability', in Atkins, Beryl T. Sue and Antonio Zampolli, eds, *Computational Approaches to the Lexicon*, 153–77, Oxford: Oxford University Press.

Churchward, Peter and Jill Willis (2019), 'The Pursuit of Teacher Quality: Identifying Some of the Multiple Discourses of Quality That Impact the Work of Teacher Educators', *Asia-Pacific Journal of Teacher Education*, 47 (3): 251–64.

Clark, Blanche (2010), 'Never Stop Learning', *Herald Sun*, 11 January: 37.

Clarke, Matthew (2014), 'The Sublime Objects of Education Policy: Quality, Equity and Ideology', *Discourse: Studies in the Cultural Politics of Education*, 35 (4): 584–98.

Cohen, Jennifer L. (2010), 'Teachers in the News: A Critical Analysis of One US Newspaper's Discourse on Education, 2006–2007', *Discourse: Studies in the Cultural Politics of Education*, 31 (1): 105–19.

Cohen, Michael I. (2021), 'Education Populism? A Corpus-Driven Analysis of Betsy Devos's Education Policy Discourse', *Education Policy Analysis Archives*, 29 (16).

Comber, Barbara (2015), *Literacy, Place and Pedagogies of Possibility*, London: Routledge.

Commonwealth of Australia (1998), *A Class Act: Inquiry into the Status of the Teaching Profession*, retrieved from Canberra: Australian Parliament Senate Employment, Education and Training References Committee.

Commonwealth of Australia (2008), *Quality Education: The Case for an Education Revolution in Our Schools*, Canberra: Commonwealth of Australia.

Commonwealth of Australia (2016), 'Parliamentary Debates, House of Representatives', 10 February: 1228.

Conboy, Martin and Scott A. Eldridge (2017), 'Journalism and Public Discourse', in Cotter, Colleen and Daniel Perrin, eds, *The Routledge Handbook of Language and Media*, 164–77, London: Routledge.

Craven, Greg, Kim Beswick, John Fleming, Trevor Fletcher, Michelle Green, Ben Jensen, Eva Leinonen and Field Rickards (2015), *Action Now: Classroom Ready Teachers*, Canberra: Commonwealth Department of Education.

Credlin, Peta (2020), 'It's a Recipe for Disaster', *Daily Telegraph*, 23 February: 87.

Dalton, Mary M. and Laura R. Linder, eds (2019), *Teachers, Teaching, and Media: Original Essays About Educators in Popular Culture*, Leiden: Brill.

Davies, Mark (2008–), 'The Corpus of Contemporary American English (COCA). Available online at https://www.english-corpora.org/coca (accessed 1 October 2021).

Davies, Mark (2016–), Corpus of News on the Web (NOW). Available at https://corpus.byu.edu/now (accessed 1 October 2021).

De Waal, Ester and Klaus Schoenbach (2010), 'News Sites' Position in the Mediascape: Uses, Evaluations and Media Displacement Effects over Time', *New Media & Society*, 12 (3): 477–96.

Devine, Miranda (2017), 'Safe Schools and Ssm Go Hand-in-Hand'. *Daily Telegraph,* 4 October.

Dinham, Stephen (2011), 'My Say', *The Age*, 22 August.

Dodd, Tim (2015), 'Are Primary Teachers Ready to Give Coding Lessons? Ian Chubb Says No', *The Australian*, 12 December: 4.

Dodd, Tim (2017), 'Falling Class Sizes Raise Education Bill', *Australian Financial Review*, 3 February: 2.

Donnelly, Kevin (2005), 'Fads No Substitute for Teaching', *The Australian*, 5 January: 13.

Donnelly, Kevin (2009), 'Education Standards Institute', *Quadrant Online*. Available at https://quadrant.org.au/opinion/qed/2009/11/education-standards-institute/ (accessed 1 October 2021).

Donnelly, Kevin (2012), 'Left Uses Schools as Recruiting Grounds for Its Gender War', *Weekend Australian*, 20 October: 16.

Donnelly, Kevin (2013), 'Set Our Curriculum Free', *The Australian*, 4 September: 14.

Donnelly, Kevin (2019), 'Failed in the Past, Failed Now, but We Just March On', *The Australian*, 26 December: 10.

Donnelly, Kevin (2021), 'Dr Kevin Donnelly: About', retrieved from https://kevindonnelly.com.au (accessed 20 January 2021).

Dowling, Andrew (2008), '"Unhelpfully Complex and Exceedingly Opaque": Australia's School Funding System', *Australian Journal of Education*, 52 (2): 129–50.

Druckman, James N. (2001), 'On the Limits of Framing Effects: Who Can Frame?', *Journal of Politics*, 63 (4): 1041–66.

Drudy, Sheelagh (2008), 'Gender Balance/Gender Bias: The Teaching Profession and the Impact of Feminisation', *Gender and Education*, 20 (4): 309–23.

Duguid, Alison and Alan Partington (2018), 'Absence: You Don't Know What You're Missing. Or Do You?', in Taylor, Charlotte and Anna Marchi, eds, *Corpus Approaches to Discourse: A Critical Review*, 39–59, London: Routledge.

Education Council (2019), 'Alice Springs (Mparntwe) Education Declaration', retrieved from https://docs.education.gov.au/documents/alice-springs-mparntwe-education-declaration (accessed 1 October 2021)

Education Queensland (2001), *The Queensland School Reform Longitudinal Study: Final Report*, Brisbane: Education Queensland.

Egbert, Jesse and Doug Biber (2019), 'Incorporating Text Dispersion into Keyword Analyses', *Corpora*, 14 (1): 77–104.

Entman, Robert M. (1993), 'Framing: Toward Clarification of a Fractured Paradigm', *Journal of Communication*, 43 (4): 51–58.

Entman, Robert M. (2003), 'Cascading Activation: Contesting the White House's Frame after 9/11', *Political Communication*, 20 (4): 415–32.

Erss, Maria and Veronika Kalmus (2018), 'Discourses of Teacher Autonomy and the Role of Teachers in Estonian, Finnish and Bavarian Teachers' Newspapers in 1991–2010', *Teaching and Teacher Education*, 76: 95–105.

Fahey, Kevin, Carol Weissert and Matt Uttermark (2018), Studying Ballot Endorsements Shows That Even in the Digital Age, Newspapers Still Matter to Voters, retrieved from https://blogs.lse.ac.uk/usappblog/2018/06/25/studying-ballot-endorsements-shows-that-even-in-the-digital-age-newspapers-still-matter-to-voters/ (accessed 1 October 2021).

Fenech, Marianne and David P. Wilkins (2017), 'Representations of Childcare in the Australian Print Media: An Exploratory Corpus-Assisted Discourse Analysis', *Australian Educational Researcher*, 44 (2): 161–90.

Fenech, Marianne and David P. Wilkins (2019), 'The Representation of the National Quality Framework in the Australian Print Media: Silences and Slants in the Mediatisation of Early Childhood Education Policy', *Journal of Education Policy*, 34 (6): 748–70.

Ferrari, Justine (2008), 'More Funds for Primary Schools', *The Australian*, 29 November: 6.

Firth, J. R. (1957), *Papers in Linguistics 1934–1951*, London: Oxford University Press.

Fisher, Roy, Ann Harris and Christine Jarvis (2008), *Education in Popular Culture: Telling Tales on Teachers and Learners*, London: Routledge.

Fitzgerald, Scott, Susan McGrath-Champ, Meghan Stacey, Rachel Wilson and Mihajla Gavin (2019), 'Intensification of Teachers' Work under Devolution: A "Tsunami" of Paperwork', *Journal of Industrial Relations*, 61 (5): 613–36.

Foucault, Michel (1972), *The Archaeology of Knowledge*, London: Tavistock.

Franklin, Bob (2004), 'Education, Education and Indoctrination! Packaging Politics and the Three "Rs"', *Journal of Education Policy*, 19 (3): 255–70.

184   *References*

Friedman, Milton (1982), *Capitalism and Freedom*, Chicago: University of Chicago Press.

Gabrielatos, Costas (2018), 'Keyness Analysis', in Taylor, Charlotte and Anna Marchi, eds, *Corpus Approaches to Discoruse: A Critical Review*, 225–58, London: Routledge.

Gabrielatos, Costas and Paul Baker (2008), 'Fleeing, Sneaking, Flooding: A Corpus Analysis of Discursive Constructions of Refugees and Asylum Seekers in the UK Press, 1996–2005', *Journal of English Linguistics*, 36 (1): 5–38.

Galtung, Johan and Mari Holmboe Ruge (1965), 'The Structure of Foreign News: The Presentation of the Congo, Cuba and Cyprus Crises in Four Norwegian Newspapers', *Journal of Peace Research*, 2 (1): 64–90.

Gamson, William A. and Andre Modigliani (1987), 'The Changing Culture of Affirmative Action', *Research in Political Sociology*, 3: 137–77.

Gamson, William A. and Andre Modigliani (1989), 'Media Discourse and Public Opinion on Nuclear Power: A Constructionist Approach', *American Journal of Sociology*, 95 (1): 1–37.

Gamson, William A. and Kathryn E. Lasch (1983), 'The Political Culture of Social Welfare Policy', in Spiro, Shimon E. and Ephraim Yuchtman-Yaar, eds, *Evaluating the Welfare State: Social and Political Perspectives*, 397–415, New York: Academic.

Germond, Basil, Tony McEnery and Anna Marchi (2016), 'The Eu's Comprehensive Approach as the Dominant Discourse: A Corpus-Linguistics Analysis of the Eu's Counter-Piracy Narrative', *European Foreign Affairs Review*, 21 (1): 135–54.

Gill, Margaret (1994), 'Who Framed English? A Case Study of the Media's Role in Curriculum Change', *Critical Studies in Education*, 35 (1): 96–113.

Gillard, Julia (2010), 'A Future Fair for All – School Funding in Australia – Address to Sydney Institute', retrieved from https://parlinfo.aph.gov.au/parlInfo/search/display/display.w3p;query=Id:%22media/pressrel/VMGW6%22 (accessed 12 February 2021).

Gillard, Julia (2011), 'Transcript of Joint Press Conference, Canberra [2 May 2011]', retrieved from https://web.archive.org/web/20110601213147/http://www.pm.gov.au/press-office/transcript-joint-press-conference-canberra-2 (accessed 4 November 2020).

Gillard, Julia (2012), 'Interview with John Laws, 2SM [Radio Broadcast, September 4 2012]', retrieved from http://pandora.nla.gov.au/pan/121064/20130626-1841/www.pm.gov.au/press-office/interview-john-laws.html (accessed 4 July 2020).

Gillard, Julia and Peter Garrett (2012), 'Transcript of Joint Press Conference – Gonski Review of Funding for Australian Schooling Report', retrieved from https://web.archive.org/web/20130330101813/http://ministers.deewr.gov.au/gillard/transcript-joint-press-conference-gonski-review-funding-australian-schooling-report (accessed 30 January 2020).

Glick, Peter and Susan T. Fiske (1996), 'The Ambivalent Sexism Inventory: Differentiating Hostile and Benevolent Sexism', *Journal of Personality and Social Psychology*, 70 (3): 491–512.

Glick, Peter and Susan T. Fiske (2001), 'An Ambivalent Alliance: Hostile and Benevolent Sexism as Complementary Justifications for Gender Inequality', *American Psychologist*, 56 (2): 109–18.

Goffman, Erving (1974), *Frame Analysis: An Essay on the Organisation of Experience*, Boston: Northeastern University Press.

Goldstein, Dana and Ben Casselman (2018), 'Teachers Find Support as Campaign for Higher Salaries Goes to Voters', *New York Times*, 1 June: 13.

Gómez, Pascual C. (2013), *Statistical Methods in Language and Linguistic Research*, Sheffield: Equinox.

Gonski, David, Ken Boston, Kathryn Greiner, Carmen Lawrence, Bill Scales and Peter Tannock (2011), *Review of Funding for Schooling: Final Report*, Canberra: Department of Education, Employment and Workplace Relations.

Gonski, David, Terry Arcus, Ken Boston, Valerie Gould, Wendy Johnson, Lisa O'Brien, Lee-Anne Perry and Michael Roberts (2018), *Through Growth to Achievement: Report of the Review to Achieve Educational Excellence in Australian Schools*, Canberra: Commonwealth of Australia.

Goodfellow, Nhada (2003), 'Extra Teachers, Smaller Classes the Primary Goal', *The Advertiser*, 29 April: 7.

Gore, Jennifer, James G. Ladwig and Bruce King (2004), *Professional Learning, Pedagogical Improvement, and the Circulation of Power*, paper presented at the Australian Association for Research in Education Annual Conference, University of Melbourne, December 2004.

Gore, Jennifer, Andrew Miller, Leanne Fray, Jess Harris and Elena Prieto (2021), 'Improving Student Achievement through Professional Development: Results from a Randomised Controlled Trial of Quality Teaching Rounds', *Teaching and Teacher Education*, 101: 103297.

Grube, Kathy (2006), 'Teachers Tackle Science: Bartlett Considers Retraining Scheme', *The Australian*, 2 September: 12.

Grundmann, Reiner and Ramesh Krishnamurthy (2010), 'The Discourse of Climate Change: A Corpus-Based Approach', *Critical Approaches to Discourse Analysis across Disciplines*, 4 (2): 125–46.

Grundy, Shirley (1998), 'The Curriculum and Teaching', in Hatton, E., ed., *Understanding Teaching: Curriculum and the Social Context of Schooling*, Sydney: Harcourt Brace.

Guerrera, Orietta, Chee Chee Leung and Annabel Crabb (2004), 'Private, Public Schools Hit PM', *The Age*, 21 January: 1.

Gulson, Kalervo N. and Christopher Lubienski (2014), 'The New Political Economy of Education Policy: Cultural Politics, Mobility and the Market', *Knowledge Cultures*, 2 (2).

Harcup, Tony and Deirdre O'Neill (2001), 'What Is News? Galtung and Ruge Revisited', *Journalism Studies*, 2 (2): 261–80.

Harcup, Tony and Deirdre O'Neill (2017), 'What Is News?', *Journalism Studies*, 18 (12): 1470–88.

Hardie, Andrew (2014), 'Cass Blog: Log Ratio – an Informal Introduction', retrieved from http://cass.lancs.ac.uk/?p=1133 (accessed 26 June 2021).

Hattam, Robert, Brenton Prosser and Kathy Brady (2009), 'Revolution or Backlash? The Mediatisation of Education Policy in Australia', *Critical Studies in Education*, 50 (2): 159–72.

Hayes, Debra, Martin Mills, Pam Christie and Bob Lingard (2006), *Teachers and Schooling Making a Difference: Productive Pedagogies, Assessment and Performance*, Sydney: Allen & Unwin.

Henderson, Paul (2006), 'Committed to Our Future', *Northern Territory News*, 27 October: 103.

Hepp, A. (2019), *Deep Mediatization*, London: Routledge.

Bethany (2006a), 'Teachers Unqualified: Survey', *West Australian*, 20 July: 9.

Hiatt, Bethany (2006b), 'Unions Hit Back at Obe "Slurs"', *West Australian*, 9 May: 15.

Hiatt, Bethany (2018), 'Expert Fears Failed School Policy Is Back', *West Australian*, 2 May: 12.

Hopkins-Doyle, Aife, Robbie M Sutton, Karen M Douglas and Rachel M Calogero (2019), 'Flattering to Deceive: Why People Misunderstand Benevolent Sexism', *Journal of Personality and Social Psychology*, 116 (2): 167.

Howard, John and Brendan Nelson (2004), 'The Australian Government's Agenda for Schools: Achievement through Choice and Opportunity' [press release], retrieved from https://parlinfo.aph.gov.au/parlInfo/search/display/display.w3p;query=Id%3A%22media%2Fpressrel%2FJDXC6%22 (accessed 1 October 2021).

Hunston, Susan (2002), *Corpora in Applied Linguistics*, Cambridge: Cambridge University Press.

Hurrell, Bronwyn (1997), 'Self-Managed Schools Backed', *The Advertiser*, 1 December: 5.

Image Bid for State Schooling (1998), 'Editorial', *The Courier-Mail*, 11 May: 5.

Iyengar, Shanto (1990), 'Framing Responsibility for Political Issues: The Case of Poverty', *Political Behavior*, 12 (1): 19–40.

Iyengar, Shanto (1991), *Is Anyone Responsible?: How Television Frames Political Issues*, Chicago: University of Chicago Press.

Jaworska, Sylvia and Ramesh Krishnamurthy (2012), 'On the F Word: A Corpus-Based Analysis of the Media Representation of Feminism in British and German Press Discourse, 1990–2009', *Discourse & Society*, 23 (4): 401–31.

Jensen, Ben and Jacqueline Magee (2019), 'Putting Learning at the Heart of Curriculum Reform', *Sydney Morning Herald*, 15 April: 19.

Jones, Carolyn (1996), 'Strategy to Raise Status of Teaching', *The Australian*, 8 February: 8.

Jones, Carolyn (1998), 'Catholics Attack over Class Sizes', *Sunday Age*, 15 March: 8.

Kelleher, Fatimah, Francis O Severin, Meera Samson, Anuradha De, Tepora Afamasaga-Wright and Upali M Sedere (2011), *Women and the Teaching Profession: Exploring the Feminisation Debate*, Paris: UNESCO.

Kelly, Fran (2013, 23 February), 'Gonski Education Reforms: Chistopher Pyne [Interview]'. Retrieved from https://www.pyneonline.com.au/media-centre/transcripts/abc-radio-national-3 (accessed 30 April 2015).

Kelly, Paul (2014), 'Keynote Address to Symposium Marking 50 years of *The Australian*', 7–8 July, Macquarie University, Sydney, NSW, retrieved from https://youtu.be/g9EeVUSk7CU (accessed 20 January 2021).

Kemmis, Stephen (2017), *Theorising Education as a Practice*, paper presented at the Sydney School of Education and Social Work School and Teacher Education Policy Research Network Seminar Series, University of Sydney, July 2017.

Kemmis, Stephen (2019), *A Practice Sensibility: An Invitation to the Theory of Practice Architectures*, Dordrecht: Springer.

Kemmis, Stephen and Peter Grootenboer (2008), 'Situating Praxis in Practice: Practice Architectures and the Cultural, Social and Material Conditions for Practice', in Kemmis, Stephen and Tracey Smith, eds, *Enabling Praxis: Challenges for Education*, 37–62, Rotterdam: Sense.

Kemmis, Stephen, Jane Wilkinson, Christine Edwards-Groves, Ian Hardy, Peter Grootenboer and Laurette Bristol (2014), *Changing Practices, Changing Education*, Dordrecht: Springer.

Keogh, Jayne and Barbara Garrick (2011), 'Creating Catch 22: Zooming In and Zooming Out on the Discursive Constructions of Teachers in a News Article', *International Journal of Qualitative Studies in Education*, 24 (4): 419–34.

Kerr, Christian (2009), 'National Scheme to Assess Teachers', *The Australian*, 17 August: 5.

Kim, Kyung Hye (2014), 'Examining US News Media Discourses About North Korea: A Corpus-Based Critical Discourse Analysis', *Discourse & Society*, 25 (2): 221–44.

King, Rhianna (2007), 'State School Students Taught Sludge: Howard', *West Australian*, 9 February: 6.

Kipnis, Andrew B. (2013), 'Subjectification and Education for Quality in China', *Economy and Society*, 40 (2): 289–306.

Ladwig, James G., Maxwell Smith, Jennifer Gore, Wendy Amosa and Tom Griffiths (2007), *Quality of Pedagogy and Student Achievement: Multi-Level Replication of Authentic Pedagogy*, paper presented at the Australian Association for Research in Education Annual Conference, Fremantle, WA, December 2007.

Lampert, Jo, Bruce Burnett, Barbaar Comber, Angela Ferguson and Naomi Barnes (2018), 'Quality Teaching Discourses: A Contested Terrain', in Gannon, S., R. Hattam and Wayne Sawyer, eds, *Resisting Educational Inequality*, 150–8, London: Routledge.

Larsen, Marianne (2010), 'Troubling the Discourse of Teacher Centrality: A Comparative Perspective', *Journal of Education Policy*, 25 (2): 207–31.

188 References

Law, Benjamin (2017), 'Moral Panic 101: Equality, Acceptance and the Safe Schools Scandal', *Quarterly Essay*, 67: 1–81.

Lebihan, Rachel (2012), 'Learning Tops Funding', *Australian Financial Review*, 17 February: 9.

Legal Threat against Teachers (2010b), 'Editorial', *West Australian*, 13 April: 3.

Lewis, Rosie (2010), 'Happy Learners in a Class of Their Own: Top of the State', *Sydney Morning Herald*, 29 January: 5.

Lidberg, Johan (2019), 'The Distortion of the Australian Public Sphere: Media Ownership Concentration in Australia', *AQ: Australian Quarterly*, 90 (1): 12–44.

Lingard, Bob (2000), 'Federalism in Schooling since the Karmel Report (1973), Schools in Australia: From Modernist Hope to Postmodernist Performativity', *The Australian Educational Researcher*, 27 (2): 25–61.

Lingard, Bob (2010), 'Policy Borrowing, Policy Learning: Testing Times in Australian Schooling', *Critical Studies in Education*, 51 (2): 129–47.

Lingard, Bob and Shaun Rawolle (2004), 'Mediatizing Educational Policy: The Journalistic Field, Science Policy, and Cross-Field Effects', *Journal of Education Policy*, 19 (3): 361–80.

Lingard, Bob, Peter O'Brien and John Knight (1993), 'Strengthening Australia's Schools through Corporate Federalism?', *Australian Journal of Education*, 37 (3): 231–47.

Lortie, Dan (1975), *Schoolteacher: A Sociological Study*, Chicago: University of Chicago Press.

Louden, William (2008), '101 Damnations: The Persistence of Criticism and the Absence of Evidence about Teacher Education in Australia', *Teachers and Teaching*, 14 (4): 357–68.

Louw, Bill (1993), 'Irony in the Text or Insincerity in the Writer? The Diagnostic Potential of Semantic Prosodies', in Baker, Mona, Gill Francis and Elena Tognini-Bonelli, eds, *Text and Technology* (Vol. 240), 157–92, Amsterdam: John Benjamins.

Love, Robbie, Claire Dembry, Andrew Hardie, Vaclav Brezina and Tony McEnery (2017), 'The Spoken Bnc2014: Designing and Building a Spoken Corpus of Everyday Conversations', *International Journal of Corpus Linguistics*, 22 (3): 319–44.

MacMillan, Katie (2002), 'Narratives of Social Disruption: Education News in the British Tabloid Press', *Discourse: Studies in the Cultural Politics of Education*, 23 (1): 27–38.

Maddox, Marion (2011), 'A Secular Cancellation of the Secularist Truce: Religion and Political Legitimation in Australia', in Michel, Patrick and Enzo Pace, eds, *Annual Review of the Sociology of Religion* (Vol. 2: Religion and Politics), 287–308, Leiden: Brill.

Mahon, Kathleen, Susanne Francisco and Stephen Kemmis, eds (2017), *Exploring Education and Professional Practice: Through the Lens of Practice Architectures*, Dordrecht: Springer.

Mahon, Kathleen, Stephen Kemmis, Susanne Francisco and Adam Lloyd (2017), 'Practice Theory and the Theory of Practice Architectures', in Mahon, Kathleen,

Susanne Francisco and Stephen Kemmis, eds, *Exploring Education and Professional Practice: Through the Lens of Practice Architectures*, 1–30, Singapore: Springer.

Maiden, Samantha (2007), 'Numeracy Skills Crisis Grows', *The Australian*, 28 March: 1.

Margaretta, Pos (1996), 'Strike Savings Will Go Back to Schools', *Hobart Mercury*, 26 July.

Marriage Amendment (Definitions and Religious Freedoms) Act (2017).

Matthews, Charmaine (2003), 'Search for a Teacher', *Herald Sun*, 4 March: 27.

McEnery, Tony, Richard Xiao and Yukio Tono (2006), *Corpus-Based Language Studies: An Advanced Resource Book*, London: Routledge.

McLeod, Julie (1989), 'Debating English Curriculum in the 1980s: Questions About Ideology, Discourses and Commonsense', *Critical Studies in Education*, 31 (1): 107–20.

McNair, Brian, Terry Flew, Stephen Harrington and Adam Swift (2017), *Politics, Media and Democracy in Australia: Public and Producer Perceptions of the Political Public Sphere*, London: Routledge.

Milburn, Caroline (2005), 'Teacher Training "Ineffectual"', *The Age*, 18 April: 4.

Mills, Martin and Amanda Keddie (2010), 'Cultural Reductionism and the Media: Polarising Discourses around Schools, Violence and Masculinity in an Age of Terror', *Oxford Review of Education*, 36 (4): 427–44.

Mills, Nicole (2013), 'You Just Don't Get It: Teachers Slam Minister', *Northern Territory News*, 9 May: 7.

Mockler, Nicole (2008), 'Beyond "What Works": Teachers and the Politics of Identity', PhD diss., University of Sydney.

Mockler, Nicole (2013), 'Reporting the "Education Revolution": Myschool.edu.au in the Print Media', *Discourse: Studies in the Cultural Politics of Education*, 34 (1): 1–16.

Mockler, Nicole (2014), 'Simple Solutions to Complex Problems: Moral Panic and the Fluid Shift from 'Equity' to 'Quality' in Education', *Review of Education*, 2 (2): 115–43.

Mockler, Nicole (2016), 'NAPLAN and the Problem Frame: Exploring Representations of NAPLAN in the Print Media, 2010 and 2013', in Lingard, Bob, Sam Sellar and Greg Thompson, eds, *National Testing in Schools: An Australian Assessment*, 181–98, London: Routledge.

Mockler, Nicole (2017), 'Classroom Ready Teachers? Some Reflections on Teacher Education in Australia in an Age of Compliance', *Teacher Education and Practice*, 30 (2): 335–39.

Mockler, Nicole (2018), 'Early Career Teachers in Australia: A Critical Policy Historiography', *Journal of Education Policy*, 33 (2): 262–78.

Mockler, Nicole (2019a), 'Education and Media Discourses', *Oxford Research Encyclopedia of Education*, October 2019.

Mockler, Nicole (2019b), 'Shifting the Frame: Representations of Early Career Teachers in the Australian Print Media', in Sullivan, Anna M, Bruce Johnson and Michele

Simons, eds, *Attracting and Keeping the Best Teachers: Issues and Opportunities*, 63–82, Dordrecht: Springer.

Mockler, Nicole (2020a), 'Discourses of Teacher Quality in the Australian Print Media 2014–2017: A Corpus-Assisted Analysis', *Discourse: Studies in the Cultural Politics of Education*, 41 (6): 854–70.

Mockler, Nicole (2020b), 'Ten Years of Print Media Coverage of NAPLAN: A Corpus-Assisted Assessment', *Australian Journal of Applied Linguistics*, 43 (2): 117–44.

Mockler, Nicole and Susan Groundwater-Smith (2018), *Questioning the Language of Improvement and Reform in Education: Reclaiming Meaning*, London: Routledge.

Mons, Nathalie and Xavier Pons (2009), *The Reception of PISA in France: Knowledge and Regulation of the Educational System* (Wp 12), retrieved from Project KNOW and POL: http://knowandpol.eu/IMG/pdf/o31.pisa.france.pdf (accessed 1 October 2021).

Moreau, Marie-Pierre (2019), *Teachers, Gender and the Feminisation Debate*, London: Routledge.

Munro, Kelsey (2017), 'The Bigger, the Better for Class Sizes, Says Education Guru; Education – Teaching Quality', *Sydney Morning Herald*, 22 March: 9.

Murray, Paul (2006), 'Premier's Press Attack Just the Same Old Story', *West Australian*, 6 June: 18.

Northern Territory News (2015), 'Awards Pay Tribute to Those Who Inspire', 30 October: 54.

NSW Legislative Council Portfolio Committee No.3 – Education (2020), *Measurement and Outcome-Based Funding in New South Wales Schools: Informed by the Data: Evidence-Based Education in NSW*, retrieved from Sydney, https://nla.gov.au/nla.obj-2496117855/view (accessed 1 October 2021).

NSW Productivity Commission (2021), *Productivity Commission White Paper 2021: Rebooting the Economy*, Sydney: NSW Productivity Commission.

Organisation for Economic Cooperation and Development (2005), *Teachers Matter: Attracting, Developing and Retaining Effective Teachers*, Paris: OECD.

Organisation for Economic Cooperation and Development (2020), *Talis 2018 Results (Volume II): Teachers and School Leaders as Valued Professionals*, Paris: OECD.

Patty, Anna (2008), 'Ministers Agree on Merit Pay for Teachers', *Sydney Morning Herald*, 18 April.

Patty, Anna (2010), 'Catholic and State Schools Add to HSC All-Rounders', *Sydney Morning Herald*, 30 December: 3.

Pearson, Noel (2011), 'Education Guru Teaching to the Converted', *Weekend Australian*, 30 April: 18.

Pearson, Noel (2018), 'Beacons of Light at Chalkface', *The Australian*, 5 May: 17.

Penfold, Andrew (2014), 'Making a Difference in Indigenous Education', *The Australian*, 18 October: 18.

References

Pettigrew, May and Maggie MacLure (1997), 'The Press, Public Knowledge and the Grant Maintained Schools Policy', *British Journal of Educational Studies*, 45 (4): 392–405.

Phelan, Sean and Leon A. Salter (2019), 'The Journalistic Habitus, Neoliberal(Ized) Logics, and the Politics of Public Education', *Journalism Studies*, 20 (2): 154–72.

Potts, Amanda, Monika Bednarek and Helen Caple (2015), 'How Can Computer-Based Methods Help Researchers to Investigate News Values in Large Datasets? A Corpus Linguistic Study of the Construction of Newsworthiness in the Reporting on Hurricane Katrina', *Discourse & Communication*, 9 (2): 149–72.

Poulos, Elenie (2020), 'The Politics of Belief: The Rise of Religious Freedom in Australia', PhD diss., Sydney: Macquarie University.

Priestley, Mark, Daniel Alvunger, Stavroula Philippou and Tiina Soini, eds (2021), *Curriculum Making in Europe: Policy and Practice within and across Diverse Contexts*, Bingley: Emerald.

Punakallio, Ella and Fred Dervin (2015), 'The Best and Most Respected Teachers in the World? Counternarratives About the "Finnish Miracle of Education" in the Press', *Power and Education*, 7 (3): 306–21.

Quality Teaching Must Be the Focus of School Reform (2017), 'Editorial', *The Australian*, 18 April.

Raethel, Stephanie (1996), 'School Quality Control Flying Squad Scrapped', *Sydney Morning Herald*, 26 June: 3.

Raethel, Stephanie (1997), 'No Yearning for the Past from Long-Serving Teachers', *Sydney Morning Herald*, 9 December: 6.

Rawolle, Shaun (2010), 'Understanding the Mediatisation of Educational Policy as Practice', *Critical Studies in Education*, 51 (1): 21–39.

Rayner, Gordon (2018), '"My Biggest Challenge Is to Reverse the Staffing Crisis in the Teaching Profession": Secretary of State Aims to Introduce Flexible Working and Reduce Workloads to Halt Exodus of Teachers', *Daily Telegraph (UK)*, 11 May: 4.

Reid, A. (2019), *Changing Australian Education: How Policy is Taking Us Backwards and What Can Be Done About It*, New York: Routledge.

Richards, Christopher (1999), 'Query About the Quality', *The Age*, 17 November: 4.

Richardson, John E. (2007), *Analysing Newspapers: An Approach from Critical Discourse Analysis*, London: Palgrave.

Riordan, Geoff (2011), 'Politics, Personalities and the Public Interest: The Establishment of the NSW Board of Studies and the Determination of Curriculum', in Yates, Lyn, Cherry Collins and Kate O'Connor, eds, *Australia's Curriculum Dilemmas: State Cultures and the Big Issues*, Melbourne: Melbourne University Press.

Rizvi, Fazal and Bob Lingard (2009), 'The OECD and Global Shifts in Education Policy' *International Handbook of Comparative Education*, 437–53, Dordrecht: Springer.

Rizvi, Fazal and Bob Lingard (2010), *Globalizing Education Policy*, Abingdon: Routledge.

Robert, Sarah A. (2012), '(En)Gendering Responsibility: A Critical News Analysis of Argentina's Education Reform, 2001', *Discourse: Studies in the Cultural Politics of Education*, 33 (4): 485–98.

Roberts-Hull, Katie (2020), 'Teachers Need Better Resources to Plan Great Lessons', *Sydney Morning Herald*, 24 February: 14.

Rönnberg, Linda, Joakim Lindgren and Christina Segerholm (2013), 'In the Public Eye: Swedish School Inspection and Local Newspapers: Exploring the Audit–Media Relationship', *Journal of Education Policy*, 28 (2): 178–97.

Rose, Danny (2004), 'Libs Rip into Teachers for Joining Rally', *Hobart Mercury*, 28 May: 21.

Roulston, Kathy and Martin Mills (2000), 'Male Teachers in Feminised Teaching Areas: Marching to the Beat of the Men's Movement Drums?', *Oxford Review of Education*, 26 (2): 221–37.

Rowe, Emma E. and Andrew Skourdoumbis (2019), 'Calling for "Urgent National Action to Improve the Quality of Initial Teacher Education": The Reification of Evidence and Accountability in Reform Agendas', *Journal of Education Policy*, 34 (1): 44–60.

Rowe, Emma E. and Laura B. Perry (2020), 'Private Financing in Urban Public Schools: Inequalities in a Stratified Education Marketplace', *The Australian Educational Researcher*, 47(1): 19–37.

Roy Morgan (2021), Newspaper Readership. Retrieved from http://www.roymorgan. com/industries/media/readership/newspaper-readership (accessed 1 October 2021).

Ruddock, Philip, Rosalind Croucher, Annabelle Bennett, Frank Brennan and Nicholas Aroney (2018), *Religious Freedom Review: Report of the Expert Panel*, Canberra: Commonwealth Government.

Sachs, Judyth (1997), 'Reclaiming the Agenda of Teacher Professionalism: An Australian Experience', *Journal of Education for Teaching*, 23 (3): 263–75.

Safe Schools Coalition Australia (2021), 'Resources' (accessed 8 January).

Sahlberg, Pasi (2016), 'The Global Education Reform Movement and Its Impact on Schooling', in Mundy, K., A. Green, B. Lingard and A. Verger, eds, *The Handbook of Global Education Policy*, 128–44, New Jersey: John Wiley & Sons.

Savage, G. (2021), *The Quest For Revolution in Australian Schooling Policy*, London: Routledge.

Savage, Glenn C. and Bob Lingard (2018), 'Changing Modes of Governance in Australian Teacher Education Policy', in Hobbel, N. and B. Bales, eds, *Navigating the Common Good in Teacher Education Policy: Critical and International Perspectives*, 64–80, New York: Routledge.

Savage, Glenn C. and Kate O'Connor (2015), 'National Agendas in Global Times: Curriculum Reforms in Australia and the USA since the 1980s', *Journal of Education Policy*, 30(5): 609–30.

References

Savage, Glenn C. and Steven Lewis (2018), 'The Phantom National? Assembling National Teaching Standards in Australia's Federal System', *Journal of Education Policy*, 33 (1): 118–42.

Schatzki, Theodore R. (2002), *The Site of the Social: A Philosophical Account of the Constitution of Social Life and Change*, University Park, PA: Pennsylvania State University Press.

Scheufele, Bertram T. and Dietram A. Scheufele (2013), 'Framing and Priming Effects', *The International Encyclopedia of Media Studies*.

Scheufele, Dietram A. and David Tewksbury (2007), 'Framing, Agenda Setting, and Priming: The Evolution of Three Media Effects Models', *Journal of Communication*, 57 (1): 9–20.

Scholes, Laura, Jo Lampert, Bruce Burnett, Barbara M Comber, Lutz Hoff and Angela Ferguson (2017), 'The Politics of Quality Teacher Discourses: Implications for Pre-Service Teachers in High Poverty Schools', *Australian Journal of Teacher Education*, 42 (4): 19–43.

Scott, Mike (2010), 'Problems in Investigating Keyness, or Clearing the Undergrowth and Marking Out Trails', in Bondi, Marina and Mike Scott, eds, *Keyness in Texts*, 43–58, Amsterdam: John Benjamins.

Scott, Mike (2020a), Download Parser (Version 1), Stroud, UK: Lexical Analysis Software.

Scott, Mike (2020b), WordSmith Tools (Version 8), Stroud, UK: Lexical Analysis Software.

Scott, Mike and Christopher Tribble (2006), *Textual Patterns*, Amsterdam: John Benjamins.

Sellar, Sam and Bob Lingard (2013), 'Looking East: Shanghai, PISA 2009 and the Reconstitution of Reference Societies in the Global Education Policy Field', *Comparative Education*, 49 (4): 464–85.

Shann, Ed (2000), 'Building Skills Pays Off', *Herald Sun*, 16 September: 150.

Shine, Kathryn (2012), 'Seen but Not Heard: Schoolteachers in the News', PhD diss., University of Western Australia, Perth.

Shine, Kathryn (2015a), 'Are Australian Teachers Making the Grade? A Study of News Coverage of Naplan Testing', *Media International Australia*, 154 (1): 25–33.

Shine, Kathryn (2015b), 'Reporting the "Exodus": News Coverage of Teacher Shortage in Australian Newspapers', *Issues in Educational Research*, 25 (4): 501–16.

Shine, Kathryn (2020), '"Everything Is Negative": Schoolteachers' Perceptions of News Coverage of Education', *Journalism*, 21: 1694–709.

Shine, Kathryn and Tom O'Donoghue (2013a), *Schoolteachers in the News: A Historical Analysis of Coverage in the West Australian Newspaper*, Amherst, NY: Cambria Press.

Shine, Kathryn and Tom O'Donoghue (2013b), 'Teacher Representation in News Reporting on Standardised Testing: A Case Study from Western Australia', *Educational Studies*, 39 (4): 385–98.

Sinclair, John (1991), *Corpus, Concordance, Collocation*, Oxford: Oxford University Press.

Sinclair, John, Susan Jones and Robert Daley (1969), *English Collocation Studies: The Osti Report*, London: Mimeo.

Snyder, Ilana (2008), *The Literacy Wars*, Crows Nest, NSW: Allen & Unwin.

Spicksley, Kathryn (2021), '"The Very Best Generation of Teachers Ever": Teachers in Post-2010 Ministerial Speeches', *Journal of Education Policy*: 1–25.

Stacey, Meghan, Rachel Wilson and Susan McGrath-Champ (2020), 'Triage in Teaching the Nature and Impact of Workload in Schools', *Asia Pacific Journal of Education*: 1–14.

Stack, Michelle (2006), 'Testing, Testing, Read All About It: Canadian Press Coverage of the PISA Results', *Canadian Journal of Education/Revue canadienne de l'Èducation*, 29 (1): 49–69.

Stack, Michelle (2007), 'Representing School Success and Failure: Media Coverage of International Tests', *Policy Futures in Education*, 5 (1): 100–10.

Stack, M. (2016), *Global University Rankings and the Mediatization of Higher Education*, New York: Palgrave MacMillan.

Steiner-Khamsi, Gita (2004), *The Global Politics of Educational Borrowing and Lending*, New York: Teachers College Press.

Stenhouse, Lawrence (1975), *An Introduction to Curriculum Research and Development*, London: Heinemann.

Stubbs, Michael (1996), *Text and Corpus Analysis*, London: Blackwell.

Stubbs, Michael (2001), *Words and Phrases: Corpus Studies of Lexical Semantics*, Oxford: Blackwell.

Synder, I. (2008), *The Literacy Wars: Why Teaching Children to Read and Write Is a Battleground in Australia*, Sydney: Allen & Unwin.

Takayama, Keita (2008), 'The Politics of International League Tables: PISA in Japan's Achievement Crisis Debate', *Comparative Education*, 44 (4): 387–407.

Takayama, Keita (2010), 'Politics of Externalization in Reflexive Times: Reinventing Japanese Education Reform Discourses through "Finnish PISA Success"', *Comparative Education Review*, 54 (1): 51–75.

Takayama, Keita, Florian Waldow and Youl-Kwan Sung (2013), 'Finland Has It All? Examining the Media Accentuation of "Finnish Education" in Australia, Germany and South Korea', *Research in Comparative and International Education*, 8 (3): 307–25.

Tamir, Eran and Roei Davidson (2011), 'Staying above the Fray: Framing and Conflict in the Coverage of Education Policy Debates', *American Journal of Education*, 117 (2): 233–65.

Tan, Emrullah (2014), 'Human Capital Theory: A Holistic Criticism', *Review of Educational Research*, 84 (3): 411–45.

Tavris, Carol and Carole Wade (1977), *The Longest War: Sex Differences in Perspective*, New York: Harcourt Brace Jovanovich.

References

Taylor, Charlotte (2018), 'Similarity', in Taylor, C. and A. Marchi, eds, *Corpus Approaches to Discourse: A Critical Review*, 19–37, London: Routledge.

Thomas, Sue (2003), '"The Trouble with Our Schools": A Media Construction of Public Discourses on Queensland Schools', *Discourse: Studies in the Cultural Politics of Education*, 24 (1): 19–33.

Thomson, Pat, Jill Blackmore, Judyth Sachs and Karen Tregenza (2003), 'High Stakes Principalship – Sleepless Nights, Heart Attacks and Sudden Death Accountabilities: Reading Media Representations of the United States Principal Shortage', *Australian Journal of Education*, 47 (2): 118–32.

Thorp, Diana (2020), 'Teacher Bashing in Pandemic Is Contagious', *Herald Sun*, 30 April.

Thurman, Neil and Richard Fletcher (2019), 'Has Digital Distribution Rejuvenated Readership?', *Journalism Studies*, 20 (4): 542–62.

Ulmer, Jasmine B. (2016), 'Re-Framing Teacher Evaluation Discourse in the Media: An Analysis and Narrative-Based Proposal', *Discourse: Studies in the Cultural Politics of Education*, 37 (1): 43–55.

Unmarked Software (2019), TextSoap (Version 8.5).

Vonow, Brittany (2015), 'Primary Kids Show Their True Class', *The Courier-Mail*, 6 August: 10.

Waldow, Florian, Keita Takayama and Youl-Kwan Sung (2014), 'Rethinking the Pattern of External Policy Referencing: Media Discourses over the "Asian Tigers" PISA Success in Australia, Germany and South Korea', *Comparative Education*, 50 (3): 302–21.

Wallace, Mike (1993), 'Discourse of Derision: The Role of the Mass Media within the Education Policy Process', *Journal of Education Policy*, 8 (4): 321–37.

Waller, Lisa and Kerry McCallum (2016), 'Keystone Media: The Australian and Indigenous Affairs', *Media International Australia*, 161 (1): 109–19.

Warmington, Paul and Roger Murphy (2004), 'Could Do Better? Media Depictions of UK Educational Assessment Results', *Journal of Education Policy*, 19 (3): 285–99.

Webber, Nicola (2000), 'School Literacy Threat', *Herald Sun*, 5 December: 10.

Weber, Sandra (2006), 'The Public Imaginary of Education as Cumulative Cultural Text', *Journal of Curriculum and Pedagogy*, 3 (2): 72–6.

Weber, Sandra and Claudia Mitchell (1995), *That's Funny, You Don't Look Like a Teacher: Interrogating Images and Identity in Popular Culture*, London: Falmer.

Why We Are Publishing a League Table (2010a), 'Editorial', *Sydney Morning Herald*, 29 January.

Wilson, Andrew (2013), 'Embracing Bayes Factors for Key Item Analysis in Corpus Linguistics', in Bieswanger, Markus and Amie Koll-Stobbe, eds, *New Approaches to the Study of Linguistic Variability. Language Competence and Language Awareness in Europe*, 3–11, Frankfurt: Peter Lang.

Wilson, John P. (2017), 'Will We Still Be Free to Have Our Own Opinions of Same-Sex Marriage?', *The Australian*, 22 August: 12.

Winburn, Jonathan, Amanda Winburn and Ryan Niemeyer (2014), 'Media Coverage and Issue Visibility: State Legislative Responses to School Bullying', *The Social Science Journal*, 51 (4): 514–22.

Windle, Joel A. (2015), *Making Sense of School Choice: Politics, Policies, and Practice under Conditions of Cultural Diversity*, New York: Palgrave Macmillan.

Yates, Lyn. (2009), 'From Curriculum to Pedagogy and Back Again: Knowledge, the Person and the Changing World', *Pedagogy, Culture & Society*, 17 (1): 17–28.

Ydesen, Christian and Anna Bomholt (2020), 'Accountability Implications of the OECD's Economistic Approach to Education: A Historical Case Analysis', *Journal of Educational Change*, 21(1): 37–571.

Yemini, Miri and Noa Gordon (2017), 'Media Representations of National and International Standardized Testing in the Israeli Education System', *Discourse: Studies in the Cultural Politics of Education*, 38 (2): 262–76.

Zuboff, S. (2019), *The Age of Surveillance Capitalism: The Fight or the Future at the New Frontier of Power*, London: Profile Books.

Index

Abbott–Turnbull–Morrison (Liberal-National) government 36, 66, 73, 75, 79, 95, 148, 151
aboutness 21, 39, 44–5, 59–60, 86–7, 145–52
accountability 6–7, 44, 58, 65, 67, 118, 121–2, 143, 149–153, 163–7
AntConc 3.5.8 22, 30, 145
AntFileConverter 29
apprenticeship of observation 11, 53
Australian print media landscape 23, 31–5, 87

Baker, Paul 17, 18, 19, 21, 23, 27, 39, 61, 80, 104, 105
Bayesian Information Criterion 21, 39, 60, 88
Bednarek, Monika 5, 15–18, 171–2
British National Corpus (BNC) 18

Caple, Helen 5, 15–18, 171
class sizes 106, 109, 112–16, 135, 146
classroom readiness 93, 109, 139, 140, 166, 172
collocation analysis 19–20, 45
commonwealth control of education 28, 72, 77, 79–80
concordance analysis 22
consistent collocates 80–1
corpus construction 28–31
Corpus of Contemporary American English (COCA) 18
Corpus of News on the Web (NOW) 18, 21, 40, 59, 60, 67, 105
Covid-19 pandemic 2, 30, 68, 71, 120, 152, 161, 174
culture wars 69, 76, 95, 96
cumulative cultural text of teacher 7, 11, 55, 168
curriculum 43, 62–4, 90, 95–6, 134, 140–3, 148–9

density of media coverage of teachers 9, 29, 36, 166
diachronic analysis 28, 59
dichotomizing discourses 53–6, 155
direct instruction 94–6, 167
disadvantaged schools 43–4, 66, 149
discourse prosody 19, 20, 45, 51–3, 57, 85, 93, 103, 154
dispersion 21, 40, 56, 88
Donnelly, Kevin 94–6
download Parser 145

early career teachers 46, 109, 119, 138–9, 157, 160, 167, 172, 173
education policy reform 44, 114, 166, 173, 174
'education Revolution' 36, 64, 66, 70, 79, 98, 123, 166
explicit instruction (*see* direct instruction)

female teachers 47–50, 82
former teachers 82, 154
Foucault, Michel 2, 17
framing (*see* media framing)
frequency analysis 19

gendered representations 47–50, 173
Global Education Reform Movement (GERM) 143, 145
Gonski, David 137
Gonski reviews (*see* School Funding)

Hardie's Log Ratio 21, 39, 60, 88
heroic teacher, discourse of 107, 111–12, 156
homogenizing discourses 53–6, 155
Howard (Liberal-National) Government 63, 65–6, 69–72, 79, 97, 134

Indigenous education 96–7

Index

international large-scale assessments 7, 8, 42, 65, 71, 80, 89, 98, 111, 138

keyword analysis 21, 59–60

Larsen, Marianne 2, 53, 117, 121–3, 142
league tables 72–3, 78, 80, 115
local vernaculars of education policy 24, 143, 160, 162, 164
lockwords 61

male teachers 47–50, 82
marriage equality 68, 71, 73–6, 86, 147, 152, 173
media framing 1, 4 to 7, 13, 14, 104–7, 117–18, 174
media logic 9, 11, 168
mediatization 9, 10
mutual Information 20, 45
my School website 9, 70, 72–3, 79, 115, 135

National Assessment Program – Literacy and Numeracy (NAPLAN) 9, 70, 72–3, 78–80, 111–15, 115, 128, 135, 147, 149
national values' 69–71, 76, 79, 96, 137, 166
new teachers (*see* early career teachers)
news values 4–5, 14–17, 88, 118, 132, 150
newsworthiness 5, 15–16, 36, 132
NOW Corpus (*see* Corpus of News on the Web)

Organisation for Economic Co-operation and Development (OECD) 7, 71, 89, 95, 98, 138, 141, 143
outcomes-based education 90–3, 114

performance pay 64, 64, 92, 135, 143
political discourse, teachers and 77–9, 148
practice Architectures, theory of 4, 11 to 14, 17, 24, 66, 142, 165, 168–9
problem frame 8, 88, 104, 107–17
professional associations 41–2, 62–3
ProtAnt 1.2.1 22, 30, 104–5, 132
public school teachers 48, 50–1
Pyne, Christopher 78–9, 95, 136–40

religious freedom 68, 71, 3, 75–7, 86, 152, 173
Rudd-Gillard (Labor) Government 28, 36, 64–66, 70–1, 80, 98, 123, 126, 134–5, 166

Safe Schools' 73–4, 173
school autonomy 52, 71, 89, 97–9, 140
school funding 28, 43, 65–6, 135, 137, 149
Semantic prosody (*see* Discourse prosody)
Shine, Kathryn and O'Donoghue, Tom 6, 91
specialist teachers 41–3, 62–4, 71, 80, 84

t-score 20, 45
Teacher centrality, discourse of 2, 53, 76, 82, 117, 121, 126, 134
teacher education 41–4, 62–3, 81–6, 101, 108–10, 116–21, 129–42, 147, 151–4, 157, 160, 167, 172
Teacher Education Ministerial Advisory Group (TEMAG) 86, 109, 139
teacher industrialism 41–2, 50–1, 56–7, 62–3, 68–70, 81–90, 98–104, 115–17, 147, 151–2, 159–61
teacher professionalism 101–4, 134
teacher quality, discourse of 8, 24, 46, 51–53, 82, 107–10, 119–142, 161–2, 167
teacher shortage 41–2, 46, 55, 62–4, 100–3, 106–7, 110–11, 116, 139, 147, 153, 160, 167, 172–3
teacher workload 112–14
teaching standards 24, 28, 42, 56, 62, 64, 83, 85, 100, 102–3, 108, 117–18, 123, 131–2, 142–3, 150, 162
TextSoap 8.5 29
The Australian 93–7, 120
The Australian Financial Review 97–9, 120
The West Australian 90–93

What's the problem represented to be? 120, 133
Wordsmith Tools 8 20, 22, 30, 40, 88, 124, 145

Printed in the USA
CPSIA information can be obtained
at www.ICGtesting.com
LVHW012033210124
769418LV00004B/191